The Balsams Grand Resort Hotel, Dixville Notch

The Mount Washington Hotel and Resort, Bretton Woods

The Sagamore, Bolton Landing •
The Equinox, Manchester Village •

Boyne Highlands, Harbor Springs •
Treetops Resort, Gaylord •
Garland Resort, Lewiston •
Grand Traverse Resort and Spa, Acme •
The Inn at Bay Harbor, Bay Harbor •
Crystal Mountain Resort, Thompsonville •

Ocean Edge Resort and Golf Club, Brewster

The Otesaga, Cooperstown •

The American Club, Kohler •

The Hotel Hershey, Hershey •

Nemacolin Woodlands Resort & Spa, Farmington •

Seaview Marriott Resort, Absecon •

The Homestead, Hot Springs •
Wintergreen Resort, Wintergreen •
The Greenbrier, White Sulphur Springs •

Williamsburg Inn Kingsmill Resort

Hound Ears Club, Blowing Rock •

Pinehurst Resort, Pinehurst •

Chateau Elan Winery and Resort, Braselton •

Wild Dunes Resort, Charleston •
Kiawah Island Golf and Tennis Resort, Kiawah Island •

Callaway Gardens, Pine Mountain •

The Westin Resort, Hilton Head Sea Pines
The Cloister, Sea Island •

Four Seasons Resort and Club, Dallas at Las Colinas •

Amelia Island Plantation
The Ritz-Carlton, Amelia Island
Sawgrass Marriott Resort, Ponte Vedra Beach •

Barton Creek, Austin •

Turnberry Isle Resort and Club, Aventura •
Westin Innisbrook Resort, Palm Harbor •
Renaissance Vinoy Resort, St. Petersburg •
The Resort at Longboat Key Club, Longboat Key •

Hyatt Regency Grand Cypress
Disney's Grand Floridian Resort and Spa

PGA National Resort and Spa
The Breakers

Boca Raton Resort and Club, Boca Raton •

FAIRWAYS

America's Greatest Golf Resorts

Selected by the World's Leading Golf Travel Writers

A TEHABI BOOK

FAIRWAYS

America's Greatest Golf Resorts

Selected by the World's Leading Golf Travel Writers

A TEHABI BOOK

A TEHABI BOOK

Publisher: Sean Moore
Editorial Director: Chuck Wills
Art Director: Dirk Kaufman

First American Edition, 2001

2 4 6 8 10 9 7 5 3 1

Published in the United States by DK Publishing Inc.
95 Madison Avenue
New York, NY 10016

Library of Congress Cataloging-in-Publication Data

Fairways : America's greatest golf resorts.
    p. cm.
    Includes index.
    ISBN 0-7894-7500-6 (alk. paper)
    1. Golf resorts—United States—Guidebooks. 2. Golf
resorts—United States—Directories. 3. Golf courses—
United States—Guidebooks. 4. Golf courses—
United States—Directories.
    GV981 .F35 2001
    796.352'06'873—dc21
                    00-065784

The paper used in this publication meets the minimum requirements
of the American National Standard for Information Sciences—
Permanence of Paper for Printed Library Materials, ANSI z39.48-1984.

Printed and bound in Hong Kong through Dai Nippon Printing Company

Tehabi Books conceived, designed and produced
Fairways and has developed and published many
award-winning books that are recognized for their
strong literary and visual content. Tehabi works
with national and international publishers,
corporations, institutions, and nonprofit groups to
identify, develop, and implement comprehensive
publishing programs. The name Tehabi is derived
from a Hopi Indian legend and symbolizes the
importance of teamwork. Tehabi Books is located
in San Diego, California. www.tehabi.com

President: Chris Capen
Senior Vice President: Tom Lewis
Vice President of Development: Andy Lewis
Director of Sales and Marketing: Tim Connolly
Director of Trade Relations: Marty Remmell
Editorial Director: Nancy Cash
Art Director: Sébastien Loubert
Editor: Sarah Morgans
Copy Editor: Lisa Wolff
Proofreader: Camille Cloutier

Tehabi Books offers special discounts for bulk
purchases for sales promotions or premiums.
Specific, large quantity needs can be met with
special editions, including personalized covers,
excerpts of existing materials, and corporate
imprints. For more information, contact Eric
Pinkham, Director of Publishing and Promotions,
at Tehabi Books, 4920 Carroll Canyon Road,
Suite 200, San Diego, California 92121-1725.

CONTENTS

A TRAVELER'S FORECADDIE

BY DAVID G. MOLYNEAUX

UNTIL RELATIVELY RECENTLY, golf was mostly a home course game. The wealthy few played at their posh country clubs, round after round, on the familiar eighteen. I know a man who has caddied and golfed, week after week, on the same challenging country club course for more than sixty years; he knows every nuance, perhaps every blade of grass. The rest of us were confined to the local public courses, if we were lucky enough to live near one, as golf usually was way down the list of community recreational essentials.

Well, thanks to an explosion of popularity for the game of golf, no longer are we stuck with the offerings at home. These days, millions of Americans on business and vacation are packing their clubs to play fantastic courses all over the country—at luxury resorts where they don't need a membership. We are in the midst of a golf revolution that is changing America's vacation habits and its resorts, which are building fancy and fun new golf layouts at a furious pace.

THE TOP FIVE RESORTS FOR:

BEST CHALLENGE

1. THE AMERICAN CLUB
2. THE INN AT SPANISH BAY
3. THE LODGE AT PEBBLE BEACH
4. PINEHURST RESORT
5. THE MANELE BAY HOTEL

Golf resort guests have access to some of the world's most gorgeous real estate, as you will see in this book. It is an outstanding collection of the country's best golf resorts, as determined from a survey of the world's leading golf travel writers, people who make their living visiting and writing about destinations—and as often as possible playing a round of golf.

As a newspaper travel editor who is on the road as much as one-third of the year, I often pack my clubs in the hope of finding several hours on the links. When possible, my morning meetings are preceded by a quick nine or eighteen. It's my way of tossing off the airplane fatigue, getting into the rhythm of resort life, and touring what usually is the prettiest part of the resort property—from the beaches and spray of the surf on the coasts to the peaks and flora of the mountains and deserts in the interior to the lush lava fields of Hawaii.

THE TOP FIVE RESORTS FOR:

BEST BEAUTY

1. THE AMERICAN CLUB
2. TETON PINES
3. THE LODGE AT PEBBLE BEACH
4. THE INN AT SPANISH BAY
5. THE RITZ-CARLTON, KAPALUA

While the game is the same wherever you go, its play changes as you move about the six regions of the country. This book is organized by region to give you a taste of play at each resort.

Because a resort stay is made great by far more than the quality of the golf courses—and every family member may not have the same love for the game—we paid heavy attention to resort amenities. To help you select a destination for your next trip, we asked our experts to rate not only the challenge and beauty of each golf course, but also the quality of the lodgings, the cuisine, and the amenities. Useful course information is provided in Golfing boxes, which are paired with evocative tidbits in Experiencing boxes to give you a complete resort perspective at a glance.

QUAIL LODGE RESORT AND GOLF CLUB
CARMEL, CALIFORNIA

Architect: Robert Muir Graves

Tour stops: California Women's Amateur Championship, 2000

USGA Women's Amateur Regional Qualifier

Par: 71

Bentgrass/Poa Annua fairways and greens

Yardage/Rating/Slope:

Blue tees
6,516 /72.1/129

Gold tees
6,140/70.4/125

Red tees
5,451/71.8*/124*

*Women's ratings

GOLF AT A GLANCE

Each resort carries a Golfing box, which gives golfers a rundown of the important details to know about each course.

KAUAI MARRIOTT RESORT AND BEACH CLUB
KAUAI, HAWAII

Experience the irresistible combination of gracious Hawaiian hospitality and luxurious accommodations.

• Spend hours on secluded Kalapaki Beach, a quarter-mile-long white sand beach.
• Glide through the seas by kayak, windboard, or sailboat, or plunge into scuba diving, snorkeling, or fishing.
• Relax at one of Hawaii's largest swimming pools, surrounded by five soothing whirlpools and four cascading waterfalls.
• Play tennis, take a hike, ride a horse, or explore the nearby wonders of Wailua Falls and Waimea Canyon.

AMENITIES, OPTIONS

Each resort carries an Experiencing box, which offers suggestions for non-golf activities during a visit.

Our regional experts will take you to the towering pines of Hershey, Pennsylvania, built on a chocolate dream; the gentle hills of the venerable Homestead in Hot Springs, Virginia, where you have to know how to play a side hill lie; the Irish links along Lake Michigan at the American Club in Kohler, Wisconsin; the thinner air and rugged peaks of Sun Valley, Idaho; amazing Boulders in the desert of Carefree, Arizona; and prehistoric lava flows on the Big Island of Hawaii.

THE TOP FIVE RESORTS FOR:

BEST LODGING

1. THE RITZ-CARLTON, KAPALUA
2. THE BOULDERS
3. FOUR SEASONS RESORT, HUALALAI
4. THE REGENT LAS VEGAS (TIE)
4. THE AMERICAN CLUB (TIE)

"Weather is always iffy" in the Midwest, says golfer and travel writer Cynthia Boal Janssens. "Which may be why Midwesterners are so passionate about their golf. We play in rain, fog, sleet, and snow."

That's one reason that a majority of the nation's outstanding golf resorts are in the warmer climes. Resorts are, after all, travel destinations. And for six months of the year, portions of the United States are not fit for most golfers. Larry Olmsted, our Northeast regional expert and editor of the national *Golf Insider* newsletter, finds a passion for golf in his neck of the greens. "It was Northeasterners, after all, who filled the rooms at Pinehurst, The Greenbrier and the other grand resorts of the South," writes Olmsted.

More than ever, Americans are traveling to play golf, planning vacations around opportunities to experience new layouts and challenges. Even when golfers travel for other purposes—especially to a convention—they are taking their clubs in anticipation of playing a round of golf. According to the National Golf Foundation, nearly half of the vacation and business trips taken by people who play golf include at least one round on the links.

THE TOP FIVE RESORTS FOR:

BEST CUISINE

1. THE RITZ-CARLTON, KAPALUA
2. THE LODGE AT KOELE
3. MAUNA KEA BEACH HOTEL
4. THE LODGE AND SPA AT CORDILLERA
5. THE AMERICAN CLUB

On a recent trip, a resident course pro suggested that if I wanted to understand the brilliance of today's new resort golf course designs, I should play his course twice: first from the men's blue tee box, then a whole new round from the white resort box. You will play two different courses, he said.

He was right on the money. I played two very different games on the same course. The first was a tougher one that required carries over marshes, penalties for poor club selection, and accurate long iron shots to the green. The resort game, however, offered wider landing areas off the tee, fewer opportunities for trouble, and shorter irons to the greens.

THE TOP FIVE RESORTS FOR:

BEST AMENITIES

1. CRYSTAL MOUNTAIN RESORT
2. THE REGENT LAS VEGAS
3. THE AMERICAN CLUB
4. THE HYATT REGENCY BEAVER CREEK RESORT AND SPA
5. MAUNA KEA BEACH HOTEL

This is the genius of today's outstanding golf resorts that you will discover on the following pages, resort courses that challenge the golfer with a handicap in single figures, while providing great fun for the rest of us, including those who just hope to break 100.

With this book—a combination of extraordinary photos and inside tips from experienced travelers—a truly dedicated traveler could find several thousand holes of magnificent golf. The courses provide an amazing array of opportunities to mix the beauty of the outdoors with the thrill of playing the world's greatest recreational game. I've played many of these courses, but I have just as many holes to go. See you on the links.

REGAL RETREATS

BY LARRY OLMSTED

THE NORTHEAST RESORTS

The Hotel Hershey,
Hershey, Pennsylvania

Nemacolin Woodlands
Resort & Spa,
Farmington, Pennsylvania

The Otesaga,
Cooperstown, New York

The Balsams Grand Resort Hotel,
Dixville Notch, New Hampshire

The Mount Washington Hotel & Resort,
Bretton Woods, New Hampshire

The Sagamore,
Bolton Landing, New York

The Equinox,
Manchester Village, Vermont

Ocean Edge Resort & Golf Club,
Brewster, Massachusetts

Seaview Marriott Resort,
Absecon, New Jersey

NOWHERE ON THIS side of the Atlantic does the game of golf enjoy the history it has in the northeastern United States, where the sport was first introduced to Americans eager for outdoor recreation. Fittingly, the St. Andrews Golf Club in New York is the oldest club in this country, just as its Scottish namesake is the first course anywhere on Earth.

The Northeast lacks the year-round warmth of Hawaii or the Southwest, the rugged Pacific coast of California, and the sand hills of North Carolina. Its frigid winters drive golfers south to the innumerable courses of Florida, and its costly real estate has prevented anyone from erecting a ninety-hole resort challenge to La Quinta or Kiawah. But other than inexpensive land and warm winter days, the region lacks for nothing when it comes to great golf courses and the wonderful terrain on which to build them. The sometimes sunny, sometimes foggy New England coast more rivals the Scottish linksland than does anywhere else in the country. New Jersey's Pine Barrens setting equals that of the Carolinas for perfect parkland routings. The Adirondack, White, and Green mountains provide the elevation changes that form a background to a never-ending natural color palette—from the daffodils of spring to the wildflowers of summer to the red, yellow, and orange maple leaves of fall—all reflected in pristine lakes and ponds that make beautiful yet penal hazards.

A rich history of golf and a passion for the game—it was Northeasterners, after all, who filled the rooms at Pinehurst, the Greenbrier, and the other grand golf resorts of the South—have kept the spirit of golf alive and well in these parts. Steeped in the tradition of the many important tournaments played in the region, and with a huge variety of styles from which to choose, from oceanfront links to mountain courses, citizens of the Northeast are fortunate indeed. All they have to do is jump in their cars and in a matter of hours they are transported to some of the best golf resorts in the world, resorts that offer not just world-class golf but cuisine to rival that of the region's urban centers, floral bedspreads and antique furnishings, and sporting pursuits ranging from falconry to sailing to late nights of casino gaming. In many cases, these resorts are so entertaining that the fine golf is just the icing on a very sweet cake.

For those who have the appetite, few golf resorts come sweeter than the Hotel Hershey, in the nation's chocolate capital. Milton Hershey was a visionary, the son of a poor farming family, whose life was changed by youthful employment in some Pennsylvania candy factories. After heading out on his own and building a successful caramel business that made him a millionaire, Hershey turned his attention to milk chocolate, then a luxury item made only in Switzerland. He sold his caramel factory and parlayed the windfall into what at the time was one of the most technologically advanced, state-of-the-art factories in the world. A utopian philanthropist, Hershey envisioned a

"The South and West courses are tree-lined, with smaller greens and plenty of bunkers, putting a premium on placing the ball in the right spot."

—MIKE BATTISTELLI, DIRECTOR OF GOLF AND HEAD GOLF PROFESSIONAL, THE HERSHEY COUNTRY CLUB

RESORT RATING:

CHALLENGE	★★★☆
BEAUTY	★★★☆
LODGING	★★★★
CUISINE	★★★★
AMENITIES	★★★★

THE HOTEL HERSHEY

HERSHEY, PENNSYLVANIA

FACTORY TOWN

Hershey's golf history dates back to 1930, when Milton Hershey designed the Hershey Country Club and the first-ever juvenile golf course in the United States. Today Hershey is home to five championship courses, including the Hershey Hotel's on-site nine-hole course.

model town to accompany his model plant and built Hershey, with its affordable, quality homes, inexpensive public transportation, and abundance of cultural and recreational opportunities. For today's guests, the latter sums up the sweetest place on Earth in a nutshell.

To call Hershey a resort really is a bit of an understatement. The well-planned town encompasses two hotels with more than nine hundred rooms, a full-blown amusement park, three sports and performing arts venues, extensive formal gardens, more than a dozen restaurants, a first-rate chocolate factory tour, and seventy-two holes of golf, along with just about every other sporting diversion imaginable.

Milton Hershey was well traveled internationally and drew his inspiration for the Hotel Hershey from the grand hotels he had seen in Europe. When he commissioned an architect to design it, he handed him a postcard of an Italian hotel he had been impressed with, and the result is a stunning Mediterranean-themed building, complete with rotundas, reflecting pools, columns of every description, and endless amounts of white marble. The hotel has service to match, and has long enjoyed distinction as a recipient of AAA's prestigious Four Diamond award. Fresher than ever after a recent facelift, the Hotel Hershey leaves guests wanting for nothing, with spacious, well-appointed guest rooms, prompt and attentive service, a nine-hole golf course and putting green on the premises, and Hershey Gardens, twenty acres of formal flower beds with more than fourteen thousand roses. In keeping with the sweeping trend, the hotel recently added a brand-new spa.

FOR THOSE WHO MUST

The Hershey Lodge remains a

cozy, more casual alternative to

the Hotel Hershey.

THE HOTEL HERSHEY
THE HERSHEY COUNTRY CLUB

WEST COURSE
Architect: Maurice McCarthy
Par: 73
Rye fairways, Poa Annua greens
Yardage/Rating/Slope:
Back tees
6,860/72.6/130
Middle tees
6,480/71.0/129
Forward tees
5,598/68.5, 72.6*/121, 129*

EAST COURSE
Tour stops: PGA Buy.com
Hershey Open
Architect: George Fazio
Par: 71
Rye fairways, bentgrass greens
Yardage/Rating/Slope:
Back tees
7,061/74.5/136
Middle tees
6,363/71.0/133
Forward tees
5,654/67.6, 73.6*/124, 128*

SOUTH COURSE
Architect: Maurice McCarthy
Par: 70
Rye fairways, Poa Annua and
rye greens
Yardage/Rating/Slope:
Back tees
6,332/71.0/129
Middle tees
5,794/68.6/123
Forward tees
4,979/68.6*/119*
*Women's ratings

SPRING CREEK GOLF COURSE
Par: 33
Bentgrass fairways and greens
2,318 Yards

**HOTEL HERSHEY NINE-HOLE
EXECUTIVE COURSE**
Par: 34
Rye/bluegrass
fairways, bentgrass
greens
2,680 Yards

SUMPTUOUS SURROUNDINGS

The Hotel Hershey's most discriminating

guests enjoy the Mediterranean theme

and spectacular views from each of its

twenty-seven luxury suites, including the

Milton Hershey presidential suite.

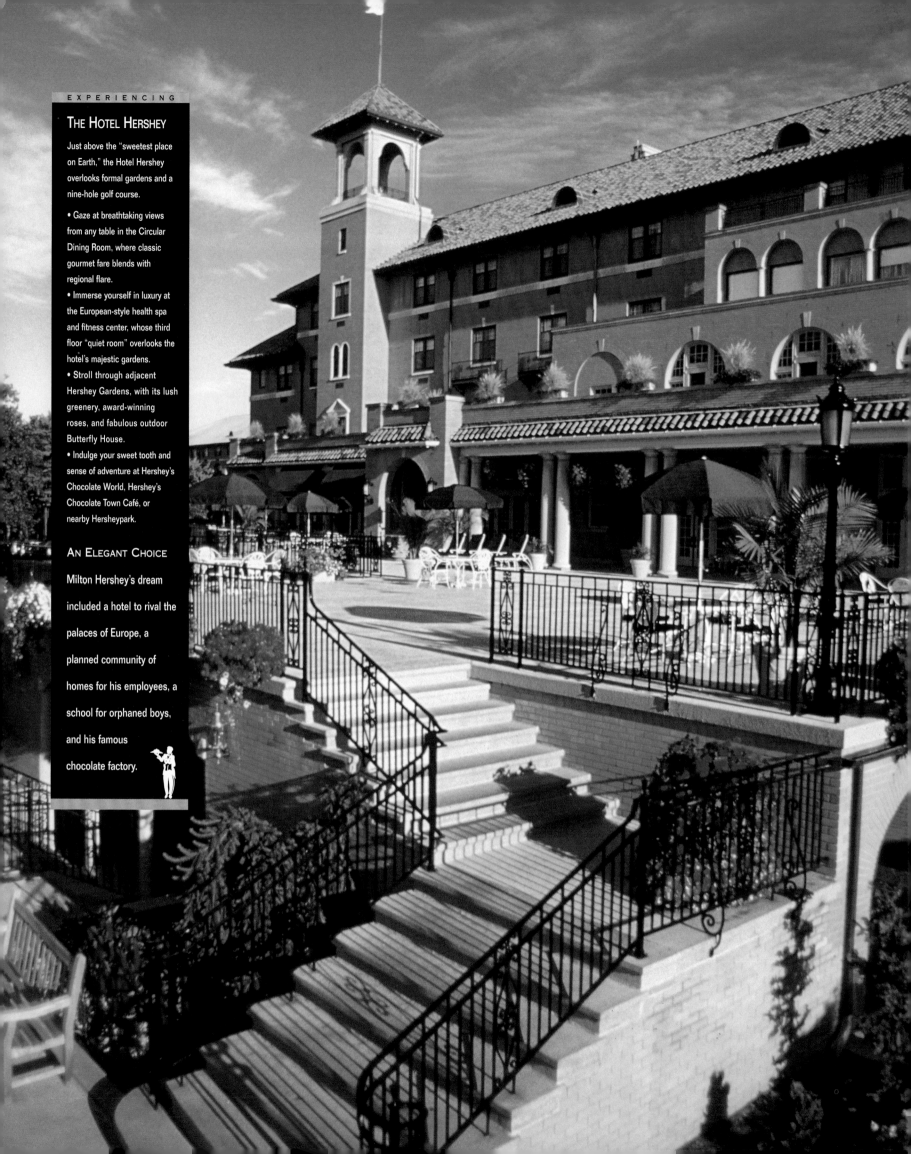

THE HOTEL HERSHEY

Just above the "sweetest place on Earth," the Hotel Hershey overlooks formal gardens and a nine-hole golf course.

• Gaze at breathtaking views from any table in the Circular Dining Room, where classic gourmet fare blends with regional flare.

• Immerse yourself in luxury at the European-style health spa and fitness center, whose third floor "quiet room" overlooks the hotel's majestic gardens.

• Stroll through adjacent Hershey Gardens, with its lush greenery, award-winning roses, and fabulous outdoor Butterfly House.

• Indulge your sweet tooth and sense of adventure at Hershey's Chocolate World, Hershey's Chocolate Town Café, or nearby Hersheypark.

AN ELEGANT CHOICE

Milton Hershey's dream included a hotel to rival the palaces of Europe, a planned community of homes for his employees, a school for orphaned boys, and his famous chocolate factory.

Hershey's dream and its manifestation as the Hershey resort of today can be best appreciated through the lens that is the Hotel Hershey's fine dining room. Mr. Hershey, in his extensive European travels, noted that in many elegant restaurants, guests who did not tip the maitre d' sufficiently were relegated to tables in far-flung corners. Since this insulted his sense of equality, Hershey charged the hotel's designer with building a formal dining room without corners. Today, the Circular Dining Room is unique, overlooking the hotel's gardens and reflecting pools and expressing the hotel's mission: to provide excellent service to each and every customer.

The Hershey Country Club is the heart of the Hershey golf experience, with three majestic eighteen-hole courses. The facility has hosted PGA and LPGA tournaments and catered to golf legends past and present. The silky-smooth Ben Hogan served as the club's pro for a decade.

The West Course represents the club's stiffest challenge. Long and difficult for its time, it has not given any ground since its creation. Its fairways are lined with old and majestic towering pines in the style of the classic U.S. Open courses, and like many older championship layouts, it bares its teeth around the small greens. To keep your ball in play is an easy feat here but to score well is something else entirely, requiring proficiency hitting lobs and chips and striking the flat stick. The East Course is carved from the same mature pine forest; dotted with more than one hundred bunkers and incorporating three man-made lakes, it presents no shortage of hazards. But despite its ample sand and prodigious length, the course plays slightly softer than its counterpart, offering easier birdie opportunities. It is the East Course that has been the site of most of the professional tournaments held at the club, and it remains the choice of the Buy.com Tour. The resort's first course was the South, by far the most resort friendly of the three and one of the most reasonably priced quality resort courses in the nation.

Guests of the Hotel Hershey do not have to board any shuttles to play golf, with a nine-hole layout on-site. The hotel's par-thirty-four course winds through a thick pine forest adjacent to the building. A second nine is available at the nearby Spring Creek Golf Club, a very short par-thirty-three that relies on its namesake hazard for defense.

Hershey may be the largest golf resort in the Northeast, but a close second is its fellow Pennsylvanian, the Nemacolin Woodlands Resort and Spa. Nemacolin is a relative newcomer to the resort business, by far the youngest of the Northeast's elite golf destinations. The resort's earliest incarnation, as a ten-room, Tudor-style lodge, was built just over three decades ago. But the area in which the resort is located is rich in history. It is the site of the Nemacolin trail, named for the Delaware Indian chief who carved it, which later became the nation's first official highway, known today as Route 40. Nearby Laurel Springs was a popular vacation home choice for Pittsburgh's aristocratic industrialists, and it was here that architect Frank Lloyd Wright was commissioned to build his most spectacular creation, Fallingwater, which can still be visited today. It was also here that the Rockwell family, owner of conglomerate Rockwell Industries, built the lodge that would become Nemacolin Resort as a country place to entertain guests, mainly for trapshooting and quail hunting. These sporting interests led to the creation of two artificial lakes and a creek for the development of fly-fishing, which remains excellent today.

TUNNEL OF TREES
Guests of the Hotel Hershey will be able to find the right course for their level of play. The East Course at the Hershey Country Club, left, provides numerous natural hazards, rolling fairways, and difficult greens.

THE SWEETEST HOLE
The West Course's signature hole is the 176-yard, par-three number 5, featuring spectacular scenery and the High Point Mansion as a backdrop.

A private golf course, now part of the resort, was also added. The property was not converted into a public access resort until 1986, when more guest rooms were added and an ambitious expansion plan was begun.

Today the fruits of that plan include a large, full-service spa, which, although recent, was ahead of its time and predates the now commonplace spa-building trend. Another golf course and a golf academy, a number of restaurants and bars, a third large lake, a lodge annex and freestanding town homes, an equestrian center with polo stadium, a tropical theme pool, a miniature golf course, an adventure sports activity center, and a complete downhill ski area have all been added. There are an astonishing

"At Nemacolin's Mystic Rock Course, the greens are so severely undulated that if you put the ball in the wrong place, you're going to three-putt for sure. . . .

RESORT RATING:

CHALLENGE	★★★⯪
BEAUTY	★★★⯪
LODGING	★★★★
CUISINE	★★★★
AMENITIES	★★★⯪

FARMINGTON, PENNSYLVANIA

NEMACOLIN WOODLANDS

RESORT AND SPA

If you want to play well, bring all facets of your game."

—DELLO NEES, DIRECTOR OF GOLF AND HEAD GOLF PROFESSIONAL, NEMACOLIN WOODLANDS RESORT

thirteen eateries, with an emphasis on game and country-style cuisine. Antelope, trout, and various types of barbecue are commonplace here, and an unusual offering is the twice-weekly wine tasting session tapping the resort's ten-thousand-bottle cellar. Nemacolin's newest addition, completed in late 1999, celebrates the property's original history: the new Shooting Academy features a thirteen-station sporting clays course, one of the most elaborate in the world, on 140 acres.

With its vast lands and facilities, there is no doubt that Nemacolin meets the definition of the phrase "full-service resort," but it is the golf that steals the show here. The Links Course has a Scottish flair, with lots of mounding and a propensity towards uneven lies, but with more dramatic elevation changes than most courses back in the old country. Expansive bunkering, excellent greens, and the requirement to play a lot of different shots make this course very worthwhile and fun to play. At most resorts, the Links could head up the roster as the marquee layout, but the star at Nemacolin is Mystic Rock.

Ooh La La

For fine wine, cordials, cocktails, and coffees, the Lautrec

Bar is an ideal spot. The Lautrec bistro offers contemporary

French cuisine with a light hand and creative flair.

To Dye for

Nemacolin Woodland's Mystic Rock Course is the star

of the show. The stunning and tough twelfth hole

illustrates architect Pete Dye's ability to create

hazards that are threatening as well as beautiful.

Into the Swing of Things

Golf pros at the Nemacolin Golf

Academy can help resort guests

raise their level of play.

NEMACOLIN WOODLANDS RESORT AND SPA

Exhilarating activities, enchanting architecture, and European hospitality await guests in the heart of the Laurel Highlands Mountains.

• Enjoy unparalleled service in a palatial château or a charming mountain-style English Tudor lodge.

• Pamper yourself among elegant furnishings, a multimillion-dollar art collection, and the Shooting Academy, the country's grandest sporting clays.

• Visit the Woodlands Spa for a relaxing massage, expert body therapy, consultation with an in-house dietitian, or gourmet cuisine.

• Browse in the specialty shops or sample award-winning eateries, from a French bistro and a 1950s-style soda shop to a western-style bar or traditional English tearoom.

BOULDERS, BUNKERS

Hole 2 on the Mystic Rock Course illustrates the features that make this course so challenging. Punctuated with giant boulders, challenging bunkers, and severely undulating greens, the Mystic Rock Course winds through Nemacolin's wooded acreage.

SADDLE UP!

Lessons, trail rides, and even

pony rides can be found at

Nemacolin's equestrian center.

RELAXING IN STYLE

Elegant public spaces like the

Château LaFayette lobby allow

vacationers a place to unwind

with a drink and conversation with

fellow resort guests.

THE OTESAGA HOTEL

THE LEATHERSTOCKING GOLF COURSE

Architect: Devereaux Emmet

Par: 72

Bentgrass fairways, bentgrass/Poa Annua greens

Yardage/Rating/Slope:

<u>Back tees</u>

6,324/71.0/124

<u>Middle tees</u>

6,053 /69.3/120

<u>Front tees</u>

5,254/69.2/116

GRAND TRADITION

The Otesega takes one back to a tranquil time of afternoon tea, piano music at dinner, and afternoons spent relaxing on the veranda. Such traditions live on in this historic five-story, Federal-style resort.

No expense was spared in shaping the course, which includes features of every design school. Vast boulders form rock-strewn wastelands suggestive of the target desert courses of Scottsdale, Arizona, while water comes frequently into play, and huge bright white bunkers transport players to Hawaii, if only in spirit. Trees, numerous streams, wetlands, and rock outcroppings all pose additional hazards. The well-conditioned course sits at the border of the temperate range where Bermuda grass begins to become common, but Dye wisely chose the superior bent variety from tee to green, with thick penal bluegrass rough. All of this adds up to a visually impressive golf course that challenges shot after shot.

Another challenging northeastern golf experience is in upstate New York, sitting at the gateway to the agricultural lands that compose the western half of the state. Golf here is overshadowed in the public eye by another sport: the Otesaga is in Cooperstown, home to the National Baseball Hall of Fame.

Like many of the Northeast's top golf resorts, the Otesaga is reminiscent of the much bigger grand resorts of the South. In fact, the entranceway to the hotel will give a déjà vu experience to anyone who has ever pulled up at Virginia's Homestead, which the red brick building with white gambrel roof resembles. Inside, the hotel has the prototypical layout common to these establishments: a grand entrance atrium where afternoon tea is served, and a long hallway full of function and sitting rooms, libraries and game rooms, leading to an elegant main dining room where almost all meals are taken. A veranda off the back of the main entrance overlooks Otsego Lake, complete with rocking chairs.

The resort is quite compressed, and does not have the sprawling grounds associated with similar properties. Guests see the Leatherstocking golf course quite clearly as they arrive, its heavily and starkly bunkered holes forming an indelible image from the road. The clubhouse, with its stunning century-old post-and-beam interior and comfortable nineteenth-hole tavern, is just a few steps across the parking lot from the hotel itself.

Visitors should be cautious not to let the short yardage influence their estimation of the formidable challenge ahead. Few layouts play as long relative to their actual yardage as the Leatherstocking, which features some of the most difficult greens of any public course. These fast, undulating, and hard-to-read putting surfaces are well protected by deep, steep-walled bunkers, and the fairways are guarded by large, jagged-walled bunkers that were ahead of their time in terms of shaping and contour, giving the course a dramatic look. The quiet countryside that surrounds the resort creates a startling counterpoint to the stunning course.

Those who are looking for another bucolic country escape would be hard-pressed to do any better than the New Hampshire resort, the Balsams. The Granite State is a microcosm of all New England, with a sampling of

THE OTESAGA

COOPERSTOWN, NEW YORK

RESORT RATING:

CHALLENGE	★★★½
BEAUTY	★★★★
LODGING	★★★½
CUISINE	★★★½
AMENITIES	★★★★

EXPERIENCING

THE OTESAGA

Originally built in 1909, the magnificent five-story Federal-style Otesaga has been completely restored to its original grandeur.

• Journey back to a time of antique toilets, pedestal sinks, oversized tubs, and old-style windows that actually open to admit the breeze.

• Enjoy simple pleasures like afternoon tea and relaxing on a veranda with breathtaking views.

• Take a short walk or trolley ride to the National Baseball Hall of Fame, the Farmer's Museum, Fenimore House art museum, or Doubleday Field, birthplace of our national pastime.

• At the Clark Sports Center, a state-of-the-art facility just a short drive away, work up a sweat with a bevy of activities.

"The greens are domed, like inverted saucers. If you don't approach shots precisely, they fall away in different directions."

—BILL HAMBLEN, PGA, DIRECTOR OF GOLF AND HEAD PROFESSIONAL, THE BALSAMS

RESORT RATING:

CHALLENGE	★★★☆
BEAUTY	★★★★☆
LODGING	★★★★
CUISINE	★★★★
AMENITIES	★★★★

EXPERIENCING

THE BALSAMS GRAND RESORT HOTEL

Opulent chandeliers and ginger jars adorn this grand hotel, but its warmth and hospitality evoke the feel of a cherished country inn.

• Discover each room's individual character, including vintage details and wrought iron accessories.
• Dress for dinner and the "viewing of the food," where every elegant dish is laid out on a long, two-tiered table.
• Don't worry about dinner reservations—you'll have your own table and waitstaff throughout your stay.

DIXVILLE NOTCH, NEW HAMPSHIRE

THE BALSAMS

GRAND RESORT HOTEL

everything unique to the region. Its southernmost tip features true cities and stretches all the way to suburban Boston. It even has a tiny slice of the seacoast that is home to lobster fishermen, and its center is filled with maple-syrup-producing forests and the White Mountains, the highest in all of New England. It is at the northernmost reaches of these mountains, just thirteen miles south of the Canadian border and a world away from the towering skylines of the Northeast's metropolises, that you will find one of the most unlikely golf resorts on the planet.

If the Balsams requires a journey to reach today, imagine the trip in 1866 when the grand mountain hotel opened its doors. There were a lot of places with easier access, as there still are, so the Balsams needed to offer something special. It is more than a resort; it is an enclave where past meets present, and in one of just over two hundred rooms set on fifteen thousand private acres, you might forget that the outside world exists.

The main draws here are peace and quiet, nature at its rawest, fine dining, elegant service of a bygone era, and one truly outstanding golf course. The Panorama Course is widely considered one of the best mountain courses in the nation, and it affords stunning views of Canada to the north and Vermont's Green Mountains to the west. Besides the challenge, golfers are rewarded with beautiful views as the course rises and falls through the mountains. The first five holes climb and drop alarmingly before the course flattens, and every natural feature, even the free-ranging moose, serves to improve the golf experience: meadows full of wildflowers, pristine mountain lakes, and views of the snow-capped peaks of the Presidential range even in summer, which have earned the Balsams the nickname Little Switzerland of the United States.

Along with the Greenbrier and Homestead, the Balsams is one of the last of the nation's grand hotels clinging to the way things used to be done. Guests at the resort pay for a full American plan that includes all activities and dining. While the golf courses are open to outside play, greens fees are waived for guests. This encourages them to play nine, twelve, fifteen, or twenty-seven holes as time or stamina permits. But all guests, even the most avid thirty-six-hole-per-day golfers, leave ample time for enjoying meals. The Balsams has won numerous awards and accolades for its lavish gastronomic presentations, and rightfully so. Nothing is skimped on or overlooked, from the pressed linen napkins to hand-shined silver to the pianist accompanying dinner nightly. The menu, which has been likened to a telephone book

LAKEFRONT LEGACY

Nestled between the White Mountains and Lake Gloriette, the Balsams

has welcomed guests to Dixville Notch, New Hampshire, since 1866.

GOLFING

THE BALSAMS GRAND RESORT HOTEL

THE PANORAMA COURSE

Architect: Donald Ross

Par: 72

Bentgrass fairways and greens

Yardage/Rating/Slope:

Gold tees

6,804/73.9/136

Blue tees

6,097/70.5/130

Silver tees

5,069/67.8/115

COASHAUKEE COURSE

Architect: Jim Smith

Par: 64

Yardage/Rating/Slope:

Gold tees

3,834/60.5/93

CLASSIC ROSS

Looking out over the

eleventh hole with its wide

fairways and unsurpassed

views of Vermont and

Canada, it's easy to see

why the Panorama Course

is so renowned.

THE MOUNT WASHINGTON HOTEL AND RESORT

MOUNT WASHINGTON COURSE

Architect: Donald Ross

Par: 71

Bentgrass/fescue fairways, Penn-Cross bentgrass greens

Yardage/Rating/Slope:

Blue tees

6,638/71.0/122

White tees

6,154/68.6/113

Red tees

5,536 /69.7/116

MOUNT PLEASANT COURSE

Architects: Cornish & Silva Golf Course Architects, with advice from Gene Sarazen and Ken Venturi

Par: 70

Yardage/Rating/Slope:

Blue/White tees

5,980/68.1/116

Red tees

4,950/67.6/109

PREPARE TO PLAY

Mount Washington's two golf courses date back to the early 1900s. Although one of many courses designed by Donald Ross, the Mount Washington Course is one of the few whose construction he personally supervised.

HISTORIC HOSPITALITY

Two hundred guest rooms and suites grace the turn-of-the-century Mount Washington Hotel, which is listed as a National Historic Landmark.

for its comprehensive offerings, emphasizes New England regional ingredients prepared in a continental fashion. Items like fresh sea scallops from the nearby Atlantic coast are combined with the produce of local farmers to create one stunning dish after another.

Despite its unique charms, the Balsams is not the only grand hotel left in northern New Hampshire's rugged White Mountains. An hour away, or just down the road by local standards, sits the Mount Washington Hotel and Resort at Bretton Woods.

The two have many similarities, yet remain as different as night and day. Like the Balsams, the Mount Washington Hotel is

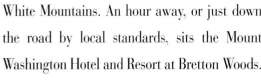

BRETTON WOODS, NEW HAMPSHIRE | **RESORT RATING:**

THE MOUNT WASHINGTON

HOTEL AND RESORT

CHALLENGE	★★★⯪
BEAUTY	★★★★⯪
LODGING	★★★⯪
CUISINE	★★★⯪
AMENITIES	★★★★

inseparable from its home, the tiny town of Bretton Woods. Like Dixville Notch, Bretton Woods has important ties to political history. It was here in 1944, at the Mount Washington Hotel, that world leaders from forty-four countries convened to create the World Bank and the International Monetary Fund, set the gold standard, and make the U.S. dollar the standard of international exchange.

The Mount Washington is a true mountain hotel, and the spectacular white building with its signature red-peaked roof sits at the base of Mount Washington, the highest peak in the Northeast. This 6,288-foot rugged granite and snow-crowned peak provides a stunning backdrop to the hotel, located on a gently sloped meadow at the mountain's base.

BLAST FROM THE PAST
The Mount Washington Cog Railway takes visitors on a three-hour, round-trip ride to the summit of the 6,288-foot mountain. At the top of the summit is the Sherman Adams Observation Center.

"This is a timeless Donald Ross Course with several small, undulating greens with false fronts. It allows the classic ground game, the old bump-and-run, pitch-and-run style."

—Douglas Ruttle, Head Golf Professional, Mount Washington Resort

BOUNTEOUS BUFFETS

Dining rooms both large and small offer gracious settings for dining and dancing. Exceptional breakfasts, buffets, and four-course dinners are served throughout the hotel.

Accommodations include the two hundred rooms and suites in the main hotel. Free shuttle service links all the properties as well as the golf courses, sports center, and restaurants. The Bretton Woods ski area, a full-service alpine resort across the road, has shared ownership with the Mount Washington Hotel and in golf season, guests can ride chairlifts to the top of this area, enjoying stunning views of the surrounding mountains, the heart of the Presidential range.

Mount Washington is one of the most visited peaks in the nation, with a road that is the reason for the oft-sighted "This Car Climbed Mount Washington" bumper stickers. Closer to the hotel is the Cog Railway, a historic coal-fired incline train that takes passengers slowly to the mountain's summit, where a museum and weather station await.

But the hotel tempts guests to remain on the property with a dozen red clay tennis courts, trail rides from the hotel's restored Victorian stables, fly-fishing in nearby rivers and streams, and golf on the fine Mount Washington Course. All eighteen holes have a distinctively Scottish flair, as they are set on a relatively flat plain and wind along a small river, with sandy soil and thick, fescue-like rough. Despite its proximity to the highest mountain in the region, the course has little elevation change other than the first hole, a short downhill par-three that literally begins on a tee box outside the hotel's back door.

A classic Donald Ross design can be found on the banks of the huge Lake George in New York's Adirondack Mountains. If the mountain hotels of New England are self-contained escapist getaways, then the Sagamore reflects the urbane

civility of the Empire State. It draws the racing aristocracy for the summer meets at nearby Saratoga and is set amid the bustling area of Lake George, with its endless array of entertainment and dining options. But despite the frenetic surroundings, the Sagamore offers peace and quiet, an enclave of civility on a private island on the lake.

The bridge linking the Sagamore to the small resort village of Bolton Landing may be only some one hundred yards long, but the exclusive island is a world away from the amusement parks, souvenir shops, and family-style

REFINEMENT

Guests are known to roam the public spaces of

the Mount Washington Hotel, seemingly

transformed by the warm elegance of the place.

FOUR-SEASON BEAUTY

Hiking, biking, fishing, photography, skiing, and

snowboarding—the resort presents a year-round slate of

activities worthy of its pristine surroundings.

OLD-FASHIONED CHARM

Sweeping verandas and wicker furniture

help visitors ease back to an earlier era,

where the pace of life was less hectic.

"The course is in hilly terrain, cut through tall pines and birches, so play it in three stages. Drive well off the tee and into the fairway to avoid the boulders and woods. . . .

RESORT RATING:

CHALLENGE	★★★★
BEAUTY	★★★★½
LODGING	★★★★½
CUISINE	★★★★
AMENITIES	★★★★½

For an unlevel lie, take one more club than normal and make a slower, easier swing. Then keep the ball below the hole—our greens are very fast and you'll have a better putt."

—THOMAS E. SMACK, DIRECTOR OF GOLF AND HEAD PROFESSIONAL, THE SAGAMORE

restaurants that dot the lakeshore. Beyond the gates leading to the Sagamore's island lies a grand hotel, whose guests spend their days on croquet courts, playing tennis, sunning by the pool, or boating in the huge lake.

Instead of trying to replicate a European hotel feel, the Sagamore celebrates its rustic Adirondack setting with lodge furniture, a comfortable pub, and hallways lined with art and photographs depicting the natural beauty and history of the Northeast. However, grand hotel elegance is not forsaken, and in the hotel's jacket-and-tie-required fine dining room, Trillium, meals to rival those of the best urban restaurants are turned out nightly, accompanied by an award-winning wine list. The more casual

THE SAGAMORE

BOLTON LANDING, NEW YORK

Sagamore Dining Room evokes the feel of the southern grand hotels, with buffet tables groaning under their loads at breakfast, lunch, and dinner.

The Sagamore is a pure golf course, calling for continuous execution and strategy, and while difficult to score well on, it is beautiful and rewarding. The first hole sets the tone with the best view on the course, a downhill tee shot that drops more than eight stories to the fairway before climbing back steeply uphill to a green that causes nearly all first timers to leave their approach shots one to two clubs short. The view from the elevated tee overlooks the lake, with the towering Adirondacks in the background, one of the more memorable views in all of golf.

Though the Sagamore is the resort's only golf course, it is the kind of course that can be played over and over again, revealing a new subtlety and inviting players to try to unlock its secrets. When guests can tear themselves away from the course, which is difficult, the resort offers fine dining and relaxed elegance in its glamorous lakeside setting.

MOONLIGHT, MOUNTAINS, AND MEMORIES

Shelving Rock Terrace, with panoramic views of Lake George

and the Adirondacks, provides the perfect setting for elegant

weddings, banquets, and other special occasions.

THE SAGAMORE

The Adirondack Mountains and Lake George provide a breathtaking backdrop for this national historic landmark.

• Stay in the historic English Colonial Main House, a charming Adirondack-style suite, an executive retreat, or even a castle.

• Enjoy afternoon tea in the Veranda, a glass-enclosed lodge overlooking the lake.

• Take a lunch or dinner cruise on *The Morgan*, the resort's seventy-two-foot replica 19th-century touring vessel.

• Gaze at the panoramic view while working out in the Sagamore Spa, with its full range of amenities and treatments, healthy cuisine, state-of-the-art equipment, and comprehensive classes.

ISLAND RETREAT

While at the Sagamore, guests can take advantage of the resort's

numerous facilities. Besides golf, there are tennis, racquetball, a full-

service spa, a fitness center, a swimming pool, whirlpools, and saunas.

Outlet shopping and a number of historic sites are just minutes away.

A TOUCH OF NATURE

In the Lodge Suites, a touch of the

mountains comes indoors. Each

Adirondack-style suite has its own wet

bar, dining area, terrace, and wood-

burning fireplace.

THE SAGAMORE
BOLTON LAKE, NEW YORK

Architect: Donald Ross

Tour stops: Qualifier for
United States Senior Open
Championship

Par: 70

Bentgrass fairways and greens

Yardage/Rating/Slope:

Blue tees
6,950/73.8/137

White tees
6,492/72.9/133

Red tees
5,211/73.0/122

SEE FOR MILES

White birches and
evergreens line the
Sagamore fairways, along
with heather brought by
Donald Ross from
his native Scotland.

THE EQUINOX
GLENEAGLES GOLF COURSE

Architect: Walter Travis,
renovated by Rees Jones
Par: 71
Bentgrass fairways and greens
Yardage/Rating/Slope:

Blue tees
6,423/71.3/129

White tees
6,069/69.1/125

Red tees
5,082/65.2/117

HISTORIC IMPRESSIONS

Mount Equinox has stood

sentinel duty over the resort

since the Patriots plotted

revolution in the historic

Marsh Tavern.

The sophisticated town of Saratoga Springs is well worth a visit, whether or not the horses are running, and the resort setting of Lake George and nearby Adirondack State Park leaves guests with no shortage of sightseeing options.

Vermont's Equinox, also with one course, succeeds with another classic designer and another wonderful tourist town. But unlike the vast majority of leading resorts in the region, the Equinox forgoes the grand resort feel for rustic country elegance—and the most varied range of unusual activities in the country.

While many American golf resorts and courses take great pains to emulate Scotland, the birthplace of the game, the Equinox actually has Scottish ties. Until very recently, the resort was owned by Guinness PLC, the brewing giant that also owns the Equinox's former sister property, the Gleneagles, in Scotland. It was from the Gleneagles, truly one of the world's greatest resorts, that the Equinox imported many of its fantastic offerings, which have continued under new ownership.

Inside the hotel, the Equinox exudes New England charm, with rustic furniture, colonial décor, and framed displays of antique fishing equipment. The most popular eatery is the lobby tavern, whose menu and décor, like the resort itself, successfully blends the history of the state as a British colony with its current status as a sporting and outdoor paradise. The Equinox is the most relaxed of the Northeast's golf resorts, where wool sweaters, tweed jackets, and jeans are common, and suits and ties rare.

The dramatic elevation changes of the Gleneagles Course, downhill on holes 1 and 10 and steeply uphill back to the clubhouse on 9 and 18, bookend two innovative nines and offer some of the best views in New England during prime fall foliage season. The white steeple of the colonial church in downtown Manchester, Mount Equinox, and the hotel itself all form scenic viewpoints during the round. The course opens with a straightforward downhill par-four to get golfers into a nice rhythm, then climbs along wooded ridges with some blind shots and unique holes through the pine and birch trees, including the "road hole," a long and memorable par-five requiring a strong tee shot and a second shot played over a public roadway. The design uses the mountainous terrain to the utmost advantage and will be everything first-time visitors expected when they closed their eyes and pictured the Vermont countryside. After the round, golfers can visit the clubhouse pub overlooking the ninth green and enjoy an authentic draft Guinness stout or Harp lager.

Just as the Equinox captures the essence of stereotypical Vermont, it is impossible to think of Massachusetts, the Bay State, without picturing clambakes, lobsters, and the rugged coastline of Cape Cod. The Cape's only true destination golf resort is Ocean Edge. There are a handful of exclusive, truly championship-caliber courses on the

THE EQUINOX

MANCHESTER VILLAGE, VERMONT

RESORT RATING:

CHALLENGE	★★★⯪
BEAUTY	★★★⯪
LODGING	★★★★
CUISINE	★★★★
AMENITIES	★★★★

EXPERIENCING

THE EQUINOX

From its early days as the Marsh Tavern, the Equinox's colonial New England hospitality remains unaltered.

• Bask in the elegantly appointed rooms and antique furnishings of the main hotel or the Charles Orvis Inn.

• Enjoy fine dining and entertainment in a four-diamond restaurant or an authentic colonial tavern, the Equinox's original structure, dating back to 1769.

• Find everything you'd expect from a world-class fitness spa, plus individualized services like body composition analysis, private training, and private exercise classes.

• Fly a bird of prey at the nation's first British School of Falconry, or master 4 x 4 driving techniques at the Land Rover Driving School.

• Visit nearby Manchester Village, with its four miles of marble-paved sidewalks and designer outlet stores.

RESORT RATING:

CHALLENGE	★★★⯨
BEAUTY	★★★★
LODGING	★★★⯨
CUISINE	★★★⯨
AMENITIES	★★★★

BREWSTER, MASSACHUSETTS

OCEAN EDGE RESORT

AND GOLF CLUB

"It doesn't pay to be aggressive here; it's not power golf. There are a lot of grass and sand pot bunkers that you need to avoid. You can't just hit the driver off of every tee."

—Dale Morrison, Head Golf
Professional, Ocean Edge Golf Club

narrow neck of land, but only one public layout worthy of the description, and it is for this reason that the course at Ocean Edge has been chosen to host the New England PGA championship five years in a row.

The course is an homage to the Scottish style, with sixty-four punishing sand traps, many of them small but deep pot bunkers in the classic tradition. The greens are quite undulating and, in the truest British Isles sense, are almost indistinguishable from their surroundings when viewed from the fairway. The design is not long, but the well-placed bunkers and a trio of freshwater ponds are placed so as to frustrate the long-ball hitter playing the back tees. The course winds throughout the resort, which features golf course and waterfront villas as the bulk of its lodging, but mercifully, these structures are set well back from the course and screened with thick foliage, avoiding the real estate atmosphere so common these days.

Within the resort are a dozen hard and clay tennis courts, a true destination golf school offering a variety of multi-day instructional packages, and a private beach—a rare commodity indeed in these parts. Ocean Edge is laid out more like a village than a typical resort: regular guest rooms are in a building next to the mansion and are perfect for singles or couples, while a broad range of villas, in two groups, along the bay and adjacent to the golf course fairways, are perfect for families and larger groups. These buildings are spread across nearly four hundred acres, dividing each cluster of villas into its own little neighborhood. The resort's main restaurant, Ocean Grille, is inside the mansion and is the obvious choice for sampling the fresh seafood of the region, expertly prepared, its selections ranging from Rhode Island oysters to Maine lobsters and, of course, New England clam chowder. The other choice is Nickerson's Pub, where the region's British colonial history can be relived over cocktails and a game of billiards. With the frequently heavy traffic that clogs the few roads of the Cape, Ocean Edge is a perfectly located respite from the hustle and bustle, a golf resort with an excellent course that is also a comfortable base from which to explore one of the most historic areas in the country.

The Seaview Marriott resort is unlike any other in the Northeast. While most of the region's premier destinations are in the mountains, it is on the ocean. While most are rural, it is just outside Atlantic City, easily reached from New York and Philadelphia. While most are relaxed, escapist destinations, Seaview is full of pomp and circumstance, still an important player on the world golf stage.

The resort has won industry accolades for every aspect of its operation, from its white-glove hotel service to its exquisite golf. After a recent and extensive renovation, the hotel's guest rooms are in fine shape and match the quality of the resort's other facilities, which include a brand new Elizabeth Arden Red Door Spa and a Nick Faldo Golf Institute.

OCEAN EDGE RESORT AND GOLF CLUB

Architects: Geoffrey Cornish
and Brian Silva
Tour stops: 1986–1991 New
England PGA Championship
Par: 72
Bentgrass fairways and greens
Yardage/Rating/Slope:
Blue tees
6,665/71.9/129
White tees
6,127/68.7/125
Red tees
5,168/70.6/123

SCOTTISH HAZARDS

With its fifty-six Scottish-
style pot bunkers, the
Ocean Edge has a
reputation for being one of
New England's most
challenging layouts.

OCEAN EDGE RESORT AND GOLF CLUB
BREWSTER, MASSACHUSETTS

This historic resort on Cape Cod Bay offers every imaginable New England activity.

• Enjoy meals in the mansion or clambakes on the beach.

• Discover the Cape's deep-sea fishing, whale watching, horseback riding, and island cruises.

• Play croquet on the lawn, try your hand at sand sculpting, or sign up for lessons at the two tennis complexes.

• Cycle, walk, or jog on the Cape Cod Rail Trail, a shaded twenty-six-mile paved path running through Ocean Edge to the Cape Cod National Seashore.

• Join a guided power walk or explore the tidal flats with a Massachusetts Audubon Society guide.

BREWSTER LANDMARK

The Ocean Edge is the premier golfing vacation destination on Cape Cod, and offers villas along the course's fairways for families and large groups.

"The Bay Course is a classic Donald Ross design, influenced a lot by winds off the Atlantic."

—JOHN KONYA, HEAD GOLF
PROFESSIONAL, SEAVIEW MARRIOTT

The Bay Course, where Sam Snead won the first of his major titles, is so named because its links hug the coastline of Reed's Bay. The course features small tabletop greens, tricky undulating targets in the Scottish fashion, protected by the water and a daunting array of more than one hundred large sand bunkers throughout the course. The course is short by modern standards, but besides the sand and water, the wind whips in incessantly off the bay, causing club selection to frequently vary by two or even three clubs. Golfers are required to consider club selection and placement carefully every time they step on the tee box, even on longer holes, and then employ the full range of shots, including frequent accurate long irons.

RESORT RATING:	
CHALLENGE	★★★⯪
BEAUTY	★★★★
LODGING	★★★⯪
CUISINE	★★★
AMENITIES	★★★

ABSECON, NEW JERSEY

SEAVIEW MARRIOTT

RESORT

Off the fairways, the hotel excels with first-class service and a wide range of amenities, including swimming pools, tennis courts, nature trails, and a jogging path winding through the resort's nearly seven hundred pine-filled acres. The hotel's main dining room turns out fabulous meals at breakfast, lunch, and dinner, and the newest offering is a healthy spa menu to go with the new full-service spa.

The Northeast's myriad offerings for classic resort life and challenging play pose a dilemma for any traveler who does not have the time to sample them all.

PLENTY TO DO

Although Atlantic City and its boardwalk are tempting, you don't have to leave the Seaview for something to do. The complex contains golf, tennis, a health club, jogging trails, and swimming pools.

FOOD WITH A FLAIR

A variety of restaurants and lounges let

you relax over a fine meal or enjoy a

light bite in a casual setting.

SEAVIEW MARRIOTT RESORT

The Seaview Marriott is a haven for both outdoor enthusiasts and those seeking exciting night life.

• Spend a day sampling the wide variety of water sports activities, including snorkeling, sailing, jet skiing, water skiing, relaxing on the beach, and lounging beside the pool.

• Take a short drive into Atlantic City, just minutes away, for some of the most exciting night life on the East Coast.

• Enjoy an afternoon of the most indulgent pampering imaginable at the Elizabeth Arden Red Door Spa.

THE WIND FACTOR

The classic Donald Ross design and

fierce Atlantic winds add an extra

dimension to golf on the Bay Course,

challenging pros and amateurs for

more than half a century.

NEW JERSEY NUGGET

The Seaview Marriott Resort makes its home on 670 secluded acres

bordering tranquil Reed's Bay in southern New Jersey. The resort features

two eighteen-hole championship golf courses, the Bay Course and Pines

Course, and is just minutes away from Atlantic City's exciting night life.

SEAVIEW MARRIOTT RESORT
ABSECON, NEW JERSEY

BAY COURSE

Architect: Donald Ross

Tour stops: Shoprite LPGA Classic

Par: 71

Bentgrass fairways and greens

Yardage/Rating/Slope:

Blue tees

6,247/70.7/122

White tees

6,011/69.5, 73.9*/120, 126*

Red/Gold tees

5,017/68.4*/114*

PINES COURSE

Architects: Howard Toomey,
William Flynn

Par: 71

Bentgrass fairways,
bentgrass greens

Yardage/Rating/Slope:

Blue tees

6,731/71.7/128

White tees

6,211/70.1, 76.0*/126, 131*

Red tees

5,276/69.8*/119*

*Women's ratings

JUST LIKE THE MASTERS

With forecaddies clad in white overalls and green caps, and a course layout similar to Augusta's, the Pines Course may be New England's version of the famed Augusta Nationals.

DECISIONS, DECISIONS

When the outdoor settings are this inviting, the biggest decision of the day may be whether to dine inside or out.

TRANQUIL SURROUNDINGS

The four-story resort features 297 rooms and 37 suites, each one graciously appointed and attentively detailed to make guests feel welcomed and pampered.

GRAND TRADITION

BY LYNN SELDON

PASS THE GRITS and praise the golf gods. The South has risen as one of the best places to stay and play.

When you visit the South, you might hear the story of a wealthy old southern gentleman who was once asked why he so seldom traveled. He replied, "Kind sir, why should I travel when I'm already here?" He must have been a golfer.

Everything about the South is different, and golf is no exception. From the mountains to the ocean to palm-tree-lined fairways, golf with a southern accent is well worth the trip. In the northern part of the region, the mountains of Virginia and West Virginia await duffers with time-tested layouts and resorts, while Virginia's tidewater region continues to rise to prominence as a golf mecca. North Carolina offers the famed Sandhills region, more mountain golf, and lots of hacker history, while South Carolina's coastal courses and accommodations feature southern hospitality at its finest.

Down in Georgia, more of the nation's peachiest coastal golf awaits, while inland golf featuring gardens and a winery provide unique allure. The Sunshine State has more courses than any other state in the nation, but the quality as much as the quantity is what keeps golfers coming back for more. Finally, over in Texas, the Lone Star state adds its own spicy flavor to golf with a southern accent.

Many vacationers may not consider golf a part of the package when planning a trip to historic Williamsburg, Virginia—but there, the sport has developed an impressive history of its own. Since it first opened in 1963, the Golden Horseshoe Golf Club, located minutes from colonial Williamsburg, has ranked among Virginia's premier golf courses, garnering *Golf* magazine's prestigious Gold Medal award for over a dozen consecutive years.

The club draws its name from the legendary 1716 expedition in which Governor Alexander Spotswood led a team of explorers to the pristine western Virginia frontier. Upon their return, Spotswood presented each brave explorer with a tiny golden horseshoe, acknowledging his bravery and support.

The Golden Horseshoe may be ranked among the elite, but its three courses—the Gold Course, the Green Course, and the nine-hole Spotswood Course—are designed for golfers of every skill level, from the occasional golfer to the seasoned pro. The award-winning Gold Course, the facility's oldest, is on 125 acres of wooded beauty and rolling greens, peppered with dramatic hazards. Renowned golf architect Robert Trent Jones, Sr. called the Gold Course his finest design, and for decades, critics have agreed.

After a round of golf, vacationers can relax at the Williamsburg Inn, conveniently located near the historic area. Designed with eighteenth-century portico columns, arches, and green awnings, the inn offers the finest in southern

GO FOR THE GOLD

The sixteenth hole of the Gold Course features

an island green that slopes from back to front

and is surrounded by five bunkers.

WILLIAMSBURG INN
GOLDEN HORSESHOE
GOLF COURSES

GOLD COURSE

Architects: Robert Trent Jones,
Sr., Rees Jones

Par: 71

Bermuda 419 fairways,
Penncross bentgrass greens

Yardage/Rating/Slope:

Gold tees

6,817/73.6/138

Blue tees

6,522/72.4/135

White tees

6,248/70.7/129

Red tees

5,168/66.2, 70.6*/120, 127*

GREEN COURSE

Architect: Rees Jones

Tour stops: 1998 USGA Senior
Women's Amateur
Championship, 1999 USGA
State Team Championships

Par: 72

Bermuda fairways, Penncross
bentgrass greens

Yardage/Rating/Slope:

Green tees

7,120/74.3/132

Blue tees

6.722/72.5/128

White tees

6,244/70.4/124

Gold tees

5,348/69.3, 70.8*/109, 124*

*Women's ratings

GREEN, BUT NOT MEAN

Wider fairways make the

Green Course more

forgiving than the Gold, but

golfers still face numerous

challenges. The finishing

hole is a perfect example,

with a pond to be carried, a

narrowing fairway, and

numerous oval and

pot bunkers.

comfort and hospitality. Guests can enjoy afternoon tea in the lounge, stroll along the inn's tree-lined terraces, or compete in a leisurely game of croquet, lawn bowling, or tennis.

Of course, all that exercise can bring on a twenty-first-century appetite—and the Williamsburg Inn serves up the best in colonial cuisine. At the King's Arms, Shields, Christiana Campbell's, and Josiah Chowning's taverns, visitors can enjoy food reminiscent of the Revolutionary War era, tasting everything from peanut soup to cavalier's lamb. For fine dining, the inn's elegant Regency Dining Room, with its silk draperies and gleaming crystal chandeliers, is the perfect choice.

"Big hitters should probably hit an iron off the Gold course tee to position their next shot onto the green."

—DEL SNYDER, AMBASSADOR OF GOLF/HEAD TEACHING PROFESSIONAL, GOLDEN HORSESHOE GOLF COURSES

WILLIAMSBURG INN

WILLIAMSBURG, VIRGINIA

RESORT RATING:	
CHALLENGE	★★★★
BEAUTY	★★★★⯪
LODGING	★★★★⯪
CUISINE	★★★★⯪
AMENITIES	★★★★⯪

Just a stone's throw away along the banks of the James River is Kingsmill Resort. This acclaimed plantation-style resort—named for English colonist Richard Kingsmill, who first settled the land in 1736—offers an impressive blend of the old and the new. Historical monuments and restored buildings are sprinkled throughout the greens and the unspoiled wilderness, but the resort's on-site golf courses and other amenities are decidedly modern.

Kingsmill boasts four state-of-the-art courses: the Woods Course, the River Course, the Plantation Course, and the nine-hole Bray Links Course. The newest, the Woods Course, was completed in 1995. Named for its wooded surroundings, the course contains deep ravines, fairway bunkers, and elevated greens designed

EXPERIENCING

THE WILLIAMSBURG INN

The Williamsburg Inn offers elegant lodging and attentive personal service in the heart of Virginia's restored eighteenth-century capital.

• Dine among gleaming crystal chandeliers and silk draperies inspired by the Prince of Wales' royal pavilion at Brighton, England, in the award-winning Regency Dining Room.

• At the Craft House at the Inn peruse the fine-quality reproduction furniture, china, linens, and accessories that have been officially licensed by the Colonial Williamsburg Foundation.

• Travel back in time to Colonial Williamsburg where history comes alive on every corner, from costumed shopkeepers and afternoon tea to a moving flag-lowering ceremony with the Fife and Drum Corps.

"At Kingsmill Resort and Club, we love to introduce new players to golf. With four sets of tee boxes on every course, everyone can find a course design . . .

RESORT RATING:

CHALLENGE ★★★★

BEAUTY ★★★☆

LODGING ★★★☆

CUISINE ★★★☆

AMENITIES ★★★★

and length that fits their game."

—RICHARD CROMWELL, DIRECTOR OF GOLF, KINGSMILL RESORT AND CLUB

HAUTE CUISINE

Dining at Kingsmill can range from casual venues like Moody's Tavern or Regattas' Café and Market to the elegant Bray Dining Room, all of which overlook the James River.

WILLIAMSBURG, VIRGINIA

KINGSMILL RESORT

to test—but not torture—the best player. The famous River Course, home to the Michelob Championship on the PGA Tour, combines rolling hills with thick woods and water. Fans of the tour will recognize the River Course's signature seventeenth hole, with its heart-stopping view of the James River. In addition, golfers wanting to improve their game can attend the Kingsmill Golf Academy, which emphasizes one-on-one training.

At Kingsmill, it's often said that "golf is everything, but it's not the only thing." In addition to golf, the resort features a recently expanded marina; thirteen tennis courts; a full-service Sports Club that includes racquetball courts, whirlpools, and an aerobics studio; and

Williamsburg's only spa, where visitors can relax and indulge in the latest modern-day luxuries.

The resort also offers complimentary transportation to and from nearby Busch Gardens, Water Country USA, and Colonial Williamsburg. Those who come, however, may not ever want to leave. Kingsmill's deluxe accommodations will make visitors feel right at home: Many of the four hundred villa-styled rooms include full-service kitchens, fireplaces, and outdoor decks. And each of the resort's five restaurants, specializing in mid-Atlantic cuisine and tidewater delicacies, is equally superb. The restaurants range from casual to elegant, and all have breathtaking river views, a testament to the way Kingsmill Resort can transform even the most ordinary of events—dining—into the most idyllic getaway.

Those yearning to escape from it all need look no further than Wintergreen Resort, nestled in Virginia's Blue Ridge Mountains, high above the magnificent Shenandoah Valley. Located only forty-three miles southwest of Charlottesville, this mountainside retreat has become, since its inception in 1976, a recreational haven.

SOUTHERN COMFORTS

Southern hospitality and an unhurried attitude give Kingsmill its relaxed and welcoming atmosphere.

SEEING DOUBLE

The classic park-style design of the Woods course contains a unique double green with a bunker in the center, shared by the par-three twelfth hole and the par-four fifteenth.

STUNNING SHELTER

Even when it is too cold outside to lounge poolside, guests at Kingsmill Resort can have a swim.

KINGSMILL RESORT
KINGSMILL GOLF CLUB
WILLIAMSBURG, VIRGINIA

RIVER COURSE
Architect: Pete Dye
Tour stops: PGA Michelob
Championship
Par: 71
Bermuda fairways,
bentgrass greens
Yardage/Rating/Slope:
<u>Gold tees</u>
6,853/73.3/137
<u>Blue tees</u>
6,081/69.9/130
<u>White tees</u>
5,001/65.3/120
<u>Red tees</u>
4,646/67.5/116

PLANTATION COURSE
Architects: Arnold Palmer,
Ed Seay
Par: 72
Bermuda fairways,
bentgrass greens
Yardage/Rating/Slope:
<u>Gold tees</u>
6,543/71.3/119
<u>Blue tees</u>
6,092/68.9/114
<u>White tees</u>
5,503/66.1/107
<u>Red tees</u>
4,880/67.9/116

WOODS COURSE
Architect:s: Tom Clark,
Curtis Strange
Par: 72
Bermuda fairways,
bentgrass greens
Yardage/Rating/Slope:
<u>Gold tees</u>
6,784/72.7/131
<u>Blue tees</u>
6,393/70.9/126
<u>White tees</u>
6,030/69.0/121
<u>Red tees</u>
5,140/68.7/116

HAZARDS ABOUND

Kingsmill is replete with

foreboding water

hazards and traps.

ON THE MENU

An assortment of restaurants and lounges

accommodate every taste, from continental cuisine

at Café Verandah to casual elegance at Devil's Grill.

GOLFING

WINTERGREEN RESORT

DEVIL'S KNOB COURSE
Architect: Ellis Maples
Par: 70
Bluegrass fairways and greens
Yardage/Rating/Slope:
Blue tees
6,576/72.4/126
White tees
6,003/69.8/119
Red tees
5,101/68.6/118

STONEY CREEK COURSE
Architect: Rees Jones
Par: 72
Bentgrass/rye fairways,
bentgrass greens
Yardage/Rating/Slope:
Monocan/Shamokin
Champ tees
7,005/74.0/132
Blue tees
6,740/72.6/126
White tees
6,341/71.6/121
Red tees
6,500/71.8/127
Yardage/Rating/Slope:
Monocan/Tuckahoe
Champ tees
6,951/74.0/130
Blue tees
6,645/72.4/126
White tees
6,244/71.1/121
Red tees
5,462/71.6/129
Yardage/Rating/Slope:
Shamokin/Tuckahoe
Champ tees
6,998/73.8/130
Blue tees
6,681/72.2/124
White tees
6,273/70.8/119
Red tees
5,594/72.4/128

DEVILISH CARRY

The eighth hole at Wintergreen Resort's Devil's Knob Course requires

that golfers carry a water hazard and a bunker to hit the green.

INDOOR-OUTDOOR SPORTS FACILITIES

The Wintergreen Spa and Fitness Center

offers something for everyone, with indoor

and outdoor pools, hot tubs, whirlpools,

massage facilities, and spa treatments.

Wintergreen is the perfect blend of national park, ski mountain, and golf resort—making it the ideal vacation spot for families and others with diverse interests. Nature lovers will relish the resort's thirty miles of hiking trails, which wind through pristine hills, rivers, and meadows spotted by deer and wild daisies. And those who want to experience it all can, depending on the season, golf in the morning and ski or snowboard in the afternoon, then in the evening catch the local symphony.

The array of activities is staggering—but not overwhelming. Part of Wintergreen's magic lies in its casual, refreshing atmosphere. The resort has maintained its pledge to environmental sensitivity, leaving over half its acreage

WINTERGREEN RESORT

WINTERGREEN, VIRGINIA

in a natural state, safe from future development. The result: jagged, majestic mountains, roaming wildlife, scattered wild-flowers, and breathtaking, unobstructed views.

Wintergreen's commitment to environmentalism extends even to the design of its extraordinary golf courses. Its first course, the award-winning Devil's Knob, was built onto the existing mountain. At 4,000 feet in elevation, each green is tucked into the landscape with logical landing areas, rather than carved out of the mountain, making for an awe-inspiring yet challenging game. Stoney Creek, its second course, was built into the Blue Ridge valley and is characterized by its long, immaculate fairways with views of the towering mountains above. Finished in 1988, Stoney Creek is named for the natural creeks that wind through the property and often become part of the game.

The Homestead, located to the west in mountainous Hot Springs, Virginia, offers a far more elegant resort experience—one of fine dining, incomparable southern hospitality, and rich tradition. Today it is known as the

"The three nines are very distinct. Monocan is open and long, Shamokin plays through the woods, and Tuckahoe has elevation changes."

—MIKE MAYER, HEAD GOLF PROFESSIONAL, STONEY CREEK COURSE

RESORT RATING:

CHALLENGE	★★★½
BEAUTY	★★★★
LODGING	★★★½
CUISINE	★★★
AMENITIES	★★★★

EXPERIENCING

WINTERGREEN RESORT

High in Virginia's Blue Ridge, Wintergreen is the ultimate vacation spot—peaceful and refreshing yet with recreational opportunities as diverse as the landscape.

• Splash in sky-blue pools, test your mettle on championship golf and tennis courses, or work out in the Wintergarden Spa and Fitness Center.
• Attend symphony concerts or stage plays, visit artists' studios or wineries, or spend an afternoon soaking up the area's rich history in antique stores or museums.
• Pick up a trail map, lace up your boots, and head for the thirty miles of marked hiking paths, some joining the famous Appalachian Trail.
• Take a lesson at the equestrian center or a trail ride through the valley, or sample the diverse waterfront activities at Lake Monocan.

"Here you have to know how to play side hill lies. A ball above your feet tends to go left and below tends to go right. Take a few practice swings to see where the club grounds out; . . .

RESORT RATING:

CHALLENGE	★★★★
BEAUTY	★★★★✩
LODGING	★★★★
CUISINE	★★★★
AMENITIES	★★★★

HOT SPRINGS, VIRGINIA

THE HOMESTEAD

that's where you want the ball to be in your stance."

—JEFF WOODZELL, HEAD GOLF PROFESSIONAL, THE OLD COURSE AT THE HOMESTEAD

EXPERIENCING

THE HOMESTEAD

Breathtaking scenery, quiet elegance, and more than two hundred years of exceptional attention to detail make this National Historic Landmark resort a delightful destination.

• Explore a dazzling array of recreational activities, including golf, tennis, horseback riding, carriage rides, fly-fishing, shooting sports, hiking, mountain biking, falconry lessons.

• For a quieter pastime, try traditional afternoon tea or shopping in the many fine boutiques.

grand dame of resorts, but the Homestead had humble beginnings. Founded in 1766, the first building, a tiny inn, was constructed to accommodate the stream of prominent visitors—Thomas Jefferson among them—who traveled to Virginia's hot springs nearby in search of healing, pleasure, and social activity. The resort acquired several of the hot springs, and it remained primarily a health facility until 1892, when it was expanded to include one of the first European-style spas in America, a golf course, tennis courts, and other recreational facilities.

Today, the Homestead continues to lead the way in luxury and innovation while maintaining its elegant southern tradition. Guests can enjoy horse-drawn carriage rides through the

mountains, go horseback riding, relax in the original yet fully modern European bath and spa—or play golf on one of three award-winning courses.

The resort's finest course is the Cascades, one of the nation's premier mountain courses. Well-known for its long, narrow fairways, fast greens, and twelve breathtaking waterfalls, the Cascades is host to numerous national tournaments. It is a superior course, but one accessible to all players. Golfers will also enjoy the Old Course. Originally built as a six-hole course in 1892, it expanded in 1913 to eighteen holes. The Old Course's number-one tee is the nation's oldest tee still in continuous use.

Only one thing may rival golf at the Homestead—dining. The resort specializes in "white-linen dining," and has one of the best

ACCLAIMED MOUNTAIN COURSE

Beginning with the 1928 U.S. Women's Amateur, the acclaimed

Cascades course has hosted six USGA Championships and

consistently ranks among the top fifty courses in America.

GOLFING

THE HOMESTEAD

CASCADES COURSE
Architect: William Flynn
Tour stops: 2000 U.S. Mid-
Amateur Championship
Par: 70
Kentucky bluegrass fairways,
bentgrass greens
Yardage/Rating/Slope:
Blue tees
6,679/73.0/137
White tees
6,256/70.8/131
Red tees
4,967/70.3*/124*

OLD COURSE
Architect: Donald Ross
Par: 72
Kentucky bluegrass fairways,
bentgrass greens
Yardage/Rating/Slope:
Blue tees
6,211/69.0/129
White tees
5,796/66.9/125
Red tees
4,852/67.7*/116*

LOWER CASCADES COURSE
Architect: Robert Trent Jones, Sr.
Tour stops: American Junior Golf
Association ClubCorp
Championship
Par: 72
Kentucky bluegrass fairways,
bentgrass greens
Yardage/Rating/Slope:
Blue tees
6,579/72.2/127
White tees
6,200/70.4/124
Red tees
4,686/66.2*/110*
*Women's ratings

NATIONAL TREASURE

Stepping right from the

pages of colonial America,

the Homestead boasts a

golf course with the oldest

tee in continuous use

in the U.S.

THE GREENBRIER

Two hundred years of outstanding service and amenities have made this historic Allegheny Mountain estate a favorite destination for generations of families.

• Relax and rejuvenate amid beautiful accommodations ranging from well-appointed guest rooms to luxurious suites and guest houses that pamper your most demanding tastes.

• With more than fifty activities to choose from, you can try something different every day, from fly-fishing, falconry, and skeet or trap shooting to white-water rafting and horseback riding.

• Relax your mind, tone your body, and revitalize your spirit in the Greenbrier Spa and Mineral Baths, where the temperature is set to your preference and tubs are filled with Alvon Springs mineral water or the sulphur waters of White Sulphur Springs.

• Experience time-honored traditions like afternoon tea and concerts in the upper lobby or a wild night of dancing at Slammin' Sammy's or the Old White Club.

A MAGICAL DESTINATION

For more than eighty years, royalty, celebrities, and people from all walks of life have come to play golf at the Greenbrier, resting serenely at the base of the Allegheny Mountains.

wine lists in the world. At the Homestead, the emphasis is on quality: Only three chefs have served guests since the turn of the century, and each day, the best ingredients are flown in from all over the world. Guests can choose from twelve restaurants.

Just over the state line in West Virginia, another old-style spa and golf resort awaits. For guests who wish to be pampered, there's no better place than the Greenbrier, located in White Sulphur Springs. There, the hotel staff always outnumbers guests, ensuring that every need is quickly met and every question answered. The Greenbrier's commitment to excellence and outstanding guest service have earned it the coveted Mobil Five-Star and AAA Five Diamond awards—distinguishing it as one of the world's premier resorts.

Designated as a National Historic Landmark, the resort was first founded as a spa on the site of the famous White Sulphur Springs, where centuries ago, visitors came to relax in the soothing sulphur waters. Today, the renowned Greenbrier Spa continues in its tradition of hydrotherapy, offering seventeen different sulphur and mineral treatments that promise to soothe and revitalize. Guests will relish lounging by the indoor Olympic-sized pool in the Rhododendron Lounge after a bath and massage, or lingering in the sauna or whirlpool. For the visitor whose primary concern is health, the resort even offers the Greenbrier Clinic, a medical diagnostic facility that provides guests a complete health evaluation.

Once rejuvenated, guests can enjoy an array of activities offered at the resort—and none is as popular as golf. The resort has three championship courses. The Old White Course opened in 1913 and is modeled after well-known Scottish holes, offering golfers an experience imbued with a sense of tradition. The newly redesigned Meadows Course is both challenging and beautiful, but the Greenbrier Course is the resort's finest. With its sweeping views of the Allegheny Mountains, the Greenbrier remains the only course in the world to have hosted both the Ryder and Solheim Cup matches.

At Greenbrier, however, it's not just about enjoying the game—guests are encouraged to improve it as well. The Greenbrier Sam Snead Golf Academy was founded to help golfers develop the combined techniques of legend Sam Snead, the resort's golf professional emeritus, with the John Jacobs Golf Group's highly regarded system of instruction.

Golfing isn't the only area in which guests can learn at the Greenbrier. The resort, renowned for its sumptuous American cuisine, also offers gourmet-cooking classes, taught by Greenbrier chefs, for those who hope to replicate the restaurant's meals at home. The classes teach guests how to cook in a professional kitchen, and even offer pointers on menu planning and entertaining.

"Bring your air game: there's not much roll on the soft bentgrass fairways, though the Old White course may be played with run-up shots to the greens."

—ROBERT HARRIS, HEAD GOLF PROFESSIONAL AND DIRECTOR OF GOLF, THE GREENBRIER

THE GREENBRIER

WHITE SULPHUR SPRINGS, WEST VIRGINIA

RESORT RATING:	
CHALLENGE	★★★★
BEAUTY	★★★★
LODGING	★★★★
CUISINE	★★★★
AMENITIES	★★★★

PLAY HARD, THEN RETREAT
Golf at the Greenbrier can be so consumingly challenging that the only way to wind down from the thrill is to soak in a tub of steaming, effervescent water from the nearby sulphur springs.

THE GREENBRIER
WHITE SULPHUR SPRINGS, WEST VIRGINIA

THE GREENBRIER COURSE
Architect: Jack Nicklaus
Tour stops: 1979 Ryder Cup,
1994 Solheim Cup
Par: 72
Bentgrass fairways and greens
Yardage/Rating/Slope:
Gold tees
6,675/73.1/135
Blue tees
6,377/71.7/134
White tees
6,031/69.1, 75.5*/121, 136*
Red tees
5,095/70.3*/120*

MEADOWS COURSE
Architect: Bob Cupp
Par: 71
Bentgrass fairways and greens
Yardage/Rating/Slope:
Gold tees
6,807/73.3/130
Blue tees
6,420/70.5/122
White tees
5,829/67.8, 73.4*/122, 128*
Red tees
5,001/68.0*/111*

OLD WHITE COURSE
Architect: C. B. Macdonald
Par: 70
Bentgrass fairways and greens
Yardage/Rating/Slope:
Gold tees
6,652/72.1/130
Blue tees
6,365/70.7/127
White tees
6,033/69.1, 74.4*/124, 129*
Red tees
5,179/69.7*/119*
*Women's ratings

VYING FOR THE TITLE

Greenbrier's trio of courses

strive to outdo each other

in playability and show-

stopping views of

the Alleghenies.

Much as they may enjoy cooking, however, most guests on vacation would rather enjoy a Greenbrier meal than cook one. Greenbrier presents a variety of experiences in fine dining. Along with its regular menu, the resort now offers light fare, so guests can enjoy their meals without ruining their diets. For those who want to splurge, though, the Gold Service Dinner, known as the epitome of fine dining, is the way to do it. At the Greenbrier, dining is always an event.

The ultimate in golf resort history and tradition resides at Pinehurst Resort, the southern golf mecca that's at the top of the wish list for many golf travelers. And for good reason: At Pinehurst, golf reigns supreme.

Pinehurst was originally created as a winter health retreat for turn-of-the-century vacationers. Today, a whopping eight golf courses provide variety and challenge to resort guests. Pinehurst's premier course, Pinehurst Number 2, is what every experienced golfer wants to play. Maddening frustration tinged with awe invariably comes over golfers who've been able to get onto the course. Although number 2, where the 1999 U.S. Open was played, has no water hazards, and its trees don't exactly encroach en masse on the fairways, it's incredibly difficult to get a low score on this classic course. That's because the wacky undulations and masterfully placed bunkers keep golfers on their toes.

But just setting foot on the hallowed ground of Pinehurst somehow elevates one's play. Passing the famous "Putter Boy" sundial on the way to the putting greens, visitors start to feel a part of history. The architecture of the place reinforces the thrill. The Carolina, a Victorian hotel that is the most dominant structure on the resort grounds, has a charming grace that transports guests to that idyllic time when holiday stays would be measured in months rather than days.

Inside the Carolina, guests are treated to efficient if understated service. Although the hotel was built around the turn of the last century, all its rooms have been recently renovated. The Holly Inn is the resort's oldest hotel, and recently underwent a restoration that has beautifully melded its arts-and-crafts roots with modern amenities. The resort grounds were designed by famed landscape architect Frederick Law Olmsted (designer of New York's Central Park). The Holly Inn plays off the refined version of nature Olmsted succeeded in creating: Natural wood abounds, and a delicate floral motif echoes the outdoors. Although Pinehurst does not yet have a spa (one is slated to open in early 2002), the Holly Inn's interiors and Pinehurst's rambling grounds work wonders to relieve stress.

Pinehurst's fabulous cuisine can also facilitate an escape from the trials of off-resort life. The Holly Inn serves a fine high tea. The standard finger sandwiches, petits fours, and, of course, tea are augmented by some pretty wonderful scones on weekends.

"The surfaces tend to be fairly firm, but the yardage plays just a little longer. That could be associated with lack of elevation. Just take plenty of club."
—LEW FERGUSON, HEAD GOLF PROFESSIONAL, PINEHURST RESORT AND COUNTRY CLUB

PINEHURST, NORTH CAROLINA

PINEHURST RESORT

RESORT RATING:	
CHALLENGE	★★★★★
BEAUTY	★★★★⯪
LODGING	★★★★
CUISINE	★★★★
AMENITIES	★★★★

A RICH TRADITION

Pinehurst's history bears the imprint of some of golfing's greats, including Donald Ross. A statue honors the legendary designer responsible for three of Pinehurst's eight courses.

NATIONAL HISTORIC LANDMARK

The stately Carolina has welcomed visitors to Pinehurst

since 1901. Golfers pass the famous Putter Boy

statue on their way to the putting greens.

PINEHURST RESORT
PINEHURST COUNTRY CLUB
VILLAGE OF PINEHURST, NORTH CAROLINA

COURSE NO. 1

Architect: Donald Ross

Par: 70

Bermuda/rye fairways,
G2 bentgrass greens

Yardage/Rating/Slope:

Blue tees

6,128/69.4/116

White tees

5,857/68.0/115

Red tees

5,297/70.5/117

COURSE NO. 2

Architect: Donald Ross

Tour stops: 1999 and 2004 U.S.
Open Championships

Par: 72

Bermuda/rye fairways,
G2 bentgrass greens

Yardage/Rating/Slope:

Blue tees

6,869/74.1/133

White tees

6,337/71.5/129

Red tees

5,825/74.6/130

COURSE NO. 3

Architect: Donald Ross

Par: 70

Bermuda/rye fairways,
bentgrass greens

Yardage/Rating/Slope:

White tees

5,682/67.2/115

Red tees

5,232/69.9/117

COURSE NO. 4

Architect: Tom Fazio

Par: 72

Bermuda/rye fairways,
G2 bentgrass greens

Yardage/Rating/Slope:

Blue tees

6,658/72.1/130

White tees

6,214/70.4/125

Green tees

5,677/67.8/115

Red tees

5,217/70.6/123

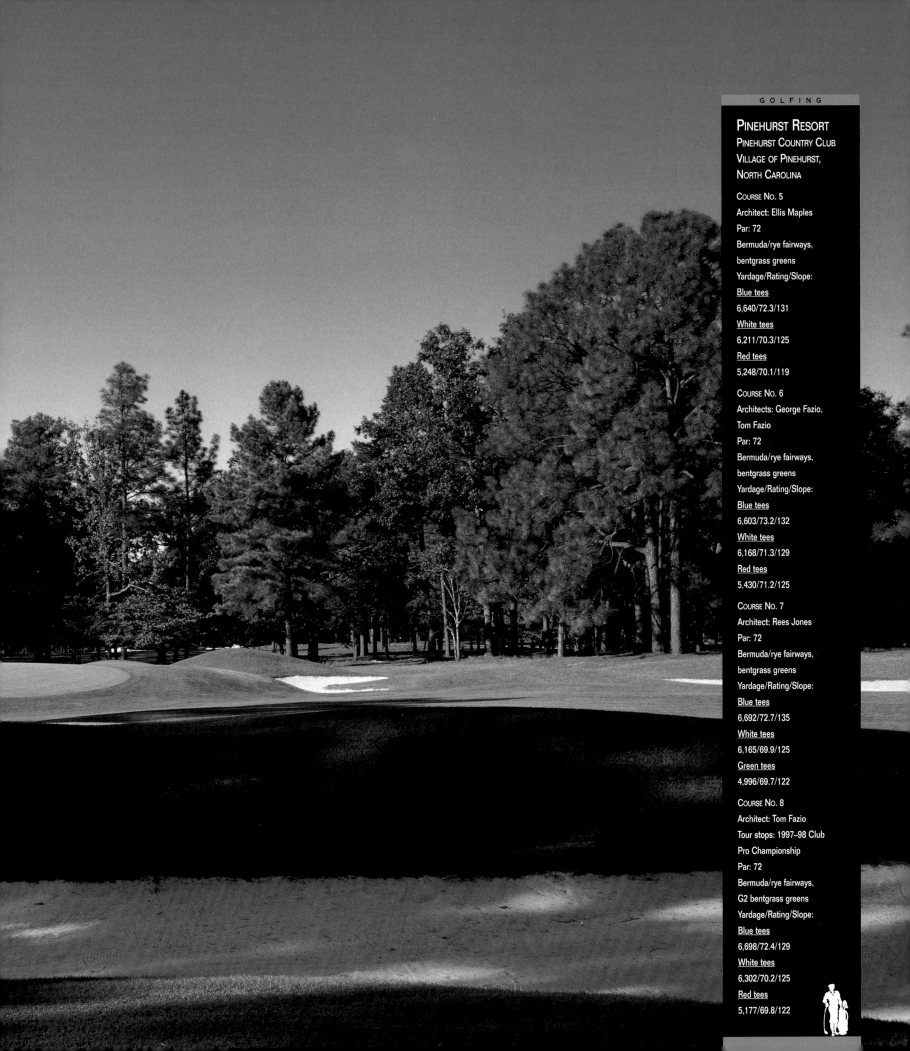

PINEHURST RESORT
PINEHURST COUNTRY CLUB
VILLAGE OF PINEHURST,
NORTH CAROLINA

COURSE NO. 5
Architect: Ellis Maples
Par: 72
Bermuda/rye fairways,
bentgrass greens
Yardage/Rating/Slope:
Blue tees
6,640/72.3/131
White tees
6,211/70.3/125
Red tees
5,248/70.1/119

COURSE NO. 6
Architects: George Fazio,
Tom Fazio
Par: 72
Bermuda/rye fairways,
bentgrass greens
Yardage/Rating/Slope:
Blue tees
6,603/73.2/132
White tees
6,168/71.3/129
Red tees
5,430/71.2/125

COURSE NO. 7
Architect: Rees Jones
Par: 72
Bermuda/rye fairways,
bentgrass greens
Yardage/Rating/Slope:
Blue tees
6,692/72.7/135
White tees
6,165/69.9/125
Green tees
4,996/69.7/122

COURSE NO. 8
Architect: Tom Fazio
Tour stops: 1997–98 Club
Pro Championship
Par: 72
Bermuda/rye fairways,
G2 bentgrass greens
Yardage/Rating/Slope:
Blue tees
6,698/72.4/129
White tees
6,302/70.2/125
Red tees
5,177/69.8/122

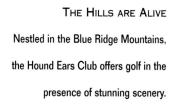

THE HILLS ARE ALIVE

Nestled in the Blue Ridge Mountains, the Hound Ears Club offers golf in the presence of stunning scenery.

GOLFING

HOUND EARS CLUB

Architects: George Cobb, Tom Jackson
Par: 72
Bluegrass fairways, bentgrass greens
Yardage/Rating/Slope:

Gold tees
6,327/70.1/127

Blue tees
6,165/69.1/125

White tees
5,639/66.8/113

Red tees
4,959/68.5/119

LIKE COMING HOME

Visitors who venture to the exclusive Hound Ears Club year after year find that coming up the drive to this isolated resort brings on a sense of calm and comfort.

The Holly Inn's Tavern offers a more total escape: The cozy restaurant has a fireplace, hand-carved bar, and warming bistro fare, just what you'd want if you were coming off the links in Scotland.

For golfers who like to feel secluded from the outside world, the small, almost isolated retreat Hound Ears Club is an ideal destination. Perched high in the Blue Ridge Mountains near the town of Blowing Rock, North Carolina, Hound Ears has just twenty-eight rooms for guests who come to golf, play tennis, hike the resort's seven hundred acres, or just relax with a book and good view.

Views of lush azalea-splashed grounds give the resort a timeless beauty. The require-

"Hitting driver on some of the par-fours is not always the best option; on some holes, the further you hit, the more narrow the fairways become."

—PETER RUCKER, HEAD GOLF PROFESSIONAL, HOUND EARS CLUB

HOUND EARS CLUB

RESORT RATING:

CHALLENGE	★★★⯪
BEAUTY	★★★★⯪
LODGING	★★★⯪
CUISINE	★★★⯪
AMENITIES	★★★⯪

BLOWING ROCK, NORTH CAROLINA

ment that guests dress for dinner speaks to a more refined era. But the Hound Ears feature that really recalls a different time is the natural grotto that serves as the resort pool. A short walk away from the lodge, the grotto evokes idealized memories of carefree childhood. Some guests might even make believe that the wildflower-draped grotto is their own discovery.

There's only a bit less to discover on the resort's golf course. The course is light on cross hazards and elevation changes, but heavy on scenery. The fifteenth hole is undoubtedly the most beautiful; it has a Garden of Eden aspect to it, with loads of flowering bushes and waterfalls. The Watauga River borders holes 2 and 11, making for a picturesque though not very threatening hazard.

EXPERIENCING

HOUND EARS CLUB

Named for a unique rock formation high above the club, Hound Ears offers a small, intimate setting in the tradition of the finest private clubs.

• Awake in the morning to find a newspaper at your door; return in the evening to find your bed turned down and a Belgian chocolate on your pillow.

• Relax in the secluded pool, nestled in a natural grotto where wildflowers cascade over the rocks and a large, cool pavilion opens to the breeze.

• Explore the beauty and tranquility of western North Carolina's Blue Ridge Mountains.

• Visit the nearby village of Blowing Rock for some wonderfully unique shopping.

RESORT RATING:

CHALLENGE	★★★★
BEAUTY	★★★★
LODGING	★★★½
CUISINE	★★★½
AMENITIES	★★★★

TREACHEROUS DUNES

Natural sand dunes come into play on the last two holes of the Links Course, both of which lie alongside the Atlantic. The par-four number 17, below, runs 405 yards from the back tees.

Dinner is a much-anticipated event at Hound Ears. Although the club is one of the few places where veal Oscar can still be found, the rainbow trout with almonds and brown butter and the grilled lamb chops are also favorites here. Finishing off the meal with the specialty dessert, ice cream pie (more like a baked Alaska), makes for a very satisfying ending to any day.

Charleston, South Carolina, is a great year-round golf destination. Wonderfully preserved and restored antebellum homes, a rich cultural history, and a nearly constant spate of interesting festivals make this charming old city a delightful one to visit.

CHARLESTON, SOUTH CAROLINA

WILD DUNES RESORT

Charleston is an easy side trip from the Wild Dunes Resort, a beachfront escape that is a great family destination.

The Boardwalk Inn is the centerpiece of Wild Dunes' accommodations. Sophisticated but by no means stuffy, the guest rooms and suites are a great home base for the activity-filled days that a stay at the resort demands. Wild Dunes provides a mind-blowing menu of activities from which to choose: A terrific tennis program, spa treatments, and a lively and varied fitness program can certainly compete for a golfer's time.

But don't miss out on a classic seaside golfing experience. Both the Links and Harbor courses have a coastal feel to them. While the Links Course fronts the Atlantic Ocean, the Harbor Course takes advantage of marshes, lagoons, and a bit of the Intracoastal Waterway.

SEASIDE ACCOMMODATIONS

Beautifully appointed rooms and suites are found

in the Boardwalk Inn, the adjacent Boardwalk

Villas, and an assortment of exclusive homes.

GOLFING

WILD DUNES RESORT

LINKS COURSE
Architect: Tom Fazio
Par: 72
Bermuda fairways and greens
Yardage/Rating/Slope:
Blue tees
6,722/73.1/132
White tees
6,131/69.7/125
Gold tees
5,359/66.4/114
Red tees
4,849/69.1/121

HARBOR COURSE
Architect: Tom Fazio
Par: 70
Bermuda fairways and greens
Yardage/Rating/Slope:
Blue tees
6,446/70.9/124
White tees
5,900/68.2/117
Gold tees
5,140/65.0/110
Red tees
4,774/68.1/117

THE SWING YOU BRING
Small classes of no more
than six students and a
three-to-one player-to-
instructor ratio make the
golf schools at Wild Dunes
a uniquely personalized
experience. Each school
day includes four to six
hours of instruction and
a complimentary
round of golf.

WILD DUNES RESORT
CHARLESTON, SOUTH CAROLINA

Whether you prefer relaxing in a beach chair or pursuing more vigorous activities, Wild Dunes offers just what you want.

• Experience classic Charleston elegance at the Boardwalk Inn, or enjoy the privacy and luxury of a spacious furnished villa or private home.

• Stroll along miles of white-sand beach, relax by the pool, or join a water workout class for exercise that feels refreshing.

• Visit nearby Charleston, with its delightful shops, venerable Old Market, and the Battery, an intriguing neighborhood of cobblestone streets, antebellum homes, and elegant gardens.

• Get out on the dance floor and learn South Carolina's official dance step, the Shag.

Sample a wide variety of dining venues, from fine dining to a café setting.

A GRAND LOCATION

The Grand Pavilion doubles as a nightspot for quiet dinners at Duney's Beach Bar and Café, or romantic walks along the beach.

OUT FOR A SPIN

Wild Dunes lends bikes to visitors who want to check out the charming neighborhoods that border the resort.

SAND SCULPTING

With its Kid's Camps and Wild Adventure Club, Wild Dunes welcomes families with an extensive menu of recreational activities, classes, and programs.

"This is a placement-type golf course with a lot of mounding, and the greens are shaped in a Donald Ross style. Due to the windy conditions and mounding that we have, . . .

RESORT RATING:

CHALLENGE ★★★★⯪

BEAUTY ★★★★

LODGING ★★★★

CUISINE ★★★

AMENITIES ★★★★

KIAWAH ISLAND, SOUTH CAROLINA

KIAWAH ISLAND

GOLF AND TENNIS RESORT

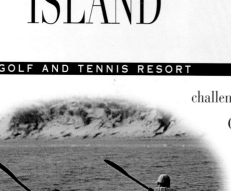

the course has been compared to links-style courses but is not built on links land."

—Mike Arthur, Head Golf
Professional, Oak Point Course

Siren Song

From nearly every point on this island retreat, the Atlantic Ocean demands rapt attention. Golfers pause in mid-swing, lovers retreat to the balcony, and adventurers board kayaks in response to its pull.

The Links Course challenges golfers with enormous, humpbacked sand dunes but goes easy on tight fairways. Golfers who lose their cool when they are dealing with water hazards should work on their visualization skills before heading to the Harbor Course: water comes into play on nearly every hole.

Soufflés at the Boardwalk Inn's Grill are a surprisingly satisfying meal after a round of golf—and they're the restaurant's specialty. A soak in any of the resort's twenty-odd pools or a more adventurous attempt at Wild Dune's other water sports (the banana boat rides are a blast) makes for interesting non-golf pursuits.

Situated over on the southern side of Charleston, Kiawah Island Golf and Tennis Resort offers the gift of getting away from it all within an easy drive of the vibrant, historic city. It is strange how the experience of staying on an island—even one separated from the mainland only by rivers—can make one truly leave all cares behind.

The resort lies along ten miles of pristine beach bordered by the Atlantic Ocean. Most of the development is contained to the west end of the island, leaving room for guests to ramble and nature to continue to flourish. Kiawah boasts almost two hundred species of birds plus dozens of different reptiles, amphibians, and mammals. It's imperative that at least one morning of a vacation on Kiawah be spent bird-watching along the near-empty stretches of pristine beach.

But that's not to downplay the resort's fabulous golf offerings. Kiawah features ninety holes of remarkable challenges. The famed Ocean Course opened in time for the 1991 Ryder Cup and earned fame for the dramatic ending of the "War by the Shore," where the Americans narrowly eked out a victory. But the panoramic views offered by the Ocean Course could not have been appreciated by those who first saw the course on television. Osprey Point has four large natural lakes, fingers of saltwater marsh, and dense maritime forests. And with three dramatic holes woven through rolling sand dunes directly along the ocean, Turtle Point requires golfers to be accurate as well as hit long. Kiawah's Cougar Point is a good course for beginning players, kissing the Kiawah River and expanses of tidal marsh. Oak Point is the most recent addition to the resort's golf line-up. Described by the resort as a Scottish-American-style course, Oak Point features the classic undulations that echo the windswept isles.

The oceanfront Kiawah Island Inn is close to the island action, but allows visitors to sink into the slow pace encouraged by that famed regional currency, Southern hospitality. The relatively new Charleston Bar is a great place to duck into to escape the sun. Its woodwork and marble-topped bar echo a more refined time, and make one wonder why the cocktail hour is a lost institution. Upstairs, rooms are pleasant enough and the amenities are definitely abundant. Views on either side of the Inn—ocean or marsh—are calming.

KIAWAH ISLAND GOLF AND TENNIS RESORT

TURTLE POINT COURSE
Architect: Jack Nicklaus
Tour stops: 1990 PGA Cup
Matches
Par: 72
419 Bermuda fairways,
TifEagle greens
Yardage/Rating/Slope:
<u>Gold tees</u>
7,054/74.0/142
<u>Blue tees</u>
6,615/71.8/134
<u>White tees</u>
6,159/69.1/125
<u>Red tees</u>
5,210/71.1/126

OSPREY POINT COURSE
Architect: Tom Fazio
Tour stops: 2000 Eastern Club
Professionals Championship
Par: 72
Bermuda fairways and greens
Yardage/Rating/Slope:
<u>Gold tees</u>
6,871/72.9/137
<u>Blue tees</u>
6,522/71.0/128
<u>White tees</u>
6,089/68.8/119
<u>Green tees</u>
5,593/66.7, 73.2*/112, 130*
<u>Red tees</u>
5,023/70.0/121
*Women's ratings

TAMED BY THE TURTLE

After meeting the challenge
at the Turtle Point Course,
Kiawah Island resort
guests often find that
some relaxation
is in order.

KIAWAH ISLAND GOLF AND TENNIS RESORT
KIAWAH ISLAND,
SOUTH CAROLINA

OAK POINT COURSE
Architect: Clyde Johnston
Par: 72
Bermuda/rye fairways and greens
Yardage/Rating/Slope:
Gold tees
6,759/73.8/140
Blue tees
6,468/72.3/135
White tees
5,952/69.8/127
Red tees
4,956/69.8/121

COUGAR POINT COURSE
Architect: Gary Player
Par: 72
Bermuda fairways,
tifdwarf Bermuda greens
Yardage/Rating/Slope:
Gold tees
6,875/73.0/134
Blue tees
6,523/70.9/130
White tees
6,090/68.5/119
Green tees
5,604/66.3, 71.6*/112, 126*
Red tees
4,776/67.6/118
*Women's ratings

OCEAN COURSE
Architect: Pete Dye
Tour stops: 1991 Ryder Cup
Matches, 1997 World Cup of Golf
Par: 72
Bermuda fairways and greens
Yardage/Rating/Slope:
Gold tees
7,296/78.0/152
Blue tees
6,552/74.5/142
White tees
6,031/71.9/134
Red tees
5,327/72.9/133

AT THE WATER'S EDGE

The Ocean Course is

Kiawah's most

challenging.

"Wind is the key factor on the Ocean Course. It's got a reputation for being a difficult course, but if you get on the right tees, it's very playable. Rather than playing one set of tees the whole way around, an option would be to play the white tees against the wind and the blue tees downwind."

—BRIAN GERARD, HEAD GOLF PROFESSIONAL, OCEAN COURSE

TINY TOTS AND JUNIOR CAMPS

Kiawah's tennis program is one of the country's most highly acclaimed, with a wide range of programs for every member of the family.

KIAWAH ISLAND GOLF AND TENNIS RESORT

On this inviting tropical island resort, quiet, privacy, endless beaches, and recreational opportunities abound.

• Stay in a lavish oceanfront home with private dock and miles of deck, a handsomely appointed villa mere steps from the first tee, or a room at the Inn, where service is abundant.

• Take advantage of the on-demand, on-island courtesy transportation available to all guests at all times.

• With two tennis complexes and a total of twenty-eight clay, Hard Tru, and hard courts, enjoy exceptional tennis and a wide range of programs, clinics, and private instruction.

• Walk or cycle along ten uninterrupted miles of wide, immaculate ocean beach, or hike, canoe, or bicycle through forest and marshes on your own or with a professional naturalist.

• Feast on exquisitely prepared and presented native foods complemented by the perfect wine or beverage and accompanied by the soft sounds of the tropics.

SILENT SHORELINE

Kiawah Island has miles of near-empty stretches of beaches and wetlands. It's the perfect setting for early-morning bird-watching.

"Planter's Row, our toughest course, is tight and tree-lined, with relatively flat greens and water hazards coming into play."

—JIM WILLIAMS, HEAD GOLF
PROFESSIONAL, PORT ROYAL GOLF CLUB

RESORT RATING:

CHALLENGE	★★★⯪
BEAUTY	★★★⯪
LODGING	★★★★
CUISINE	★★★⯪
AMENITIES	★★★★

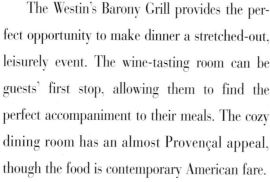

WESTIN RESORT, HILTON HEAD

HILTON HEAD ISLAND, SOUTH CAROLINA

EXPERIENCING

WESTIN RESORT, HILTON HEAD

Reminiscent of the grand turn-of-the-century hotels, the Westin Resort blends gracious hospitality with an abundance of exciting activities.

• Sample a variety of activities, from sporting events and unique shopping to galleries and live theater.

• Visit the Port Royal Golf and Racquet Club for a fully equipped health club.

Hilton Head Island is one of the few truly legendary golf spots in the country. There are seventeen courses to choose from—just on the island proper—so Hilton Head is the perfect place to buckle down and golf a lot. It's less perfect, though, for travelers seeking seclusion: things can get pretty jam-packed.

One of the resorts that do provide a measure of solitude is the Westin Resort. Placed in a twenty-four-acre pocket of preserved land, the Westin Resort offers that seaside resort experience that so many vacationers are seeking. Water sports, tennis, and golf provide diversion. Private balconies, a twelve-mile stretch of beach, and a homey, light interior atmosphere offer the opportunity for reflection.

The Westin's Barony Grill provides the perfect opportunity to make dinner a stretched-out, leisurely event. The wine-tasting room can be guests' first stop, allowing them to find the perfect accompaniment to their meals. The cozy dining room has an almost Provençal appeal, though the food is contemporary American fare.

The Port Royal Golf Club is just steps from the hotel, and offers fifty-four holes for a variety of challenges. The Barony Course's greens are so well protected that strength takes a back seat to accuracy. The Planter's Row is the perfect course for golfers to show off their short game: Pete Dye, who redesigned this course in 1994, gave the greens a heavy dose of undulation.

When guests first arrive at Sea Pines on Hilton Head Island, they may wonder if they're in the right place. Why? The resort is truly like no other.

SURROUNDED BY WATER

The Westin Resort, Hilton Head's

landscape design echoes its setting:

Water abounds everywhere one looks.

GOLFING

WESTIN RESORT, HILTON HEAD
PORT ROYAL GOLF CLUB

BARONY COURSE
Architect: George Cobb
Par: 72
Bermuda fairways and greens
Yardage/Rating/Slope:
Championship tees
6,543/71.6, 79.4*/139, 148*
Back tees
6,223/70.1, 76.2*/126, 135*
Middle tees
5,964/69.0, 75.4*/122, 132*
Forward tees
5,138/65.2, 70.7*/115, 120*

PLANTER'S ROW COURSE
Architect: William Byrd
Par: 72
Bermuda fairways and greens
Yardage/Rating/Slope:
Championship tees
6,625/72.1, 79.0*/139, 149*
Back tees
6,284/70.4, 76.5*/133, 140*
Middle tees
5,920/68.7, 75.0*/129, 134*
Forward tees
5,119/64.6, 72.0*/118, 124*

ROBBER'S ROW COURSE
Architect: Pete Dye
Par: 72
Bermuda fairways and greens
Yardage/Rating/Slope:
Championship tees
6,675/73.2, 79.8*/134, 142*
Back tees
6,329/71.4, 77.4*/129, 136*
Middle tees
6,017/70.3, 75.9*/124, 133*
Forward tees
4,902/63.9, 70.4*/114, 120*
*Women's ratings

DOCKED PLAY

Though it is surprising to

some guests, the fairway-

dense Hilton Head Island

does draw visitors for

activities other

than golf.

SEA PINES

HARBOUR TOWN GOLF LINKS
Architects: Pete Dye, Jack
Nicklaus
Tour stops: MCI Classic, The
Heritage of Golf
Par: 71
Bermuda fairways,
tif-Eagle Bermuda greens
Yardage/Rating/Slope:
<u>Heritage tees</u>
6,900/74.0/136
<u>Men's tees</u>
6,119/70.0/126
<u>Ladies' tees</u>
5,019/69.0/117

OCEAN COURSE
Architect: George Cobb,
renovated by Mark McCumber
Par: 72
Bermuda fairways and greens
Yardage/Rating/Slope:
<u>McCumber tees</u>
6,906/72.8/133
<u>Championship tees</u>
6,493/71.4/130
<u>White tees</u>
6,172/69.7/125
<u>Ladies' tees</u>
5,325/65.6/115

SEA MARSH COURSE
Architect: George Cobb,
renovated by Clyde Johnston
Par: 72
Bermuda fairways and greens
Yardage/Rating/Slope:
<u>Championship tees</u>
6,515/70.0/120
<u>Men's tees</u>
6,169/69.0/117
<u>Ladies' tees</u>
5,054/69.8/123

SECLUSION

The Hardwood Villas at Sea Pine offer a more private lodging experience. Sprinkled along the tip of the island, an assortment of guest villas offers endless choices in size, location, and amenities.

A MODERN LOOK FOR A CLASSIC COURSE

All three Sea Pines golf courses were built and opened in the 1960s, but the classic Ocean Course was renovated in 1995, enhancing its appeal among modern players. Mark McCumber's updates are showcased on the picturesque fifteenth hole.

KITE FLYING AND CRAB CATCHING

While golf and tennis keep the "big kids" busy, there's something special for the little ones, too: a Fun for Kids! program of entertainment, activities, and special events.

Instead of glittering high-rise hotels there are elegant low- to mid-rise villas nestled discreetly into the low-country landscape. Instead of paved beaches with commercial boardwalks and shorefront bars there are unspoiled sands, dotted only with footprints and wildlife. Farther inland, visitors won't see streetlights or even curbs, but tropical palm trees, towering pines, the occasional fairway—and maybe even an alligator, sunning itself in a marsh.

Outdoor enthusiasts will find Sea Pines their perfect vacation playground, as they indulge in everything from water sports to ecotours. Most guests, however, come for the award-winning tennis and championship golf. The resort features twenty-three tennis courts and a top-

"Harbour Town is a classic shot-maker's course requiring every shot in the bag. If your game has a weakness, it will be exposed."

—JOHN FARRELL, HEAD GOLF PROFESSIONAL, SEA PINES RESORT

SEA PINES

HILTON HEAD ISLAND, SOUTH CAROLINA

RESORT RATING:

CHALLENGE	★★★★
BEAUTY	★★★★
LODGING	★★★½
CUISINE	★★★½
AMENITIES	★★★★

notch tennis academy. The Sea Pines Racquet Club, run by tennis great Stan Smith, has been the proud host of the Family Circle Cup since 1972.

Tennis may be rivaled only by golf at Sea Pines. Since its first course was built in 1960, the resort—which now boasts three championship courses and a renowned golf academy—has become a golfing mecca. Its most famous course, Harbour Town Golf Links, opened in 1969 for the inaugural Heritage Golf Classic (now the MCI Classic, The Heritage of Golf), and has hosted the event ever since. Modeled after old Scottish courses, Harbour Town is known for requiring perfectly positioned shots.

At the end of the day, guests will look forward to unwinding in the community's quiet, luxurious accommodations. Options range from one-bedroom villas to private houses with backyard swimming pools. Whether overlooking the fairways, ocean, marshes, or forest preserve, the accommodations at Sea Pines will make every guest feel at home.

EXPERIENCING

SEA PINES

Whatever you want to do, whenever you want to do it, Sea Pines offers seemingly endless ways to have a good time.

• Take in the quiet pleasures of kayaking down a marsh-lined creek or catching crabs on an ebb tide.
• Stroll along the docks and breathe in the fresh salt air of South Beach, patterned after a quaint New England fishing village and the place to go for fresh seafood and charming shops.
• Play tennis where the pros play, on courts that have hosted the Family Circle Cup tennis tournament since 1972.
• Enjoy fabulous feasts of seafood, cool drinks by the harbor, and succulent shrimp cooked just so in the many restaurants and lounges.

"The Château Course is generous off of the tee, with greens that hold the ball really well. Woodlands, on the other hand, is a more scenic course but demands accuracy, . . .

BRASELTON, GEORGIA

CHATEAU ELAN

WINERY AND RESORT

with tree-lined fairways on nearly every hole"

—JEFF SARAZEN, HEAD GOLF PROFESSIONAL, CHÂTEAU ELAN

EXPERIENCING

CHATEAU ELAN WINERY AND RESORT

Originally designed as a winery, this majestic French-style château has grown into a world-class resort with a wide array of amenities and activities.

• Select luxurious accommodations ranging from country French décor at the inn, two- or three-bedroom Petit Château golf villas, or themed rooms and adjacent facilities at the full-service European-style health spa.

• Learn about winemaking, tour the lush vineyards, and taste award-winning wines at Georgia's premier winery.

Those who long for a change of pace, who seek European-style elegance and a day-in-the-country experience, will find Château Elan Winery and Resort as charming as its moniker. Located in the rolling green hills of Braselton, Georgia, just thirty minutes north of Atlanta, the resort has in recent years emerged as the South's premier winery. As the first winery of its kind in the region since Prohibition, its wines have garnered hundreds of national and international awards. And though the wine alone is enough to tempt any connoisseur, Château Elan offers much more: It has expanded since its opening in 1985 to include an inn, two championship golf courses, seven restaurants, a luxurious spa, a residential community, and an equestrian show center.

Guests arriving at Château Elan will immediately be swept away by the sixteenth-century French-style architecture, which includes a pitched roof, wrought iron, and Cornish moldings. The luxurious 272-room inn succeeds in being grand in style and taste—but its understated, muted pastel colors and French-country furnishings keep it from being ostentatious or intimidating.

The centerpiece of the resort is the winery, modeled after an old French-style château. A complimentary wine-tasting tour—which includes a video presentation and a tour of the winemaking facility, cask room, and bottling facility, concluding with a wine tasting—is offered there.

Since 1989, guests have flocked to the resort for a second reason: golf. That year, the award-winning Château golf course was unveiled, testing even the most experienced golfers with its contoured fairways, numerous bunkers, and water hazards. Along with the Château Course, Château Elan boasts the Woodlands Course, a stunning course that skirts water ten times during play; and a nine-hole walking course, perfect for beginners, children, and golfers who don't have time to play a full eighteen holes.

After a rewarding day of golf, Château Elan's acclaimed spa will beckon. The enormous thirty-room structure provides dozens of treatments, including its famed herbal body wrap. Guests who choose this exhilarating, aromatic wrap will feel smooth and soothed—so relaxed, they may want to stay in one of the spa's designated overnight rooms.

More boisterous visitors will gravitate toward one of the resort's real treats: Paddy's Irish Pub. Complete with authentic furnishings, the pub serves authentic Irish food, Irish cheer—and Irish beer, of course. But for those who prefer another type of fare, Château Elan features six other restaurants that offer everything from fine French cuisine to an American grill.

With all the fine dining and other amenities, guests won't want to leave. But when they must, they can always take a part of the resort with them to savor—a bottle of red, white, or blush wine.

CALLAWAY GARDENS

MOUNTAIN VIEW COURSE

Architect: Dick Wilson

Tour stops: PGA Buick
Challenge

Par: 72

Bermuda fairways and greens

Yardage/Rating/Slope:

Championship tees
7,057/73.9/136

Regular tees
6,630/72.1/129

Ladies' tees
5,848/74.3/131

LAKE VIEW COURSE

Architects: J. B. McGovern,
Dick Wilson

Par: 70

Bermuda fairways and greens

Yardage/Rating/Slope:

Regular tees
6,051/68.6/123

Ladies' tees
5,347/71.1/121

GARDENS VIEW COURSE

Architect: Joe Lee

Par: 72

Bermuda fairways and greens

Yardage/Rating/Slope:

Championship tees
6,392/70.7/121

Regular tees
6,108/69.2/117

Ladies' tees
5,848/72.7/123

SKY HIGH

A hot-air balloon festival brightens

the skies over Callaway Gardens

every Labor Day weekend.

HAVEN FOR WILDLIFE

Renowned for a commitment to horticulture and the environment, Callaway

Resort expands its efforts beyond the gardens. The eighteen-hole golf

courses feature the use of bluebird houses near the 150-yard markers.

FEATHERED FRIENDS

Swans grace the waters around

Callaway Gardens, adding to the

atmosphere of pristine preservation.

Nestled farther south in Pine Mountain, Georgia, only an hour southwest of Atlanta, lies Callaway Gardens, a truly unique family resort. With its acres of gardens, greenhouses, trails, and golfing greens, the casual and cheery resort has something for everyone—especially nature buffs.

Callaway Gardens was founded in 1952 for the purpose of creating a wholesome family environment that offers beauty, relaxation, inspiration, and a better understanding of the living world. One of its most popular features is the educational Cecil B. Day Butterfly Center, a glass-enclosed conservatory that houses more than one thousand free-flying butter-

"Mountain View's tree-lined fairways require accuracy off the tee, setting up mid- to long-iron approaches to small, well-bunkered greens."

—Bud Robison, Head Golf Professional, Callaway Gardens

CALLAWAY GARDENS

PINE MOUNTAIN, GEORGIA

RESORT RATING:	
CHALLENGE	★★★⯪
BEAUTY	★★★★
LODGING	★★★
CUISINE	★★★⯪
AMENITIES	★★★★

flies and hummingbirds.

For a game of golf, Callaway Gardens offers a nine-hole warm-up course and three championship courses. Mountain View, its finest course, hosts the PGA's Buick Challenge each year. Its tight, tree-lined fairways will test even the most experienced player. The resort's original course, Lake View, is known for its nine water holes and the serpentine bridge that crosses Mountain Creek Lake to the fifth hole.

Just like its activities, the resort's dining and accommodations are also family-friendly and relaxed. Guests at Callaway Gardens can choose from seven restaurants featuring everything from hearty buffet and continental-style cuisine to fine dining. Similarly, the accommodations range from comfortable yet elegant rooms to charming country cottages and deluxe mountain villas. At Callaway Gardens, the goal is to please everyone.

The Cloister in Sea Island, Georgia, offers another wonderful family escape. Located along five breathtaking miles of private white-sand beach, this resort aims to please everyone—from the harried young mother to the serious golfer.

EXPERIENCING

CALLAWAY GARDENS

Nestled in the foothills of the Appalachians, Callaway Gardens combines breathtaking gardens and a wide range of sports facilities.

• Stroll through the Cecil B. Day Butterfly Center, a haven of free-flying butterflies and hummingbirds, complete with a cascading waterfall.
• Try tennis, fly-fishing, racquetball, the lakeside jogging and fitness trail, or the state-of-the-art fitness center.
• Join horticulturists, naturalists, and volunteers for ongoing courses, workshops, and demonstrations.

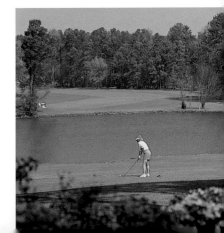

RESORT RATING:

CHALLENGE	★★★★
BEAUTY	★★★★☆
LODGING	★★★★☆
CUISINE	★★★★☆
AMENITIES	★★★★

SEA ISLAND, GEORGIA

THE CLOISTER

SOMETHING IN COMMON

What do golfing and a health spa have in common? At the Cloister, with fifty-four holes and nearly as many spa treatments, both offer exercise, ocean views, and the vacation of a lifetime.

Part of the Cloister's charm lies in its laid-back, accommodating atmosphere: Unlike most other vacation destinations, the resort offers all-inclusive packages that cover accommodations, all meals, use of Beach Club facilities, and many other amenities that can help guests unwind.

For many guests, the best way to begin unwinding is on the golf course. The Cloister boasts the acclaimed Plantation Course, and the Seaside Course at the St. Simons Island Club, adjacent to the hotel and operated by the Cloister. In 1999, the notable Seaside course was reopened after being masterfully blended from two nine-hole courses into one seamless, contemporary eighteen-hole course. Framed by tidal creeks, dunes, and saltmarshes, Seaside was developed in the tradition of Scottish links and is noted for its astonishingly open vistas. The Plantation Course was also recently expanded from two nine-hole courses into one eighteen-hole course, reflecting the resort's effort to boost its already celebrated reputation in the golfing community.

But no vacation at the Cloister would be complete without a session at the Sea Island Spa. The calming, soothing waters of the Atlantic and the brisk salt air have inspired many of the spa's techniques and treatments, including beachside aerobics, organized shoreline walks, and journaling by the sea. The spa emphasizes body and mind, encouraging guests not only to get in shape but also to reflect, meditate, and renew their spirits. To help guests relax, the spa assigns a personal spa concierge to each person who chooses one of the many packages offered, bringing southern hospitality to a whole new level. Upon request, the spa concierge will plan every aspect of the guest's itinerary, from making meal reservations to planning transportation—allowing visitors to fully rejuvenate.

At the Cloister, the daytime might be for relaxation, but the night is for dancing. Dancing is one of the resort's signature activities. Guests of all ages will enjoy twisting and turning to the latest music and old classics alike in one of the many club rooms. For those with two left feet, the Cloister offers private ballroom dance lessons along with a range of special dance programs throughout the year.

Nestled into the marshes and woods of Amelia Island, Florida, is Amelia Island Plantation, a pristine golf paradise that guests will love to share with the many striking species of birds that live there. Here the choices of accommodations—from sumptuous hotel rooms to secluded, spacious villas—and dining is also reflected in the golf itself.

Three exquisitely designed golf courses lie amid the marshes and unspoiled seashore. The entire area is a bird sanctuary, and is home not only to saltwater birds like the brown pelican, herring gulls, sandpipers, and royal terns, but also to visitors like the painted bunting and northern cardinal.

THE CLOISTER
SEA ISLAND GOLF CLUB

PLANTATION COURSE

Architect: Rees Jones

Par: 72

Bermuda fairways and greens

Yardage/Rating/Slope:

Championship tees

7,058/73.9/135

Women's Championship tees

5,863/74.8/131

Back tees

6,549/71.4/130

Middle tees

6,068/71.4/130

Forward tees

5,194/69.8/124

SEASIDE COURSE

Architect: Colt & Alison,

Tom Fazio

Par: 70

Bermuda fairways and greens

Yardage/Rating/Slope:

Men's Championship tees

6,945/73.1/131

Women's Championship tees

5,779/73.9/131

Back tees

6,550/71.1/126

Middle tees

6,006/68.7/120

Forward tees

5,048/69.3/119

RETREAT COURSE

Architect: Joe Lee, renovated by

Davis Love III

(To be completed in August 2001)

PLEASURABLE PURSUITS

The Cloister's Seaside

Course offers golfers

Scottish-links-style play

with unfettered views

to the sea.

THE CLOISTER
SEA ISLAND, GEORGIA

Nestled amid lush gardens
on the southern portion of
Sea Island, the Cloister offers
premier sports in a
luxurious setting.

• Relax by the pool or sign up
for scuba or snorkeling lessons
at the Beach Club, an
oceanside haven on five miles
of private beach.
• Strengthen your spirit and
relax your mind at the Sea Island
Spa, where oceanfront facilities
combine with personal attention
for a luxurious experience.
• Saddle up at the stables
and ride on the beach,
through marsh flats, or amid
lush woodlands.
• Try skeet and sporting clays at
the shooting school, or visit the
tennis center practice court
where balls are collected and
returned any way you choose.
• For something really out of the
ordinary, try a vintage yacht
cruise, a plantation supper, a
ballroom dance clinic, a birding
expedition, or a wine cellar tour.

REGAL RESIDENTS

Ancient live oaks grace the

grounds of the Cloister

at Sea Island.

TEACHING AND TRAINING

The health spa's staff provides

guidance and leads classes in

aerobics, tai chi, kick boxing,

and yoga.

PAST GLORIES, NEW LEGENDS

Famed designer Rees Jones

reshaped and blended the two

orginal separate nine-hole

courses into one, creating the

stunning Plantation Course.

The three courses each touch plenty of water, the marshes, and the forested interior of the island. Seven holes, in fact, play alongside the Atlantic. The Oak Marsh and Ocean Links venues take golfers from the seashore inland over tidal creeks and meandering marshland beneath majestic, Spanish moss-laden live oaks that have been around since the eighteenth century. Oak Marsh is the more difficult of the two courses, with its inland fairways cut by creeks

"You'd better bring your knockdown shot if you play Amelia because seven of the fifty-four holes are directly on the oceanfront and the wind plays a key role. . . ."

and a small, raised green on eight, as well as the surprisingly satisfying sixteenth hole, which is not only accessible to the novice, but also a challenge to more skilled golfers. Ocean Links, with five holes along the Atlantic shore, brings the sea winds into play along many of its narrow

RESORT RATING:

CHALLENGE	★★★★
BEAUTY	★★★★
LODGING	★★★½
CUISINE	★★★½
AMENITIES	★★★½

AMELIA ISLAND PLANTATION

AMELIA ISLAND, FLORIDA

You have to have a shot capable of staying low and out of the wind."

—ED TUCKER, DIRECTOR OF GOLF, AMELIA ISLAND PLANTATION

COMMITTED TO THE LAND

Amelia Island Plantation's staff naturalist and on-site nature center add to its renown for environmental consciousness.

fairways and tiny greens, demanding precision shots and deft club selection and offering, in exchange, some dramatic views of the ocean.

Long Point lies between the Atlantic to the east and the Intracoastal Waterway on the leeward side of the island. Here, the topography provides rolling fairways alongside fifty-foot-high sand dunes, with numerous commanding views of the island.

Accommodations at the Amelia Island Plantation are spread out over the entire area, and a walk to the Amelia Links Clubhouse and Restaurant from any room or suite just begs for

a detour onto the boardwalk for a quick nature tour. Not to be missed is the sunset from Walker's Landing or Drummond Point Park on the western side of the resort.

For those with quiet, exquisite taste, the Ritz-Carlton on Amelia Island offers the perfect sanctuary. The resort is situated on a generous stretch of pristine shoreline off the coast of northeastern Florida—and its relaxed elegance, attentive staff, and tropical charm make guests feel like they've entered a tropical paradise. In many senses, they have.

SALT AIR AND ACTIVITY

Golfers finish the sixth hole of the Ocean

Links Course at Amelia Island Plantation.

AMELIA ISLAND PLANTATION

Miles of uncrowded beach, world-renowned golf and tennis, fine dining, and luxurious accommodations await you at Amelia Island Plantation.

• Sample specially prepared delicacies at a variety of restaurants overlooking the Atlantic Ocean.

• Play tennis at Racquet Park, where the legends compete and an outstanding staff offers a wide range of instruction.

• Visit the nature center or join a naturalist for a leisurely kayak trip through the marsh or a stroll through the centuries-old maritime forest.

• Take a beachside gallop, go deep-sea fishing, or swim laps in pristine salt waters on the resort's three-and-a-half-mile unspoiled beach.

PRIVATE ENCLAVES

With more space, features, and

amenities than hotel rooms, the Villas at

Amelia Island Plantation allow guests to

choose the size and location of

accommodation that suits them best.

SEASIDE GOLF

Massive sand dunes, crashing surf, and

salty air set the stage for seven holes on

the Ocean Links and Long Point courses.

AMELIA ISLAND PLANTATION
AMELIA ISLAND, FLORIDA

OAK MARSH COURSE
Architect: Pete Dye
Par: 72
Tifway-419 Bermuda/
rye fairways, Tifdwarf
Bermuda/bentgrass/
Poa Trivialis greens
Yardage/Rating/Slope:
Blue tees
6,502/71.7/130
White tees
5,824/68.6/123
Red tees
4,983/69.9/124

OCEAN LINKS COURSE
Architects: Pete Dye,
Bobby Weed
Par: 70
Tifway-419 Bermuda/
rye fairways, Tifdwarf
Bermuda/bentgrass/
Poa Trivialis greens
Yardage/Rating/Slope:
Blue tees
6,301/70.3/134
White tees
5,669/67.8/126
Red tees
4,550/66.4/115

LONG POINT COURSE
Architect: Tom Fazio
Par: 72
Tifway-419 Bermuda/
rye fairways, Tifdwarf
Bermuda/bentgrass/
Poa Trivialis greens
Yardage/Rating/Slope:
Blue tees
6,775/73.0/135
White tees
6,086/70.8/127
Red tees
4,927/70.2/123

GOLFING THE MARSH

Tight fairways, small
greens, and water hazards
call for accuracy and
strategy on the Oak
Marsh Course.

RITZ-CARLTON, AMELIA ISLAND

On a mile and a half of pristine beach off the northeast coast of Florida, you'll find warm southern hospitality, coastal charm, and magnificent natural beauty.

• Whether you stay in a standard room or suite, pamper yourself with five-diamond amenities, from twenty-four-hour services to marbled baths and your own balcony by the sea.

• Sample the shopping in historic Fernandina Beach, a charming Victorian town with excellent boutiques, antique shops, bookstores, and restaurants.

• Visit the oceanside Beach Club, where an elegant restaurant and colorful gardens edge a sculpted pool and ocean-view whirlpool.

• Trust the Ritz-Carlton to arrange everything you desire, from kayaks to wave runners and fishing trips to horseback rides along the shore.

TAI CHI AT SUNSET

While some relax by the pool or beach, others stay active with classes offered by the Fitness Center and Day Spa.

PURE GOLFING PLEASURE

Just steps from the hotel, the on-site Amelia Island Golf Club offers eighteen holes of championship golf, excellent fare at the 19th Hole Bar and Grill, and the latest technology in professional instruction.

OPPOSING ATTRACTIONS

Meticulously landscaped gardens surround the free-form pool and ocean-view whirlpool, drawing visitors to enjoy the views and bask in the sun. But the windswept dunes and rustic boardwalk exert an opposite pull, calling for beach exploration and fun in the surf.

Guests are free to do as little or as much as they choose at the Ritz-Carlton. The lobby gives way to spectacular panoramic views of the resort's lush gardens, rolling sand dunes, and the Atlantic Ocean beyond. Those who want to enjoy the scenery and hobnob with other vacationers can enjoy an afternoon cup of tea or cocktails in the lobby lounge, chat by the fire, or participate in a friendly game of billiards.

The real sporting activity, however, lies outside on the resort's eighteen holes of golf. The Golf Club of Amelia Island skirts the hotel with its meticulously maintained greens and seaside fairways and has the distinction of being the only PGA tournament course on the island.

"The back nine has more marshland than the front nine, requiring well-placed drives to give you better shots onto the large, undulating greens. Stay out of the natural areas ...

AMELIA ISLAND, FLORIDA

RITZ-CARLTON, AMELIA ISLAND

RESORT RATING:	
CHALLENGE	★★★★
BEAUTY	★★★★
LODGING	★★★★½
CUISINE	★★★★½
AMENITIES	★★★★

The first nine holes wind through four-hundred-year-old oaks and tall pines, while water and marshes dominate the back nine. The flawless design tests avid golfers while keeping it fun for the occasional player.

Those guests wanting to explore will want to check out Fernandina Beach, a quaint seaside village located just minutes down the shore. The Victorian community, with its ornately painted homes and cobblestone streets, is listed on the National Register of Historic Places, and offers an array of boutiques, cafés, and art galleries.

you won't be able to retrieve or hit your ball from the marsh."

—KEITH GIBSON, HEAD GOLF PROFESSIONAL, THE GOLF CLUB OF AMELIA ISLAND AT SUMMER BEACH

DAZZLING FOOD AND VIEWS

An assortment of restaurants offer diverse menus and ocean views. The award-winning Grill features fine dining.

Many visitors to the Ritz-Carlton, however, will never want to leave. All of its 449 rooms and suites have balconies and marble baths—and the hotel offers twenty-four-hour in-room dining. But the real treasure of the resort is found in its restaurants. Along with earning the AAA Five Diamond award overall, the resort's most prestigious restaurant, the Grill, is a Five Diamond recipient, making it one of the top three restaurants in Florida. The cuisine consists of the freshest seafood, meats, and wild game, flown in from all over the world.

RITZY PLAYTIME

The signature Ritz Kids program offers a variety of activities, including cooking classes, under expert supervision.

WATERWAYS

Ritz-Carlton, Amelia Island's fitness center and day spa house an indoor pool and whirlpool, water aerobics, and steam, sauna, and massage rooms.

RITZ-CARLTON, AMELIA ISLAND
THE GOLF CLUB OF AMELIA ISLAND AT SUMMER BEACH AMELIA ISLAND, FLORIDA

Architects: Mark McCumber, Gene Littler

Tour stops: 1998 Senior Liberty Mutual Legends of Golf

Par: 72

Bermuda/rye fairways, Bermuda/bentgrass greens

Yardage/Rating/Slope:

Gold tees
6,692/72.9/136

Blue tees
6,119/70.2/128

White tees
5,741/68.5/118

Red tees
5,039/70.4/124

PLAY ON DISPLAY

The Golf Club at Amelia Island borders the Ritz-Carlton, making play an entertaining view for resort guests.

"The Stadium Course places an emphasis on an accurate approach shot to the green and a very good short game."

—JIM POOLE, HEAD GOLF PROFESSIONAL, TPC AT SAWGRASS STADIUM COURSE

RESORT RATING:

CHALLENGE	★★★★⯨
BEAUTY	★★★★
LODGING	★★★⯨
CUISINE	★★★⯨
AMENITIES	★★★⯨

EXPERIENCING

SAWGRASS MARRIOTT RESORT

This quietly elegant seaside resort blends boundless recreational activities with astonishing beauty.

• Pamper yourself with the privacy and comforts of stunning furnished villas, lavish suites, and well-appointed guest rooms.

• See the sights, do some shopping, or enjoy hours of fascinating exploration in America's oldest city, nearby St. Augustine.

• Work out at the health club, then relax in a hot steam room or sauna any time of the day or night.

• Enjoy spectacular views of the Atlantic Ocean from a variety of restaurants and lounges.

• Take a swing at tennis on seventeen championship courts featuring four different surfaces.

For adventurous eaters, the Blind Tasting menu is a must, for they will be surprised and delighted with the chef's favorite cuisine.

Sawgrass Marriott Resort in Ponte Vedra Beach, Florida, is the second largest golf resort in the United States, and winner of the Gold Medal Award by *Golf* magazine. The stars of the five championship courses at Sawgrass are two TPC courses, the Stadium Course and the Valley Course. Surrounded by the Atlantic on one side and the Intracoastal Waterway on the other, the resort grounds abound with alligator-filled lagoons, water oaks adorned with moss, stately magnolias, and twisted palms.

PONTE VEDRA BEACH, FLORIDA

SAWGRASS MARRIOTT

RESORT

This sense of being waist-deep in nature extends to the golf courses themselves.

The Stadium Course, like all the Sawgrass links, brings water into play with nearly every shot, and as if that weren't enough, the fairways are studded with moguls and pot bunkers. The Stadium Course was the first to employ the staggered grass mounding along the playing areas, which serves as natural bleachers for tournament spectators. It demands accuracy and patience on nearly every hole, with large sand waste and water hazards to penalize imprudent gamblers. The split fairway of the eleventh hole presents equally hazardous play on both sides, and features a bunker that is over two hundred yards long stretching from the edge of the tee box to the fairway.

A SUNNY WELCOME

The lobby at Sawgrass Marriott Resort

provides a pleasant public space for

guests to congregate and relax.

GOLFING

SAWGRASS MARRIOTT RESORT
SAWGRASS COUNTRY CLUB

Architect: Ed Seay
Par: 72
Tifway 419 fairways,
tifdwarf greens

EAST/WEST
Yardage/Rating/Slope:
Gold tees
7,002/75.4/149
Blue tees
6,589/73.2/144
White tees
6,034/70.4/137
Red tees
5,128/71.6*/121*

WEST/SOUTH
Yardage/Rating/Slope:
Gold tees
6,891/74.9/147
Blue tees
6,504/72.8/137
White tees
6,038/70.5/133
Red tees
5,121/71.4*/121*

SOUTH/EAST
Yardage/Rating/Slope:
Gold tees
6,991/75.5/150
Blue tees
6,611/73.4/145
White tees
6,062/70.7/136
Red tees
5,176/71.6*/122*
*Women's ratings

TARGETS

The seventeenth hole on

the TPC Stadium Course

is a killer. It's target-style

greens require nerve

and precision.

SAWGRASS MARRIOTT RESORT
PONTE VEDRA, FLORIDA

TPC AT SAWGRASS STADIUM COURSE

Architect: Pete Dye

Tour Stops: The Players
Championship

Par: 72

Bermuda/rye fairways,
bentgrass greens

Yardage/Rating/Slope:

<u>Championship tees</u>

6,954/75.0/149

<u>Blue tees</u>

6,514/72.3/139

<u>White tees</u>

5,815/69.0/130

<u>Forward tees</u>

5,000/64.9/120

TPC AT SAWGRASS VALLEY COURSE

Architects: Pete Dye, Jerry Pate

Tour Stops: 1997–1998 Senior
Tour Qualifying School

Par: 72

Bermuda/rye fairways,
bentgrass greens

Yardage/Rating/Slope:

<u>Championship tees</u>

6,864/72.8/130

<u>Blue tees</u>

6,524/71.3/127

<u>White tees</u>

6,092/69.4/123

<u>Forward tees</u>

5,126/65.0/115

LAY OF THE LAND

Landscaping that echoes
the Intracoastal Waterway
makes for dramatic
interplay between resort
and environment at the
Sawgrass Marriott.

THE BREAKERS

This Italian Renaissance–style hotel in the heart of Palm Beach evokes the classic, sensual allure and relaxed formality of St. Tropez, the French Riviera, and the Italian coast.

• Walk a few steps from the main hotel to the luxurious spa and fitness center, where you can soak a few feet from the ocean in an outdoor Jacuzzi or sign up for classes on an upper deck ocean terrace.

• Reserve a pool-deck or beachfront cabana at the Mediterranean-style beach club, situated on one-half mile of pristine, private beach.

• Sample the extensive activities and water sports, from the award-winning tennis facility to deep-sea fishing, fly-fishing, snorkeling, and scuba diving.

• Sign up for a historical tour or shopping trip, or visit the Breakers Gardens and its magical Children's Secret Garden.

OUT OF THE ASHES

The Breakers survived two tragic fires and stands today as one of Florida's finest resorts. It offers a wealth of activities for young and old, and some of the finest dining in this corner of the country.

The Valley Course is just as challenging. Hills, valleys, water on every hole, waste bunkers, and mounds demand tough decisions. This course is remarkably free of rough, however, so every shot seems makable. The finishing hole will make or break many rounds. A long iron approach finds a slim but deep green closely guarded by imposing mounds, sand traps, and a water barrier confined by railroad ties. All the courses at Sawgrass reward accurate shot placement and close attention to the winds.

The Breakers in Palm Beach is an unabashedly opulent golf resort that hearkens back to the nineteenth century, and to the playgrounds of the privileged on the Riviera. Built by oil and railroad magnate Henry Morrison Flagler, who also left his mark by connecting Key West to the mainland via rail, the Breakers first opened as the Palm Beach Inn in 1893. The resort boasts a Mobil Five-Star, AAA Five Diamond rating, and with good reason. American, Mediterranean, and English cuisine, a magnificent health spa, the vaulted ceilings and arches of the public areas, and extravagantly furnished quarters with romantic ocean views are all what one would expect from a resort that looks like it arose from the pages of an F. Scott Fitzgerald novel. Today its splendor is undiminished, and its shimmering white Mediterranean-style architecture overlooks a golf course designed in the old-fashioned style, with a more modern course a few minutes away.

The Ocean Course, Florida's oldest golf course, is located right on the grounds of the resort. It has been recently revitalized to keep it in line with the superior standards of the rest of the resort, whose life spans three centuries. To be sure, the old-world flavor of the layout is intact, with deeply recessed, randomly placed and shaped bunkers and fairways that sidestep around them. There are thirteen water hazards among the eighteen holes, and the large, undulating greens afford plenty of run-up areas for approach shots. Greens have close-cropped "surrounds" that allow some easy recovery shots, but any completely missed green will land a golfer in trouble with a very tough chip shot. The key throughout is to keep the ball in play, as anything landing in the rough is rough indeed.

The second course, the Breakers, lies about fifteen minutes from the hotel and has a more contemporary design, with abundant foliage and many water hazards. Located near a very nicely appointed residential development, this course is long in the fairways and forgiving in the roughs, and invites high, hard hitters to stand in and swing away.

Along Florida's Gold Coast is another grand resort, steeped in seventy-five years of history. As evening sunlight illuminates the coral-colored, nine-hundred-room Cloister Hotel, and as guests stroll through its lush and diverse tropical landscape, they will soon realize that Boca Raton Resort is a truly unique place stocked with wonderful, modern amenities.

PALM BEACH, FLORIDA

THE BREAKERS

RESORT RATING:

CHALLENGE	★★★⯪
BEAUTY	★★★⯪
LODGING	★★★★⯪
CUISINE	★★★★⯪
AMENITIES	★★★★

"This course is very fair if you keep the ball in play, but if you hit off-line it becomes pretty difficult. Out of eighteen holes you must negotiate thirteen water hazards. . . .

The greens are large and undulating, with plenty of run-up areas, but if you miss the green you have a very tough chip."

—Tim Collins, Head Golf Professional, Breakers West Country Club

Non-Stop Action

The Breakers is at the center of vibrant Palm Beach, giving guests endless options for activity.

THE BREAKERS
PALM BEACH, FLORIDA

BREAKERS WEST COURSE
Architect: William Byrd,
redesigned by Ken Green
Par: 71
Bermuda fairways,
Tifdwarf greens
Yardage/Rating/Slope:
Blue tees
6,905/73.7/135
White tees
6,340/70.7/131
Gold tees
5,690/67.5/123
Red tees
5,420/72.1/131

BREAKERS OCEAN COURSE
Architect: Alexander Findley,
restored by Brian Silva
Par: 70
Bermuda fairways,
TifEagle greens
Yardage/Rating/Slope: (This
course is not yet rated.)
Blue tees
6,146
White tees
5,730
Red tees
5,149

A FACE LIFT

For more than a century,
golfers challenged
Alexander Findley's Ocean
Course, a tribute to the
style of Donald Ross. The
2000 redesign was placed
in the hands of Brian Silva,
considered the undisputed
expert at revitalizing
Ross-style courses.

SMALL-FRY DIVERSIONS
The Breakers' Coconut Crew
Summer Camp features topical
"theme weeks" to keep the
younger generation occupied.

TASTE AND VIEW THE OCEAN
The casually elegant Seafood Bar
features the freshest seafood
available. Small fish and other
marine life swim amid coral
stones inside the beautiful
aquarium bar counters.

BOCA RATON RESORT AND CLUB

RESORT COURSE
Architect: William Flynn,
redesigned by Gene Bates
Tour stops: 2000 EMC Skills
Challenge
Par: 71
419 Bermuda fairways,
champion tifdwarf
Bermuda greens
Yardage/Rating/Slope:
Gold tees
6,253/69.3/128
Blue tees
5,902/67.6/124
White tees
5,602/66.4/119
Green tees
5,160/64.3, 68.7*/107, 122*
Red tees
4,577/65.5*/112*

COUNTRY CLUB COURSE
Architect: Joe Lee
Par: 72
419 Bermuda fairways,
champion tifdwarf greens
Yardage/Rating/Slope:
Gold tees
6,714/72.7/133
Blue tees
6,361/70.9/128
White tees
5,776/68.1/121
Red tees
5,298/71.8*/127*
*Women's ratings

TOWERING PRESENCE

Rising alongside the

historic Cloister building,

the twenty-seven-story

tower offers incredible

views of the ocean, golf

course, Lake Boca Raton,

and majestic fountains that

dot the grounds.

Located thirty-five minutes south of Palm Beach, the resort is considered one of the premier playgrounds for golfers who prefer a more decadent getaway. Thirty tennis courts, a half-mile-long private beach, and a full-service marina give adults lots of options for daytime fun. The opulence of this old-world resort has set the stage for a seemingly endless stream of distinguished as well as celebrity guests: It has been said that the Boca Raton Resort and Club membership list reads like a veritable who's who of the jet-set community.

Great golf is easy to come by on the newly renovated Resort Course. By restoring the original tees and bunkers of this traditional Scottish-style course, designers have created a venue that requires the clarity and focus of a seasoned golfer. Water is featured more prominently than ever before—add to this an elevated eighteenth hole and you'll end your game with a stunning vista of the beautiful resort grounds. Novices who have trouble on the newly resculpted Country Club Course can always try a lesson or two at Boca's Nicklaus/Fick school or the Dave Pelz Short Game Golf School. The Country Club Course is truly a gem, in that its ultra-shorn Champions Bermuda greens allow the ball to roll smoothly albeit quickly. Caution: The new, deeper greenside bunkers give way suddenly to sand, so remember that precision is the key on this course.

The lush grounds of Boca Raton are a fragrant, colorful tribute to the history and tradition of the resort. Chefs at Nick's Fishmarket or the Top of the Tower Italian restaurant opt to pick their herbs fresh from Boca's own herb garden, which features over twenty varieties of greens, including edible nasturtiums. After-dinner entertainment includes, among other things, an extraordinary magic and comedy club. In essence, Boca Raton is a small tropical utopia. Guests might feel as if they are enjoying a golf vacation in some other country—and will be pampered by a staff that knows how to cater to the wants and needs of kings and queens.

The PGA National Resort and Spa, in Palm Beach Gardens, Florida, honors golf's greats with five exquisitely designed courses. Reclining among the swales and palm trees of eastern Florida, the courses bear the imprint of legends like Jack Nicklaus, Arnold Palmer, and others. Nicklaus, in fact, designed the Champion Course, a difficult power course with the toughest finishing holes anywhere. The fifteenth, sixteenth, and seventeenth holes are called "the Bear Trap," after Nicklaus, and demand long, accurate drives to avoid the water hazards. The concave fairways and greens offer spectators good viewing and add to the sculpted beauty of the place. The golfer who assails this course must rely on alternating doses of power and finesse, with the least difficult holes in the front nine. The eleventh hole marks the beginning of some very challenging hitting, with long bunkers to avoid on 13; water to the right of 14, which can't be seen from the tee; and those "Bear Trap" holes lying in ambush for even the pros.

BOCA RATON, FLORIDA

BOCA RATON

RESORT AND CLUB

RESORT RATING:

CHALLENGE	★★★
BEAUTY	★★★⯪
LODGING	★★★★
CUISINE	★★★★
AMENITIES	★★★★

"The Resort Course is target-oriented, so accuracy, proper alignment off the tees, and precise approach shots are important."

—BOB COMAN, DIRECTOR OF GOLF OPERATIONS, BOCA RATON RESORT AND CLUB

EXPERIENCING

BOCA RATON RESORT AND CLUB

At this legendary resort in fabled Palm Beach County, the historic Cloister building, intimate Beach Club, and twenty-seven-story tower rise alongside majestic Lake Boca Raton.

• Sample the diverse recreational options, variety of dining and entertainment facilities, and comprehensive activities programs that give Boca Raton its wide appeal.

• Choose from a wide array of amenities, including two championship golf courses, thirty tennis courts, several pools, and state-of-the-art fitness centers.

• Enjoy an assortment of watersports activities along a half-mile stretch of private beach.

• Visit the marina to arrange for deep-sea fishing, sailing, scuba diving, snorkeling, or windsurfing lessons.

"The courses range in design and difficulty but accuracy is a must on all of them. Keeping the ball in play is the key."

—JANE BRODERICK, HEAD GOLF PROFESSIONAL, PGA NATIONAL RESORT AND SPA

RESORT RATING:

CHALLENGE	★★★★⯪
BEAUTY	★★★⯪
LODGING	★★★⯪
CUISINE	★★★⯪
AMENITIES	★★★⯪

EXPERIENCING

PGA NATIONAL RESORT AND SPA

PGA National Resort and Spa offers five championship golf courses, the Academy of Golf, a world-class spa, and so much more.

• Experience the ultimate in relaxation and rejuvenation at the spa's Waters of the World, a collection of outdoor mineral pools in the ancient tradition of health via water.

• Pamper yourself with more than a hundred other spa services, including soothing massages, cleansing facials, toning skin treatments, and full salon services.

• Improve your tennis game with state-of-the-art facilities and instructions for all skill levels at the tennis club.

• Play croquet at one of the nation's largest croquet clubs, with five full-size tournament-quality lawns.

The General Course, designed by its namesake, Arnold Palmer, is more reminiscent of the great Scottish courses, with long, undulating fairways sprinkled with dozens of grass bunkers, nearly fifty sand bunkers, and many water hazards. As with the Champion Course, the most difficult holes are in the back nine, with 17 being the toughest. The best way to negotiate this course is the way Arnold would: don't negotiate, attack. This approach will reward those who aren't made timid by the bunkers, but be careful of the wind.

The Estate Course has as its trademark nearly ninety sand bunkers, whereas the Squire Course, named after Gene Sarazen, is the shortest and narrowest of the five courses.

PALM BEACH GARDENS, FLORIDA

PGA NATIONAL RESORT

AND SPA

This one tests a golfer's accuracy, with fairway woods and irons necessary on many tee shots, and careful iron placement to hold the greens. The Haig Course is accessible to players of any skill level. Its trademark rosebushes at the 150-yard markers commemorate Walter Hagen and remind the day's players of his advice to "stop and smell the roses." Without water hazards to worry about, even high-handicap golfers can avoid the bunkers safely by playing around them.

Turnberry Isle Resort and Club is a secluded, three-hundred-acre setting in the North Miami enclave of Aventura. The Mediterranean architecture of the hotel fits perfectly into the tropical greenery and pool gardens that abut the Intracoastal Waterway. The guest rooms themselves are a very nice surprise, with terra-cotta floors, French doors opening onto private terraces, Oriental rugs, rich wood furnishings, and bathrooms complete with televisions! The flooring not only looks refreshing, but adds a very practical touch, since it makes even the rooms "golf-shoe friendly."

SOUND FUNDAMENTALS

A typical three-day program at PGA National's Academy incorporates high-speed, split-screen videos and biomechanical computer analysis with personalized instruction.

PGA NATIONAL RESORT AND SPA

CHAMPION COURSE
Architect: Tom Fazio,
George Fazio, Jack Nicklaus
Tour stops: 1982–2000 PGA
Seniors Championship
Par: 72
Bermuda fairways, tifdwarf
Bermuda greens
Yardage/Rating/Slope:
Black tees
7,022/74.7/142
Blue tees
6,373/71.1/129
Red tees
5,377/71.1/123

GENERAL COURSE
Architect: Arnold Palmer
Par: 72
Bermuda fairways, tifdwarf
Bermuda greens
Yardage/Rating/Slope:
Blue tees
6,768/73.0/130
White tees
6,270/70.4/125
Red tees
5,324/71.0/122

ESTATE COURSE
Architect: Karl Litten
Par: 72
Bermuda fairways, tifdwarf
Bermuda greens
Yardage/Rating/Slope:
Blue tees
6,784/73.4/131
White tees
6,328/70.7/124
Red tees
4,903/68.4/118

HAIG COURSE
Architects: Tom Fazio,
George Fazio
Par: 72
Bermuda fairways, tifdwarf
Bermuda greens
Yardage/Rating/Slope:
Blue tees
6,806/73.0/130
White tees
6,352/70.6/125
Red tees
5,645/72.5/121

EXEMPLARY ACCOUTREMENTS

The PGA National Resort is one of South Florida's premier vacation destinations, just minutes from ocean beaches, deep-sea fishing, and famous Worth Avenue shopping.

NO ORDINARY RESORT

As the official home of the Professional Golfers' Association of America, PGA National Resort has a reputation to uphold. Five championship courses, designed by golfing legends more than meet the challenge.

PGA National Resort and Spa

Palm Beach Gardens, Florida

Squire Course
Architects: Tom Fazio,
George Fazio
Par: 72
Bermuda fairways, tifdwarf
Bermuda greens
Yardage/Rating/Slope:
Blue tees
6,806/73.0/130
White tees
6,352/70.6/125
Red tees
5,645/72.5/121

King of Courses

Named after Gene
Sarazen, the golf great who
earned the nickname "the
Squire," PGA National's
Squire Course is the
shortest and narrowest
of the resort's
five courses.

TURNBERRY ISLE RESORT AND CLUB

Secluded on three hundred tropical acres, this haven of privilege provides a soothing retreat atmosphere in a stunning Mediterranean-style hotel.

• Enjoy the ultimate in luxury and comfort, from fresh orchids and fruit to exquisite wood furnishings, plush Oriental rugs, French doors to your private terrace, and a bathroom complete with TV and sunken whirlpool tub.

• Utilize the full-service marina for deep-sea fishing or a chartered yacht trip, or dock your boat there and enjoy all the privileges of hotel guests.

• For unlimited recreational activities, take advantage of the championship golf courses, tennis clubs, or Turnberry's own private beach with its colorful cabanas, shimmering pools, and wide variety of water sports.

• From gourmet cuisine to seaside casual, sample the fare at five restaurants and six lounges, each with its own distinctive style.

WATERWAY ACCOMMODATIONS

Located on the Intracoastal Waterway, the Marina and Yacht Club is an integral part of Turnberry Isle. While most accommodations are found in the main Country Club hotel, an additional seventy rooms and suites are available at the Yacht Club.

WELL-GUARDED GREENS

The imprint of Robert Trent Jones, Sr. is evident on both of Turnberry Isle's courses, where greens are often ringed by sand and water.

FIRST-RATE PAMPERING

The amenities here are beyond extraordinary, with two color televisions, dual-line telephones, fax machines, marble-topped minibars, walk-in closets with safes and umbrellas, and spectacular views from every room.

In keeping with the European motif and the plush appointments, the Spa at Turnberry is located in a three-story fitness center with twenty-six treatment rooms brought spectacularly together by a majestic spiral staircase and cascading waterfall, all beneath a glass dome skylight. Gourmet dining, a private marina, world-class tennis facilities, sailing, and swimming further fill in a glorious picture that is only completed by golf.

At Turnberry's two golf courses, the North and South, prudence dictates club selection, as water stands close guard to the fairways and greens of most holes. To be sure, a few of the fairways are tailor-made for long hitters, most notably the North course's ninth and

"With no way around the water on most holes, the South Course plays to the longer hitter. The North Course is narrower, making accuracy a must, but nearly every player . . .

AVENTURA, FLORIDA

TURNBERRY ISLE RESORT

AND CLUB

RESORT RATING:	
CHALLENGE	★★★★
BEAUTY	★★★★
LODGING	★★★★
CUISINE	★★★★
AMENITIES	★★★⯪

fourteenth holes, but the par-threes stand out as some of the most varied and challenging around. The prevailing wind tends to be a factor, especially on the North Course's eleventh hole. Here the proximity of the building to the par-three hole causes a "chute" effect that can make club selection vital to staying out of trouble in one of the six bunkers in front of the green.

The Hyatt Regency Grand Cypress resort is a not simply a self-contained golf resort; it can transport its guests far and wide while setting them firmly in Orlando, Florida. The

can find a way around the water on most holes."

—David Podolan, Director of Golf, Turnberry Isle Resort

Turnberry at Its Finest
The Veranda, acclaimed the "best gourmet dining experience in Miami" by Zagat, features a menu that combines South Florida ingredients with Cuban, Caribbean, and Latin American cuisine.

first thing guests see of the place is the tall central atrium, with enough greenery to re-create the rainforest. The Mediterranean-style rooms are airy and bright, with French doors opening onto private patios. New-world cuisine is the order of the day at the restaurants—the Black Angus prime rib at the White Horse Saloon is a worthy highlight. But it's the golf on the resort's four Jack Nicklaus–designed courses that commands attention.

TURNBERRY ISLE RESORT AND CLUB
AVENTURA, FLORIDA

SOUTH COURSE
Architect: Robert Trent Jones, Sr.
Par: 72
Bermuda fairways,
tifdwarf greens
Yardage/Rating/Slope:
Blue tees
7,003/73.7/136
Gold tees
6,458/71.0/118
White tees
6,078/68.7/111
Red tees
5,581/71.3/116

NORTH COURSE
Architect: Robert Trent Jones, Sr.
Par: 70
Bermuda fairways,
tifdwarf greens
Yardage/Rating/Slope:
Blue tees
6,403/70.3/127
Gold tees
5,970/68.3/110
White tees
5,589/66.3/105
Red tees
4,991/67.9/107

NO WAY AROUND

At just over seven

thousand yards, the South

Course plays to the long

hitter and finishes

on the famous

island green.

"A lot of times you can't see the bunkers from the tees, but Grand Cypress has equipped its golf carts with the Pro Shot GPS system. Like having your own caddie, . . .

RESORT RATING:

CHALLENGE	★★★★½
BEAUTY	★★★★
LODGING	★★★★½
CUISINE	★★★★
AMENITIES	★★★★½

HYATT REGENCY

GRAND CYPRESS

ORLANDO, FLORIDA

it gives you a close-up of all the greens and shows exactly where the pin placement is."

—BILL ROWDEN, DIRECTOR OF GOLF, GRAND CYPRESS GOLF CLUB

PERSONAL SPA SERVICES

Great golf and in-room spa services are two of the hallmarks at Grand Cypress resort. Therapeutic massage, natural body treatments, and a private tai chi session are all available in the privacy of your room.

With three nine-hole courses and the eighteen-hole New Course at hand, guests can begin, say, on the East Course nine and suddenly feel as if they are walking in the Carolinas among the leafy green trees and swales of the Piedmont. This course is the most generous of the four, with fewer bunkers and more forgiving greens. The greens also lie unguarded in the front, which invites those easy run-up shots.

The North and South nines are more challenging. Accuracy is rewarded here among the terraced fairways and on the platformed greens, which are surrounded by ominously large bunkers. The North Course, particularly, features sinuous mounds that call for some exacting shots. The seventh and eighth holes also present very difficult approach shots, with a shallow green on 7 and a well-guarded, elevated green on 8. Approaches on these holes must be high-angle, well-struck shots to hold the green. The South nine also challenges on some of the approaches, with a severely sloping green on 5 and a high plateau green on 6. Several fairways on these courses are ledged, which offers a nice sense of definition to the playing terrain and improves a golfer's perspective. The North and South courses are somewhat reminiscent of Scotland, with their long mounds topped by love grass and wildflowers.

But to return to the old world and play golf the old-fashioned way, the eighteen-hole New Course is the perfect vehicle. Here the Scottish influence is far more definitive, and at times golfers can imagine they are actually playing those venerable holes across the Atlantic, but in much better weather. The course is designed to resemble the terrain at the Old Course at St. Andrews, with its spacious, rolling greens, bridges, and stone walls, cut often by the twisting burns and grassy mounds and tufts so characteristic of Scotland. But the resemblance doesn't end there. Very little water comes into play here, and the course is mostly clear of trees, but the fairways are pocked with pot bunkers, those nightmarishly beckoning sand hazards that can run as much as twelve feet deep. Each of the Grand Cypress courses, but especially the New Course, will call for every shot in the golfer's bag, and leave one at the end with the assurance of having played the game in its entirety.

Golfers looking for diversity will eventually find their way to the Westin Innisbrook Resort and its stellar courses on Florida's Sun Coast just a few miles south of Tarpon Springs. The Westin Innisbrook's courses are laid out on the six-hundred-acre resort, where guest suites are housed in twenty-eight lodges nestled among seventy-two holes of championship golf, and offer views of the fairways, greens, clubhouses, and pools. The grounds are surprisingly hilly for this part of Florida, and the courses take full advantage of the varied terrain. The fact that the fairways wend their way through sixty acres of natural lakes and a splendid nature preserve only adds to the richness of the experience.

HYATT REGENCY GRAND CYPRESS
GRAND CYPRESS GOLF CLUB
ORLANDO, FLORIDA

Architect: Jack Nicklaus
Tour stops: Shark Shootout,
1992 PGA Skills Challenge,
2001 LPGA J.C. Penney Classic

NEW COURSE
Par: 72
Bermuda/bentgrass/rye fairways
and greens
Yardage/Rating/Slope:
Blue tees
6,773/72.2/122
White tees
6,181/69.6/116
Red tees
5,314/69.8/117

NORTH 9 / SOUTH 9 COURSE
Par: 72
Bermuda/bentgrass/rye fairways
and greens
Yardage/Rating/Slope:
Blue tees
6,444/72.7/131
White tees
5,933/70.5/125
Red tees
5,318/71.1/119

SOUTH 9 / EAST 9 COURSE
Par: 72
Bermuda/bentgrass/rye fairways
and greens
Yardage/Rating/Slope:
Blue tees
6,373/72.1/131
White tees
5,811/69.7/125
Red tees
5,116/70.2/114

NORTH 9 / EAST 9 COURSE
Par: 72
Bermuda/bentgrass/rye fairways
and greens
Yardage/Rating/Slope:
Blue tees
6,374/72.2/130
White tees
5.878/70.0/125
Red tees
5,056/69.1/114

WORLD-CLASS FACILITIES

A range of services are available at the equestrian center, the first U.S. riding facility to be approved by the British Horse Society.

SIMPLE RELAXATION

Art lovers will enjoy a walking tour of Grand Cypress's impressive collection of Oriental and modern art, including pieces by Dutch sculptor Jits Bakker.

WESTIN INNISBROOK RESORT

Architect: Larry Packard
Tour stops: 2000 Tampa Bay Classic

COPPERHEAD COURSE
Par: 71
Bermuda/rye fairways,
Bermuda/bentgrass greens
Yardage/Rating/Slope:
Black tees
7,230/75.6/134
Silver tees
6,180/70.4/128
Jade tees
5,605/71.8/130

ISLAND COURSE
Par: 72
Bermuda/rye fairways,
Bermuda/bentgrass greens
Yardage/Rating/Slope:
Black tees
7.017/74.1/132
Silver tees
6,166/70.7/121
Jade tees
5,578/73.0/129

HIGHLANDS NORTH COURSE
Par: 71
Bermuda/rye fairways,
Bermuda/bentgrass greens
Yardage/Rating/Slope:
Black tees
6,405/70.5/125
Silver tees
5,530/67.4/117
Jade tees
4,955/68.4/118

HIGHLANDS SOUTH COURSE
Par: 71
Bermuda/rye fairways,
Bermuda/bentgrass greens
Yardage/Rating/Slope:
Black tees
6,635/72.0/127
Silver tees
5,690/67.2/119
Jade tees
4,975/68.9/121

GRADE SCHOOL FOR GOLF

The Troon Golf Junior Institute offers individualized instruction, supervised practice, playing lessons, and fundamental rules and etiquette that will last a lifetime.

COPPERHEAD CLASSIC

The Copperhead Course, above, is home to the Tampa Bay Classic, an event especially popular with locals because the proceeds go to area charities.

NEARBY ATTRACTIONS

Although the Westin Innisbrook Resort has a wide range of activities, nearby Tampa has a lure of its own, with Busch Gardens and the Florida Aquarium.

Could golfers playing the Copperhead or the nearby Eagle's Watch course become so engrossed in their game and the lush beauty that they fail to notice they're being watched by the eagles that have called the Innisbrook courses home for the past twenty-five years? Perhaps not. An early-morning walk or jog through the nature preserve to watch the birds and scout the course layout may be the perfect way to begin a day.

Out on the courses, golfers find accuracy their best ally. Fairways and greens present a variety of challenges, including the uphill-downhill fairway on Copperhead's fifth hole, severe doglegs, and sloping greens. The green at the Island Course's last hole, which slopes to the

"Unlike typical Florida courses, we have rolling hills and tree-lined fairways that require straight drives for a decent score."

—CHUCK EADE, DIRECTOR OF GOLF, WESTIN INNISBROOK RESORT

PALM HARBOR, FLORIDA

WESTIN INNISBROOK

RESORT

RESORT RATING:	
CHALLENGE	★★★★
BEAUTY	★★★★
LODGING	★★★½
CUISINE	★★★
AMENITIES	★★★½

water, is especially dicey. Off the resort grounds, Eagle's Watch's majestic course is distin-guished by tricky green design, including the island green on the ninth hole, where the wind supplies an invisible hazard to even the best-placed shot. The eighth hole is a long, winding hole along the water leading to a small, well-bunkered green protected by a huge long-needle pine tree to the right side. If your approach shot disappears in that tree, it's best to take a drop.

Yet another Florida Gulf Coast gem is the Resort at Longboat Key Club. This beachfront resort faces the Gulf of Mexico and its striking white sand beaches, glorious blue water, and romantic sunsets. Guests who come here hoping to get away from a harried routine of important decisions find there are still many choices to make once they settle in. Which restaurant should they choose for dining, for instance? And once fed, will it be tennis at one of the thirty-eight tennis courts? A day on the beach, or windsurfing? Or perhaps the fitness center with its pool, Jacuzzi, steam rooms, and aerobics classes, or in March, a spring training baseball game in nearby Sarasota?

EXPERIENCING

WESTIN INNISBROOK RESORT

This all-suite resort boasts championship golf, a pool and water slide complex, and a range of dining options to satisfy every taste.

• Enjoy water sports and fishing in the resort's pools and beautiful Palm Harbor beaches.

• Take time for a great workout at the health club and fitness center, followed by a relaxing massage at the Innisbrook Spa.

• Savor steaks, ribs, and chops in a steakhouse atmosphere, relax in a traditional pub, or visit the cantina for a wide variety of tequilas and delicious Mexican appetizers.

"To play well here, you need to be a good long-distance putter, because the greens are large and you're going to have some rather lengthy putts."

—David Matthews, Director of Golf, The Resort at Longboat Key Club

RESORT RATING:

CHALLENGE	★★★☆
BEAUTY	★★★★
LODGING	★★★☆
CUISINE	★★★☆
AMENITIES	★★★☆

THE RESORT AT

LONGBOAT KEY CLUB

LONGBOAT KEY, FLORIDA

EXPERIENCING

THE RESORT AT LONGBOAT KEY CLUB

The Resort at Longboat Key Club offers the flawless white sands of the Gulf of Mexico, just minutes away from the international shops, restaurants, and galleries of St. Armands Circle.

• Awaken to fresh juice and coffee in your luxurious suite, complete with its own kitchen and private balcony.

• Enjoy complimentary tennis at one of the largest tennis facilities on Florida's west coast, located along the aquamarine waters of a quiet lagoon.

• On the golf course, utilize the ParView global positioning system to view pin placement, keep score electronically, receive storm alerts, or order lunch from your cart.

• Wind the afternoon down with a dip in the pool, a soak in the Jacuzzi, and a massage in the privacy of your suite or the fitness center.

Golf is the choice most make when they plan a trip to the Resort at Longboat Key Club. Longboat Key itself stretches eleven sun-drenched miles between the Gulf of Mexico and Sarasota Bay, providing a tropical setting for two courses. Islandside, the westernmost course, abuts the gulf within walking distance of the resort. Each of its eighteen holes is studded with water hazards and graced by over five thousand palm trees and stunning pink and white blooming oleanders lining the fairways. The elevated greens combine with steady winds off the water to provide a challenge on almost every approach shot, and the narrow fairways are deceptively long. Since this championship layout is very creatively squeezed into a surprisingly tight area, that steady breeze seems to shift from hole to hole as the course changes direction often within the space of a few holes. A series of interlocked lakes and canals is woven throughout the terrain, and requires careful attention to that wind and some thoughtful club selection. The key to staying out of trouble is to avoid going long on most shots.

The Harbourside Course is actually three nine-hole courses, and offers a quite different challenge than Islandside. This particular course is a soft, or spikeless, facility. Laying alongside Sarasota Bay a few miles from the resort, Harbourside plays through stands of live oak, palmetto, southern pine, and several varieties of palm and fig trees. These are virgin stands that will swallow up an errant shot forever, and while the vistas seem spacious, it's often because the fairways are lined up side by side. Water and bunkers frame most of the narrow fairways as well as the greens, so the low round will favor accuracy over power.

Four hundred years after the first Conquistadors landed near Tampa Bay, the St. Petersburg waterfront skyline was graced with the luxurious Vinoy Park Hotel. Built as a luxury hotel in 1925, the resort was restored to its original splendor in the early 1990s as the Renaissance Vinoy Resort, with exquisitely stenciled wall borders and beams, large, sumptuously furnished rooms, and breathtaking views of the bay and downtown St. Petersburg. Listed on the National Registry of Historic Places and a member of the Historic Hotels of America, this 360-room facility is a true resort, with a private golf course, spas, tennis facilities, croquet courts, swimming pools, restaurants, and even a private marina.

Nestled among pine vales, palm trees, lakes, beach bunkers, and even reaching out into the bay itself, the Renaissance Vinoy Golf Club lies just a mile and a half from the hotel. Open only to Vinoy club members and Renaissance Vinoy Hotel guests, the course demands disciplined club selection to negotiate its narrow fairways, creative bunkering, and saltwater hazards. But perhaps its most memorable features are the two double greens, the island green, and a finishing hole ranked as one of the most difficult in the world.

THE RESORT AT LONGBOAT KEY CLUB

HARBOURSIDE COURSE
Architect: William Byrd
Par: 72
Bermuda 419 fairways,
tifdwarf Bermuda greens

Red/White Yardage/Rating/Slope:
Blue tees
6,749/72.7/131
White tees
6,231/69.9/124
Gold tees
5,806/67.9/118
Red tees
5,469/71.3/125

White/Blue Yardage/Rating/Slope:
Blue tees
6,812/73.1/132
White tees
6,260/70.7/126
Red tees
5,335/70.3/126

Blue/Red Yardage/Rating/Slope:
Blue tees
6,709/72.6/130
White tees
6,109/70.1/124
Red tees
5,198/69.5/123

ISLANDSIDE COURSE
Architect: Bill Mitchell
Par: 72
Bermuda 419 fairways,
tifdwarf Bermuda greens
Yardage/Rating/Slope:
Blue tees
6,792/73.8/138
White tees
6,153/70.2/128
Red tees
5,198/68.6/121

BONDING

The winds from the Gulf of

Mexico and extra-large,

well-bunkered greens may

make Longboat Key Club's

courses too challenging for

most junior golfers. But it's

never too early for them to

watch and learn.

RENAISSANCE VINOY GOLF CLUB
ST. PETERSBURG, FLORIDA

Architects: Donald Ross, Ron Garl

Par: 70

Bermuda 419/rye fairways,
tifdwarf Bermuda/
Poa Trivialis greens

Yardage/Rating/Slope:

<u>Gold tees</u>
6,284/70.2/118

<u>Blue tees</u>
5,928/68.6, 73.5*/115, 132*

<u>White tees</u>
5,692/67.4, 72.1*/112, 129*

<u>Red tees</u>
4,818/63.1, 67.7*/101, 119*

*Women's ratings

PRESERVATION

Because of the
Renaissance Vinoy's prized
location on Tampa Bay,
special care was taken to
preserve the pristine
environment during
renovation of
the golf club.

EXPANSION PROJECT

Typical for its time, the original hotel had 375 small rooms. The present facility boasts 360 spacious, modernized rooms, accomplished by merging three rooms into two in the main building and adding a 102-room tower.

But golf isn't the only nearby pleasure in this sunny urban paradise. A leisurely walk takes a visitor to the white sand beaches, to shopping at the Pier, or to any of several nearby museums. Historic Al Lang Field, the venerable baseball spring training home for over eighty years to the Boston Braves, New York Yankees, St. Louis Cardinals, and now to Tampa Bay's own Devil Rays, is also in the neighborhood.

Disney's Grand Floridian Resort and Spa in Lake Buena Vista is a great option for golfing families or golfers with children in tow. It's touted as the most luxurious spot in town, a hotel that is brimming with turn-of-the-century opulence and a rather charming (in that Disney

"If you want to hit your driver on every hole, you can. But if your control is not there that day, play conservatively and just keep the ball in play."

—RANDY MOSLEY, DIRECTOR OF GOLF, RENAISSANCE VINOY GOLF CLUB

RENAISSANCE VINOY RESORT

RESORT RATING:

CHALLENGE	★★★
BEAUTY	★★★☆
LODGING	★★★★☆
CUISINE	★★★★
AMENITIES	★★★

ST. PETERSBURG, FLORIDA

sort of way) Victorian style. One could spend the entire vacation happily enjoying the perks of this mind-bogglingly complete resort—taking in a spa treatment or lounging on the waterfront of Lake Buena Vista in the warm tropical breeze—without even stepping foot on the resort's half dozen golf courses.

But golf at the Grand Floridian is not to be missed. For those who appreciate a beautifully designed course, there couldn't be a more exciting place to enjoy golf—but don't be fooled, these courses are as challenging as they are attractive. Lake Buena Vista has a Napoleon complex: It seems to compensate for its relative shortness with a bullying difficulty. The greens are well bunkered, and an unforgiving bermuda rough gives way to a pine forest more foreboding than an alligator-filled swamp.

EXPERIENCING

RENAISSANCE VINOY RESORT

This classic waterfront resort, originally built in 1925 and fully restored in 1992, combines the style and glamour of an earlier era with the modern convenience of exceptional amenities.

• Relax by the pool, where attendants bring you cool sparkling spritzer bottles and chilled scented towels.
• Hear about the resort's rich heritage, its celebrated guests, and extravagant balls, then top off your tour with luncheon in the original dining room.
• Escape to the Grand Canyon or listen to New Age music in the "floatarium," an egg-shaped relaxation chamber with audio and video capabilities.

GOLFING

DISNEY'S GRAND FLORIDIAN RESORT AND SPA
WALT DISNEY WORLD GOLF

PALM COURSE
Architect: Joe Lee
Tour Stops: National Car Rental
Golf Classic
Par: 72
Tifway-419 fairways,
Tifdwarf greens
Yardage/Rating/Slope:
<u>Blue tees</u>
6,957/73.9/138
<u>White tees</u>
6,461/71.6/130
<u>Gold tees</u>
6,029/69.5/126

MAGNOLIA COURSE
Architect: Joe Lee
Tour Stops: National Car Rental
Golf Classic
Par: 72
Tifway-419 fairways,
Tifdwarf greens
Yardage/Rating/Slope:
<u>Blue tees</u>
7,190/74.9/136
<u>White tees</u>
6,642/72.3/130
<u>Gold tees</u>
6,091/69.4/125

LAKE BUENA VISTA COURSE
Architect: Joe Lee
Tour Stops: 1996–97 LPGA Tour
Par: 72
Tifway-419 fairways,
Tifdwarf greens
Yardage/Rating/Slope:
<u>Blue tees</u>
6,819/73.0/133
<u>White tees</u>
6,268/70.1/129
<u>Gold tees</u>
5,919/68.6/123

SPECIAL OCCASIONS

The Grand Floridian has been the site of numerous celebrations and special events such as this one that united Disney's Michael Eisner, Burt Reynolds, and several of Walt Disney World's most distinguished residents.

MOUSE COUNTRY

No matter where you look, the scene evokes Disney magic. Even directional signs and tee markers remind guests that this is the "house the mouse built."

Water comes into play most on the Palm Course. Precision drives are more crucial on these fairways than they are, for instance, on the adjoining Magnolia Course. (Magnolia is the home of the infamous "Mouse-Trap," a cute but costly bunker shaped like Mickey's head that fronts number 6.) At Osprey Ridge, however, novices and seasoned players alike find that there are so many options for going from the tee to the putting green, they might have trouble

just keeping pace. For the golfer who is always searching for something new and unique, they'll find a surprise waiting for them at Eagle Pines. Modeled after the Old Marsh Course in Palm Beach, its concave fairways follow the inherent landscape of Florida's wetlands, with plenty of

LAKE BUENA VISTA, FLORIDA	RESORT RATING:	
	CHALLENGE	★★★★
DISNEY'S GRAND FLORIDIAN	BEAUTY	★★★⯪
	LODGING	★★★★
	CUISINE	★★★⯪
	AMENITIES	★★★★⯪
RESORT AND SPA		

bunkers and native grasses waiting to capture errant shots. Settling down at the Bonnet Creek Golf Club after a morning of putting and driving (and perhaps having used a sand wedge a bit more often than usual), visitors will notice that even the clubhouse is decorated in a fun, exaggerated, signature Disney style.

Grand Floridian guests can dine on the French Provençal cuisine of chef Roland Muller at Citricos, a restaurant that features an on-stage kitchen designed so that diners can see the entrees being prepared. The three-hundred-vintage wine list can be a bit daunting, but the

knowledgeable waitstaff is always ready to rescue even the most perplexed guest.

The gently rolling north Texas hills near Irving, Texas, are the setting for the world-class Four Seasons Resort and Club, Dallas at Las Colinas. Southwestern cuisine at several restaurants and lounges is all accentuated by that uniquely warm hospitality that is pure Texas. By all means, don't miss the Sunday brunch at Café on the Green, with a live jazz trio and an amazing buffet.

EXPERIENCING

DISNEY'S GRAND FLORIDIAN RESORT AND SPA
LAKE BUENA VISTA, FLORIDA

Nestled on acres of picturesque shorefront near the Magic Kingdom, this grand resort boasts a Disney-style theme: the opulent Victorian elegance of turn-of-the-century Florida.

• Visit Disney's legendary theme parks, with easy access via watercraft, motor coach, and monorail service from the hotel's Grand Lobby.

• Enjoy an abundance of water-oriented activities, from sunning on the beach to parasailing above Bay Lake for a view of the Magic Kingdom usually reserved for eagles.

• Enjoy everything from a soothing seaweed body wrap to a couple's massage at the full service spa and health club.

GOLFING

DISNEY'S GRAND FLORIDIAN RESORT AND SPA

WALT DISNEY WORLD GOLF
LAKE BUENA VISTA, FLORIDA

EAGLE PINES COURSE
Architect: Pete Dye
Tour Stops: 1994 PGA. 1995
LPGA. 2001 Senior Tour
Par: 72
Tifway-419 fairways,
Tifdwarf greens
Yardage/Rating/Slope:
Talons tees
6,772/72.5/135
Crest tees
6,302/70.1/129
Wings tees
5,520/66.6/119

OSPREY RIDGE COURSE
Architect: Tom Fazio
Par: 72
Tifway-419 fairways,
Tifdwarf greens
Yardage/Rating/Slope:
Talon tees
7,101/74.4/131
Crest tees
6,680/72.3/129
Wings tees
6,103/69.5/123

A DISNEY VACATION

Disney's Grand Floridian offers first-class pampering, picture-postcard views, and architectural details that evoke a bygone era. In the heart of Walt Disney World Resort, three theme parks combine with five world-class golf courses to make this a destination the whole family will love.

"At Palm and Magnolia, you play where the pros play. The Arnold Palmer Course has a tremendous amount of history. Osprey Ridge and Eagle Pines are outstanding designer courses, and Lake Buena Vista feels like a tropical paradise."

—KEVIN WEICKEL, HEAD GOLF PROFESSIONAL, WALT DISNEY WORLD GOLF

THE MAIN EVENT

The Grand Floridian has one amenity no

other golf resort can boast: Walt Disney

World is just a monorail-ride away.

"You use every club in your bag when you play the Cottonwood Valley Course. Cottonwood is fairly forgiving, with generous fairways and lots of room around the greens, . . .

RESORT RATING:	
CHALLENGE	★★★★
BEAUTY	★★★☆
LODGING	★★★★☆
CUISINE	★★★★
AMENITIES	★★★★

IRVING, TEXAS

FOUR SEASONS RESORT & CLUB

DALLAS AT LAS COLINAS

but it's still a challenging, PGA tour-caliber golf course."

—Scott McClinton, Head Golf Professional, Cottonwood Valley Course

IDEAL LOCATION

The Four Seasons Resort and Club is located within the heart of Las Colinas, where winters are mild and summers are warm, dry, and sunny.

But the real story at the Four Seasons is golf, and it all starts with guest suites that look out over the Tournament Players Course, one of the top TPC courses in the country, and one of two eighteen-hole championship courses at the resort. While the TPC fairways are lined with hundreds of stately trees of many varieties, entrances to the greens are very much open to the wind, and the course as a whole rewards finesse rather than power. With the toughest part of the round lying between the eighth and fifteenth holes, a player has a few holes to get into gear before facing the stiffest challenges. These take the form of several doglegs and a long water hazard running beside the fair-

ways, as well as some of the larger and more cunningly placed bunkers on the course. Because the water hazard is flanked on both sides by the fairways, any crosswind eventually presents an interesting obstacle. By the second to the last hole, where a picturesque lake offers a gratifying view of the hotel on the far side, golfers can well understand why this course has been a *Golf* magazine Silver Medalist from 1994 through 2000.

The other course at Four Seasons Resort and Club, Cottonwood Valley, is not only a world-class, pro-level setting, but has also repeatedly been recognized as the top "women-friendly" golf course in the country. The first green is whimsically shaped like the state of Texas, while the shape of the sand bunker bears a strong resemblance to Oklahoma. The Cottonwood Valley Course has been redesigned in recent years, drastically reducing the size and number of bunkers to coordinate with the design of the TPC Course. More than four hundred new trees fringe the fairways.

A FULL SPATE OF ACTIVITIES

Adjacent to the hotel, the Sports Club is the recreational centerpiece of the four–hundred–acre resort. In addition to golf and tennis, it features indoor and outdoor jogging tracks, a sports studio for specialty classes, three outdoor pools, and a children's pool.

HALF OLD, HALF NEW

Created in 1982 by Robert Trent Jones, Jr., the Cottonwood Course lost half of its holes to the new TPC Course. Nine new holes were created by Jay Morrish.

SPECIALTY SUITES

Of the 365 guest rooms at the Four Seasons Resort and Club, the most dramatic is the ninth-floor Nelson Suite, which overlooks the TPC Course.

FOUR SEASONS RESORT AND CLUB, DALLAS AT LAS COLINAS
DALLAS, TEXAS

TOURNAMENT PLAYERS COURSE
Tour stops: GTE Byron Nelson Classic
Architects: Jay Morrish with Ben Crenshaw and Byron Nelson
Par: 70
Bermuda fairways, bentgrass greens
Yardage/Rating/Slope:
Silver tees
6,899/73.5/135
Blue tees
6,500/71.4, 76.0*/129, 135*
White tees
6,004/68.9, 73.3*/122, 129*
Red tees
5,340/70.6*/116*

COTTONWOOD VALLEY COURSE
Architects: Robert Trent Jones, Jr., Jay Morrish
Par: 70
419 Bermuda fairways, bentgrass greens
Yardage/Rating/Slope:
Silver tees
6,927/73.4/133
Blue tees
6,367/70.5, 75.5*/126, 134*
White tees
5,961/68.4, 73.4*/117, 129*
Red tees
5,320/70.0*/118*
*Women's ratings

OPEN GREENS

The TPC Course is one of sixteen Tournament Players courses in the country. Entrances to its greens are wide open, providing a challenge to stiff winds.

Some say if you want to visit another country you need not go farther than Texas—hill country, that is, where you'll find the Barton Creek resort. Located just outside of Austin, it encompasses the famed Fazio Foothills golf course, the most recent addition to the already existing Fazio Canyons, Crenshaw Cliffside, and Palmer Lakeside courses. Foothills moves through beautiful slopes set against native limestone walls. Bordered by a meandering creek, the tree-lined fairways are a scenic treat for the enthusiastic golfer. Madrone trees and groves of Spanish oak set off what is widely considered the most breathtaking terrain in the whole state. From these little

RESORT RATING:		AUSTIN, TEXAS
CHALLENGE	★★★★⯪	
BEAUTY	★★★★⯪	
LODGING	★★★★⯪	
CUISINE	★★★★⯪	
AMENITIES	★★★★⯪	

BARTON CREEK

rolling hills one might pause in the middle of a game to admire the state capital shimmering in the distance, but great golf and pretty vistas are not the only luxuries guests will find at Barton Creek. Visitors can stay fit by visiting the European spa, playing a game of tennis, or working out in the exercise studio.

Vacationers can have a casual luncheon at Barton Creek Lakeside, enjoying real Texas barbecue in a relaxed outdoor setting. Feeling hungry after a round of golf and a trip back to their comfortable Texas-sized rooms (they're incredibly spacious!), they can also cruise down to the more formal Hill Country Dining Room, which offers a uniquely health-conscious menu featuring some of Texas's best southwestern entrees.

WATERFALLS, LIMESTONE
Both the Fazio Foothills and Crenshaw Cliffside courses are accented by scenic waterfalls and limestone canyons, providing a variety of challenging holes in a stunning natural environment.

SOUTHWESTERN STYLE

Barton Creek guest rooms feature a bath and a half, individual study desks with high-speed interconnect capabilities, and a well-stocked refreshment center. Sixteen suites provide the utmost in privacy and breathtaking views.

EXPERIENCING

BARTON CREEK

Experience gracious personal attention and a wealth of recreational options in beautiful Texas hill country.

• Relax in richly furnished rooms with views of the surrounding golf courses and grounds.
• Sample a wide range of culinary delights, from authentic Tex-Mex dishes to continental cuisine.
• Bask in a lavish European-style spa with a wide array of spa treatments, indoor and outdoor swimming pools, and a full tennis complex with pro shop.
• At day's end, relax and enjoy a steam bath, dip into the pool, or wind down with drinks and a game of billiards.

A NATURAL BEAUTY

Ben Crenshaw and Bill Coore's traditional Crenshaw Cliffside layout features broad, rolling fairways and widely varied green sizes. White-tailed deer delight golfers nearly as much as does the course's playability.

GOLFING

BARTON CREEK

BARTON CREEK
COUNTRY CLUB
AUSTIN, TEXAS

CRENSHAW CLIFFSIDE COURSE

Architects: Bill Crenshaw
and Bill Coore

Par: 71

Bermuda fairways and greens

Yardage/Rating/Slope:

Gold tees

6,678/71.0/124

Red tees

4,843/71.0/124

FAZIO FOOTHILLS COURSE

Architect: Tom Fazio

Par: 72

Bermuda fairways and greens

Yardage/Rating/Slope:

Gold tees

6,956/74.0/135

Red tees

5,207/69.4/120

FAZIO CANYONS COURSE

Architect: Tom Fazio

Par: 72

Bermuda fairways and greens

Yardage:

Pro tees

7,161

Black tees

6,690

Red tees

5,078

PALMER LAKESIDE COURSE

Architect: Arnold Palmer

Par: 71

Bermuda fairways and greens

Yardage/Rating/Slope:

Gold tees

6,657/71.0/124

Red tees

5,067/71.0/124

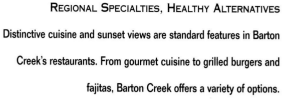

REGIONAL SPECIALTIES, HEALTHY ALTERNATIVES

Distinctive cuisine and sunset views are standard features in Barton Creek's restaurants. From gourmet cuisine to grilled burgers and fajitas, Barton Creek offers a variety of options.

TOP TEN IN TEXAS

Professional golfers rate Arnold Palmer's Lakeside design among the top ten Texas courses, and consider it to have the best Champions Bermuda greens in the state. A cascading waterfall and native flora highlight Lakeside's signature eleventh hole, above.

STEAM BATHS AND SAUNAS

The European-style spa provides an array of rejuvenating treatments including full-body massage and essential oil envelopment.

There is a down-home sense of hospitality behind the recent renovation of this classic American resort. Barton Creek likes to call its guest rooms "sanctuaries." As a member of the Audubon Cooperative Sanctuary system, the resort is committed to preserving a harmonious relationship with its landscape. This arrangement is not just good for the environment: Barton Creek's golfing visitors benefit at least as much from the proven stress-reducing power of nature—especially after a tough go at Fazio Foothills. In the end, a stay at what looks and feels like a stately Texas mansion will have Texas deep in the hearts of visitors.

The South has plenty to offer to golfers in all seasons. Its tremendous diversity necessitates that travelers return to this graceful region year after year.

"The links-style Crenshaw Course has large, undulating greens and open fairways; Palmer Lakeside has lake views and several canyon carries; and our original Fazio Foothills requires precision approach shots to small greens. Fazio Canyons is probably the most difficult course, with large greens and native areas outside the cart paths."

—Tim Oates, Head Golf Professional, Barton Creek

CHOICE OF LOCATION

Dining options are versatile and varied, ranging from authentic Tex-Mex to continental cuisine, and served in charming dining rooms, outdoor settings, or the privacy of a guest room.

LAKESIDE LINKS

BY CYNTHIA BOAL JANSSENS

MANY OF ERNEST Hemingway's early stories were about the summers he spent in northern Michigan. In these tales, he described its pristine wilderness and raw beauty. Much time has passed since Hemingway summered on Torch Lake in the days after World War I, but were he here now surely he would have played golf. For golf in the midwestern part of America has a character all its own, just like he did.

Most particularly, golf in the Midwest is marked by the change of seasons. The links open around mid-April and can be played through October. Weather is always iffy, which may be why Midwesterners are so passionate about golf. We play in rain, fog, sleet, and snow. We play on glorious days and lousy days. Fortunately, we are blessed with lovely terrain, deciduous trees, intriguing wildlife, home-grown course designers of considerable merit, rain suits of every design, and a collection of golf resorts to be envied.

Most of the midwestern golf resorts are located to the north, where lakes, woods, mountains, and valleys vary the terrain. And for grandeur, even the great oceans can hardly match the Great Lakes as a backdrop for dramatic golf holes.

The resorts in the midwest are much like the region itself, down-to-earth and homey and many are still run by families. The pricing is reasonable, too. Midweek, especially, the Midwest can be a real buy.

Weather notwithstanding, resort golf in the region can indeed be glorious . . . when the sun shines, when a doe followed by a couple of fawns wanders right next to your fairway shot, when wild turkeys scuttle over the green, when your tee shot sails off a grand elevated tee to drop softly into a valley lined with brilliant trees. For during the fall, when crimson, orange, and purple maples, golden birches, and tawny oaks paint the landscape with bold strokes, golf in the Midwest is, quite simply, breathtaking.

However, the foremost of the Midwest's golf resorts is located not in these woods, but rather by a small town. Just a few miles from the western shore of Lake Michigan lies a quiet little community of just 1,965 residents. It is innocuous enough, with tree-lined streets, picture-book schools, and lovely brick homes. But Kohler, Wisconsin, is much more than one of America's first planned communities. It is a resort town: home of the American Club, a historic inn. It is a factory town: the home base of one of the world's best known kitchen and bath products companies. And it is home to several of the best known golf courses in America.

In Kohler, enthusiasts can find a comprehensive resort that offers distinctive accommodations, fine dining, interesting shops, an array of family activities, and golf courses of extraordinary design.

Called "An American Original," at the turn of the century the distinctive red brick American Club building

PRESIDENTIAL COMFORTS

Each of the two Presidential suites includes a spacious living room and cozy fireplace, a separate dining area and powder room, and a bedroom with adjoining master bath.

THE AMERICAN CLUB
BLACKWOLF RUN

Architect: Pete Dye
Tour stops: 1998 U.S. Women's Open

MEADOW VALLEY COURSE
Par: 72
Bentgrass fairways and greens
Yardage/Rating/Slope:

Black tees
7,142/74.7/143

Blue tees
6,735/73.0/138

White tees
6,169/70.4/132

Red tees
5,065/69.5/125

RIVER COURSE
Par: 72
Bentgrass fairways and greens
Yardage/Rating/Slope:

Black tees
6,691/74.9/151

Blue tees
6,607/73.2/146

White tees
6,110/70.9/137

Red tees
5,115/70.7/128

WILD HAZARDS

Blackwolf Run's River Course challenges players early on, requiring them to use an extra club to carry the large front bunker on the second hole.

LUXURY AND TIMELESS STYLE

Floral print draperies, plush upholstery, and fine wood furniture imbue every guest room with a residential ambience.

was originally a dormitory for Kohler factory workers. Today its rooms are decorated with Americana antiques and each bathroom is outfitted with the newest Kohler fixtures. There's nothing quite like coming in off an invigorating round on the golf course to sink into a hot whirlpool tub that features several waterfalls!

But what particularly draws visitors to the American Club is golf. Imaginative golf. Golf inspired by the company chairman and president, Herbert V. Kohler, Jr. In 1988, Kohler opened Blackwolf Run with two courses designed by Pete Dye. It immediately received accolades, and it hosted the U.S. Women's Open in 1998. And that was just the beginning.

THE AMERICAN CLUB

KOHLER, WISCONSIN

RESORT RATING:	
CHALLENGE	★★★★★
BEAUTY	★★★★★
LODGING	★★★★★
CUISINE	★★★★⯪
AMENITIES	★★★★⯪

Where the Kohler is really breaking ground is with its two new courses at Whistling Straits. This dramatic links complex consists of the open, rugged, and windswept terrain of the Straits Course, winding two miles along Lake Michigan, and the Irish Course, which is a streams-and-dunes interior course. Again, both were designed by Dye, who frequently jumped aboard tractors to sculpt the earth "just so." Some three million cubic yards of dirt were moved to create the impression of a heaving Irish links. Play here can be extremely tricky, as the hazards are horrendous.

"OUTWARD BOUND"
Hole 1 of the Straits Course showcases Pete Dye's trademark hazards—railroad-tie bunkers, desert-size sand traps, and rolling mounds of prairie grass.

Or, as Dye himself put it: "I should say this with some degree of modesty. But in my lifetime, I've never seen anything like this. Anyplace. Period."

And just to make it more memorable, in the grand tradition of golf, the Straits Course is a walking course only, though caddies are available. And you are welcome to walk the Irish Course, a rarity in these days of omnipresent power carts.

DESIGNER SHOWCASE

Guest bathrooms are luxurious, with each featuring a one- or two-person Kohler whirlpool bath and a different combination of elegant fixtures and designs.

The Whistling Straits clubhouse matches the courses in both impression and design. It looks like a fortified farmhouse with rubble stone walls, a deep slate roof, and deep-set mullioned windows. Inside it is decorated in warm tones and has big fireplaces, adding to the impression that you've been transported to Scotland or Ireland. In point of fact, this clubhouse is far more lavish than most of those in the United Kingdom!

And the final touch? A flock of Scottish Blackface sheep wanders the course, adding to its look of timelessness. You'll usually find them munching contentedly in the rough.

Kohler's facilities serve both village residents and resort guests. An array of restaurants serve extremely good cuisine (particularly the Italian food at Cucina at the Inn), a spa/fitness center/racquet club offers exercise and pampering, and a shopping mall has everything from a gourmet grocery store to a cooking school. The River Wildlife hunting lodge offers shooting, hiking, and other wilderness experiences.

Some fifty miles to the northeast across Lake Michigan from Kohler is a cluster of outstanding resorts in Michigan. Like Whistling Straits, Bay Harbor is a reclamation project, built on the site of an abandoned century-old cement plant and limestone quarry. Today it is one of America's most distinguished residential communities, carved out of 1,200 acres—likened to a "moonscape"—which stretch along five miles of Little Traverse Bay just west of Petoskey.

Just approaching Bay Harbor can cause you to catch your breath, as the views from the cliffs above are stunning. Bay Harbor is as much a small city as it is a resort. Begun just six years ago, it now includes a yacht club, an equestrian club, a shopping/dining district, a one-hundred-room inn, and the nationally recognized Bay Harbor Golf Club, all strung out along the water. It is both exclusive and pricey.

FLOWING FOUNTAINS

Four garden courtyards separate the wings of

the American Club, providing the perfect setting

for a romantic stroll or tranquil meditation.

THE AMERICAN CLUB
KOHLER, WISCONSIN

At the American Club, small-town charm blends with world-class accommodations for a relaxed resort lifestyle.

• Soak in your own whirlpool bath by Kohler, whose fixtures and faucets adorn every luxurious bathroom.

• Tour the Kohler Design Center, with its museum and factory, or visit the quaint shops and boutiques at nearby Woodlake.

• Treat yourself to fine dining at a stained-glass coffeehouse transported from England, a rustic log cabin in the woods, or a floating dining raft in the middle of a lake.

• Enjoy soothing, rejuvenating services or tennis, racquetball, and more at the Sports Core Salon and Day Spa.

• Visit River Wildlife, a private preserve and hunt club with miles of trails and a meandering river ideal for canoeing and fishing.

FORMER DORMITORY

The American Club was originally built to house the single young men who worked at the nearby Kohler plumbing factory. Today it provides luxurious lodging, recreation, and accommodations like the Whistling Straits clubhouse to visitors.

THE AMERICAN CLUB
WHISTLING STRAITS

Architect: Pete Dye
Tour stops: 1999 PGA Club
Professional Championship,
2004 PGA Championship

STRAITS COURSE
Par: 72
Fescue fairways,
bentgrass greens
Yardage/Rating/Slope:
Black tees
7,288/76.7/151
Blue tees
6,869/74.2/144
Green tees
6,450/71.9, 78.1*/137, 146*
White tees
6,140/70.5, 76.4*/134, 142*
Red tees
5,381/66.9, 72.2*/125, 132*

IRISH COURSE
Par: 72
Bentgrass fairways,
bentgrass greens
Yardage/Rating/Slope:
Black tees
7,201/75.6/146
Blue tees
6,750/73.5/141
Green tees
6,414/72.0, 77.4*/137, 142*
White tees
6,038/70.3, 75.2*/133, 137*
Red tees
5,109/70*/126*
*Women's ratings

"PINCHED NERVE"

Designed in the style of the
great seaside courses,
the Straits Course boasts
some of the most scenic
holes of golf in the country.
Hole 17, with its
expansive vistas, is
a perfect example.

"The Quarry Course, built in and around an old working quarry, calls for a more target-oriented game: you're either on the fairway or in a big quarry ditch. . . .

RESORT RATING:

CHALLENGE ★★★★⯪

BEAUTY ★★★★⯪

LODGING ★★★★

CUISINE ★★★★

AMENITIES ★★★⯪

The Preserve Course requires more distance off the tees and more accuracy getting onto the greens, which are fairly small and well bunkered."

—Brian Sanderson, Head Golf Professional, Bay Harbor Golf Club

Little wonder that Bay Harbor's twenty-seven-hole golf course has been considered a "must-play" in recent seasons, despite the heftiest greens fees in the state. (Foursomes have been known to fly in for the day, just for a round of golf.) It is a stunner. There was a quarry here, and the big pits that were left make for some mighty interesting hole designs. Golfers play atop 150-foot bluffs, through majestic northern hardwoods, and along the foot of towering cliffs (expect to hit some wayward balls that you will never, ever retrieve). And to make the view even more impressive, there is waterfrontage on most holes.

Nestled in the middle of the Bay Harbor "village" is the Inn at Bay Harbor. Here, a

BAY HARBOR, MICHIGAN

THE INN AT BAY HARBOR

couple or a family can enjoy all the amenities of a condominium suite, with big-window views over the bay. After golf, visitors might consider a dip in the pool, an aromatherapy treatment in the spa, or, for those who still have energy, a workout at the fitness center.

Bay Harbor offers several dining options. At the clubhouse, guests can choose a sandwich or salad in the Grille, a bite with the kids in the sunny, casual dining area, or an elegant dinner in the airy upstairs dining room that overlooks the bay. For fine dining, the Latitude restaurant in the Marina district is not to be missed. Here, Chef Richard Travis has created a menu of modern American food featuring Michigan's seasonal larder. The two-story dining room takes full advantage of the view over Little Traverse Bay and is the perfect spot for a romantic interlude.

About fifteen miles from Bay Harbor is Boyne Highlands, one of Michigan's best-known resorts. The Highlands has long been known for its family-friendly ski trails. Now that it has added four championship golf courses, spiffed up its lodge rooms, and built some nifty cottage-style condominiums, it has become a popular resort year around.

Bay Harbor Golf Club

MINING GOLF GOLD

Bay Harbor Club's Quarry Course, left,

has a forty-foot gorge bordered by shale

cliffs, making for unique hazards.

VICTORIAN RETREAT

Lake Michigan's Little Traverse Bay is the setting for the Inn at

Bay Harbor, an elegant summer resort that reflects the splendid

simplicity of turn-of-the-century Victorian getaways.

COZY BUT BRIGHT

The rooms at the Inn at Bay Harbor play

off of the resort's Victorian charm but

remain light and airy.

THE INN AT BAY HARBOR
BAY HARBOR GOLF CLUB
BAY HARBOR, MICHIGAN

Architects: Arthur Hills and
Stephen Kircher
Tour stops: 1999 Shell's
Wonderful World of Golf

THE LINKS COURSE
Par: 36
Bentgrass fairways and greens
Yardage/Rating/Slope:
Black tees
3,432/36.2/141
Gold tees
3,023, 2,899*/34.4/126
Red tees
2,166/34.8/113

THE PRESERVE COURSE
Par: 36
Bentgrass fairways and greens
Yardage/Rating/Slope:
Black tees
3,378/36.5/143
Gold tees
2,792, 2,729*/33.7/122
Red tees
1,921/34.6/112

THE QUARRY COURSE
Par: 36
Bentgrass fairways and greens
Yardage/Rating/Slope:
Black tees
3,348/36.0/145
Gold tees
2,972, 2,954*/34.6/130
Red tees
1,985, 1,960*/34.5/112
*Women's ratings

RECLAMATION

The designers of Bay

Harbor's Quarry Course

utilized existing man-made

changes to the land in

creating a startlingly

unique layout.

BOYNE HIGHLANDS
THE DONALD ROSS
MEMORIAL COURSE

Architect: Boyne Staff (eighteen
reproductions of Donald Ross's
greatest holes)
Par: 72
Bentgrass fairways and greens
Yardage/Rating/Slope:

Black tees
6,814/73.4/132

Blue tees
6,563/73.4/132

Gold tees
6,233/70.9/128

White tees
5,658/67.1/120

Red tees
4,929/68.5/119

SHADOW AND LIGHT

Boyne Highlands' premier

Heather Course has

received numerous

accolades for its challenge.

The fifth hole proves that

the Heather Course also

deserves praise for

its beauty.

When guests drive onto the grounds of Boyne Highlands, they might think they are somewhere in central Europe. The stone-and-timber façade of the main lodge calls to mind a Bavarian manor house. The pond out front, lined with cattails, tempts you to thrown in a line in hopes of catching dinner.

This lodge area is the hub of activity, with its restaurants and bars and the bulk of the lodge rooms. Here also is the Young Americans Dinner Theater, which has been entertaining guests with song and dance in July and August since 1978. For a more elegant and discreet dining experience, drive through the woods to the prestigious Country Club of Boyne, a membership club that is open to the public for dining. Not far from the club are the Donald Ross cottages, attractive, freestanding duplexes sheathed in cedar shakes.

The four courses at Boyne Highlands are the Heather, long considered Boyne's premier course; the highly anticipated second nine of the Arthur Hills Course, now open and considered equally superb; the unique Donald Ross Memorial Course, whose eighteen holes re-create the greatest of Ross's designs at Pinehurst, Royal Dornoch, Inverness, and others; and the well-regarded Moor Course. Those staying at the Highlands may also play the two courses at its sister resort, Boyne Mountain, and the course at Bay Harbor. When not out on the links, golfers can enjoy a quick round on the par-three executive course, sharpen their skills at one of the two driving ranges, pick up some sportswear at one of the two pro shops, take a lesson at the golf school, or tip a few at the 19th Tee Bar and Restaurant.

Heading south out of Boyne country, visitors come to Traverse City, known as the Cherry Capital of America and the home of another of Michigan's outstanding resorts, the Grand Traverse Resort and Spa in Acme.

You can hardly miss the Grand Traverse Resort: In the middle of its grounds is its distinctive, gleaming seventeen-story tower—a landmark for miles around. Grand Traverse is a full-service resort geared for all ages. Its grounds are quite wonderful, offering 1,400 acres of lakes, rivers, and woodlands to explore.

Each spring the region's cherry orchards blossom and the golf courses open. Perhaps the best known course in the state (and still one of the toughest) is the Bear, an early Jack Nicklaus design. Definitely not for the faint of heart, a round here will be long-remembered. Two years ago, The Wolverine, designed by Gary Player, expanded the resort's offerings to fifty-four holes.

If the weather turns inclement, or guests are just ready to unwind, they head over to the new Spa and Health Club. Whether you're chilling out in a yoga class or experiencing a stress relief wrap, relaxation is guaranteed. Those who wish to keep fit can play a couple of sets of indoor tennis, swim laps in the pool, or work out in the weight room.

"The landing areas are generous and the greens are spacious. Just put the ball in the landing areas and you'll have a good score."

—PAULO ROCHA, HEAD GOLF PROFESSIONAL, HILLS COURSE

BOYNE HIGHLANDS

HARBOR SPRINGS, MICHIGAN

RESORT RATING:	
CHALLENGE	★★★★⯨
BEAUTY	★★★★
LODGING	★★★
CUISINE	★★★
AMENITIES	★★★★

EXPERIENCING

BOYNE HIGHLANDS

Inspired by the grand resorts of Europe, Boyne Highlands features gracious service, impeccable style, and old-world elegance.

• Visit the Wellness Institute, home of health and healing for body, mind, and spirit; its staff of physicians provide comprehensive health assessments.

• Relax in the indoor/outdoor jet pool, with its adjoining patio, sauna, and health club.

• Explore the breathtaking expanse of forests and hills from hiking and bike trails for every skill level.

• Try the time-honored pastime of fly-fishing, or play tennis on traditional clay courts.

BOYNE HIGHLANDS
HARBOR SPRINGS, MICHIGAN

THE HEATHER COURSE
Architect: Robert Trent Jones, Sr.
Par: 72
Bentgrass fairways, Poa
Annua/bentgrass greens
Yardage/Rating/Slope:
Black tees
7,210/74.0/131
Gold tees
6,527/71.2/126
Red tees
5,245/67.8/111

THE MOOR COURSE
Architects: William Newcombe,
Everett Kircher
Par: 72
Bentgrass fairways, Poa
Annua/bentgrass greens
Yardage/Rating/Slope:
Blue tees
6,556/74.0/131
Gold tees
6,196/71.3/127
White tees
5,723/69.1/122
Red tees
5,061/70.0/118

THE ARTHUR HILLS COURSE
Architect: Arthur Hills
Par: 73
Bentgrass fairways and greens
Yardage (Note: This course has
not yet been rated)
Black tees
7,312
Gold tees
6,362
Red tees
4,811

SMALL PACKAGES

Though only a nine-hole

course, the Arthur Hills

Course packs in enough

challenge to give as

much punch as many

championship

courses.

TOWERING PRESENCE

More than six hundred rooms, tower suites, and condominiums offer magnificent views of the bay and golf courses at Grand Traverse Resort.

GOLFING

GRAND TRAVERSE RESORT AND SPA

BEAR COURSE
Architect: Jack Nicklaus
Tour stops: Ameritech Senior Open, Cherry Cup Tournament, Michigan Open
Par: 72
Bentgrass fairways and greens
Yardage/Rating/Slope:
Blue tees
7,065/76.8/146
White tees
6,176/72.7/144
Red tees
5,281/73.1/137

WOLVERINE COURSE
Architect: Gary Player
Par: 72
Bentgrass fairways and greens
Yardage/Rating/Slope:
Gold tees
7,065/73.9/144
Blue tees
6,568/71.2/135
White tees
5,986/67.8/125/72
Red tees
5,029/68.1/121

SPRUCE RUN COURSE
Architect: William Newcomb
Par: 72
Bentgrass fairways and greens
Yardage/Rating/Slope:
Blue tees
6,304/70.8/130
White tees
5,696/68.2/126
Red tees
4,726/68.2/125

SINGULAR SENSATION

The experience at Grand Traverse Resort is a singular one, especially when it's spent meeting the challenge of The Bear's eighth hole.

Summer is the resort's family season, when the lakefront condos fill with parents and children. The beach club on Grand Traverse Bay offers swimming and water sports, and children can attend Camp Traverse.

Dining options on-site include Trillium, at the top of the tower, which is one of the better restaurants in the Traverse City area, and the Sweetwater Café, geared for casual meals. The nearby Interlochen Center for the Arts provides plenty of live concert options.

Continue a bit farther south and you'll come to Crystal Mountain Resort near Thompsonville. This is a family-owned resort that has been operating for forty-five years, and it's a sentimental favorite for many. It's a perfect

"If you're coming for one round of golf, play the Bear. It's a tough, championship-caliber course and a real experience to play."

—TOM SKOGLUND, DIRECTOR OF GOLF, GRAND TRAVERSE RESORT

ACME, MICHIGAN	RESORT RATING:	
	CHALLENGE	★★★★
GRAND TRAVERSE	BEAUTY	★★★½
	LODGING	★★★½
	CUISINE	★★★½
	AMENITIES	★★★½
RESORT AND SPA		

resort for seniors who want to golf at a gentler pace, for those just taking up the game, or for those with children who are learning to play.

That's because the director of golf, Brad Dean, tabbed the state's top teaching professional in 1998, runs one of the state's best golf schools. It attracts golfers from all over the region who wish to polish up their game. The modern ten-acre golf practice center is designed to duplicate real course conditions.

Staying here is special because so many of the accommodations are in either condos or resort homes lining the two golf courses. Crystal caters to families in many ways. The kids can take a golf lesson in the morning and in the afternoon go tubing down the gentle Lower Platte River. They can go frogging, mountain biking, or kayaking.

DINNER WITH A VIEW
Diners are transported by a glass elevator to the Trillium Restaurant, high atop the Grand Traverse Resort tower. The atmosphere is elegant and inviting, the service is always excellent, and the panoramic bay views are breathtaking.

POSH PAMPERING

The Spa at Grand Traverse offers
a refreshing pool, perfect for
swimming laps, soaking up the
sun, or enjoying a cool drink.

BREEZE OFF THE LAKE

Lakeshore beaches nearby the
Grand Traverse Resort and Spa
offer a relaxing outdoor retreat.

CRYSTAL MOUNTAIN RESORT

In the heart of northern Michigan, Crystal Mountain Resort provides fresh air and solitude in a relaxing, pristine setting.

• Choose from a wide variety of accommodations, from lavishly appointed hotel rooms to fully furnished vacation homes.

• Polish your golf game at the ten-acre golf academy, with over fifty schools, clinics, and instructional programs for every level of play.

• Hike through Michigan Legacy Art Park, an interactive outdoor museum featuring live performances and contemporary sculpture.

• Enjoy a wealth of activities without leaving the resort, from tennis, swimming, and mountain bike trips to a chairlift ride to the top of the mountain.

IMPROVEMENTS

Crystal Mountain Resort runs a renowned golf school that attracts golfers from all over the country who want to make small and major changes to raise their level of play.

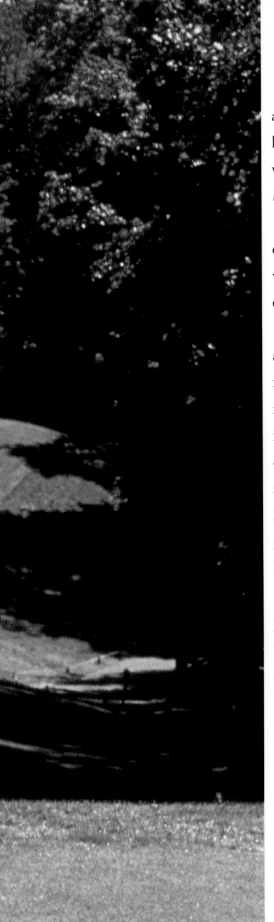

Golfing moms really like Crystal because the kids are occupied, the accommodations are homey, and they can improve their game. Crystal lures women golfers by offering several women-only golf schools. (It was ranked in the top five in America for golf instruction by *Golf for Women* magazine.)

Crystal is also home to the Michigan Legacy Art Park, a thirty-acre outdoor park where artwork is set into nature. Be sure to plan a leisurely walk through its grounds to view the sculptures, which are representative of Michigan's history and culture.

Because of Crystal Mountain's rural location in Benzie County, there are not many restaurants nearby, so lodgers mostly rely on the Wildflower Restaurant or cook for themselves. A special summer treat: Several nights a week, guests can ride a chairlift to the top of the mountain for a barbecue dinner.

THOMPSONVILLE, MICHIGAN

CRYSTAL MOUNTAIN

RESORT

RESORT RATING:	
CHALLENGE	★★★⯪
BEAUTY	★★★⯪
LODGING	★★★★
CUISINE	★★★⯪
AMENITIES	★★★★⯪

While Crystal Mountain is located in the woods, Treetops Resort sits just outside of the bustling town of Gaylord. Gaylord is the county seat of the second-fastest-growing county in Michigan, and the Gaylord Golf Mecca has been growing right along with it. Currently, there are over twenty golf courses in the region, easily accessible from Interstate 75.

Treetops actually began as a very small, family-run ski area called Sylvan Knob. In 1986, Robert Trent Jones, Sr. opened his Masterpiece Course here. He was inspired to give the resort its current name while standing on the tee of his signature number 6 hole, a par-three with a 120-foot vertical drop that looks out over the Pigeon River Valley.

In 1992, the resort opened Treetops North, just a few miles down the road. Located here are the Premier Course, designed by Tom Fazio, and the Signature, Tradition, and Threetops courses, all designed by famed golf instructor and designer Rick Smith, who is the resort's director of golf. It should be noted that Threetops is a tricky par-three cut into ravines between two of the major courses. It's famous as the site of ESPN's Par-3 Shootout each summer.

"On Mountain Ridge, with its wide fairways and deep greens, you can get away with a few missed hits, but keep the elevation changes in mind when choosing your irons. . . .

Betsie Valley is shorter but a little tighter."

—BRAD DEAN, PGA DIRECTOR OF GOLF, CRYSTAL MOUNTAIN RESORT

OUTDOOR CHARM

Picturesque settings like this one lend themselves to a variety of outdoor activities, from relaxing with a good book and enjoying the lake views to cocktails before dinner and meals alfresco.

CRYSTAL MOUNTAIN GOLF
THOMPSONVILLE, MICHIGAN

MOUNTAIN RIDGE COURSE
Architect: William Newcomb
Tour stops: 2000 Michigan Open
Qualifier, 2000 Northern PGA
Michigan Chapter Championship
Par: 72
Bluegrass fairways,
bentgrass greens
Yardage/Rating/Slope:
Blue tees
7,007/73.3/132
White tees
6,258/70.1/128
Red tees
4,956/68.2*/119*

BETSIE VALLEY COURSE
Architect: Renovation by
Ray Hearn Golf Design
Par: 71
Bluegrass fairways,
bentgrass greens
Yardage/Rating/Slope:
Blue tees
6,357/70.2/127
White tees
5,654/67.2, 72.5*/120, 15*
Red tees
4,902/68.5*/12*
*Women's ratings

A FAIRY-TALE HISTORY

What started out as the dream of local citizens has become a major year-round destination resort. The original ski area evolved into a beautiful resort, where wide fairways, breathtaking scenery, and manicured greens make golfing memorable.

"Club selection is key because of the elevation changes at Treetops. The rule is one club up or down for each ten-yard change in elevation."

—SCOTT HEAD, DIRECTOR OF GOLF, TREETOPS RESORT

RESORT RATING:

CHALLENGE	★★★★☆
BEAUTY	★★★★☆
LODGING	★★★
CUISINE	★★★
AMENITIES	★★★☆

EXPERIENCING

TREETOPS RESORT

Perched high atop Pigeon River Valley, this modern alpine retreat offers incomparable views of the Michigan scenery.

• Take in beautiful views of the golf course or woodlands from nearly every room on every level.

• Visit the Top of the Hill Club Sports Bar, featuring more than 250 bottled beers.

• Kick back and relax at the pool or a hot tub, or work up a sweat with some tennis or volleyball.

• Enjoy the cigar-friendly atmosphere and an extensive scotch selection at Fairways Grille, with its extensive menu and inviting ambience.

Driving into Treetops, you'll find the buildings scattered about in a campus-like setting. Two buildings contain lodge rooms, swimming pools, and restaurants, while another is a convention center. The pro shop is also freestanding, as is the day care center near the front entrance. For shoppers, there is a sports merchandise shop featuring golfwear in summer and skiwear in winter. At the Top of the Hill Club Sports Bar, visitors can choose from close to three hundred brands of bottled beers and fifteen varieties on tap.

Treetops Resort offers dining at both of its locations, at the Fairways Grille and the Horizon Dining Room on the main campus

TREETOPS RESORT

GAYLORD, MICHIGAN

and at the new clubhouse at Treetops North. Also at Treetops North, condominiums and home rentals are available.

East of Gaylord is Garland, a gem of a resort tucked into the pristine woods outside Lewiston. Its approach from the north on county road 489 is signaled by a log bridge that spans the road.

Garland Resort is a beautiful facility with outstanding accommodations and four golf courses to match. Its main lodge is the largest log structure east of the Mississippi, set among groomed gardens. It offers rooms, suites, and even a penthouse. Visitors can also opt to stay in one of the many villas scattered over the grounds. These "mini-houses" have four-poster beds, Jacuzzi bathtubs, and fireplaces.

WIDE-OPEN SPACES

The resort buildings at Treetops are

scattered about the grounds, creating

a campus-like setting.

TREETOPS RESORT

TRADITION COURSE
Architect: Rick Smith
Par: 70
Bentgrass/Poa Annua
fairways, bentgrass/
Poa Annua greens
Yardage/Rating/Slope:
Black tees
6,467/70.3/122
Blue tees
5,834/67.8/112
White tees
5,530/66.4/109
Red tees
4,907/67.3/109

THREETOPS COURSE
Architect: Rick Smith
Tour stops: ESPN's Par-3
Shootout
Par: 27
Bentgrass fairways,
bentgrass/Poa Annua greens
Yardage (Note: Threetops has
not yet been rated)
Black tees
1,400
Blue tees
1,297
White tees
1,124
Red tees
967

A DAY WELL SPENT

Treetops Resort began as a

ski area but now draws

visitors for its fabulous

golf offerings

TREETOPS RESORT
GAYLORD, MICHIGAN

MASTERPIECE COURSE
Architect: Robert Trent Jones, Sr.
Par: 71
Bentgrass/Poa Annua fairways
and greens
Yardage/Rating/Slope:
Black tees
7,060/75.5/144
Blue tees
6,399/72.3/135
White tees
5,817/69.5/126
Red tees
4,972/70.0/123

PREMIER COURSE
Architect: Tom Fazio
Par: 72
Bentgrass/Poa Annua fairways
and greens
Yardage/Rating/Slope:
Black tees
6,832/73.6/136
Blue tees
6,302/71.1/129
White tees
5,886/69.1/126
Red tees
5,039/70.0/125

SIGNATURE COURSE
Architect: Rick Smith
Par: 70
Bentgrass/Poa Annua fairways
and greens
Yardage/Rating/Slope:
Black tees
6,653/72.8/140
Blue tees
6,285/71.1/135
White tees
5,863/68.9/130
Gold tees
5,413/72.0/135
Red tees
4,604/67.0/123

TREELINED

It's not hard to see why

Robert Trent Jones, Sr.

thought of the name

Treetops for the

Michigan resort.

"All four courses put a premium on putting. The short game is very important. Ideally, you always want to be below the hole."

—ANDREW BRAILEY, HEAD GOLF PROFESSIONAL, GARLAND

RESORT RATING:

CHALLENGE	★★★⯪
BEAUTY	★★★★
LODGING	★★★★
CUISINE	★★★⯪
AMENITIES	★★★

EXPERIENCING

GARLAND RESORT

In the wooded confines of northern Michigan lies Garland, the largest log lodge east of the Mississippi.

• Feast on local delicacies complemented by fine wines from around the world in the elegant hunt-themed Herman's Dining Room.

• Wander among immaculately groomed grounds or miles of trails in the pristine woodlands.

• If you're a rifle, shotgun, handgun, or bow enthusiast, join a premier trophy hunt in an unparalleled setting.

• Catch glimpses of fox, white-tailed deer, wild turkeys, and nesting bald eagles in one of the few parts of Michigan where they can be seen.

• Burn off calories or build a better body in the fully equipped fitness center.

Dining is equally special. The hunting-themed Herman's Dining Room is the main restaurant (named after the founder and builder, Herman Otto), while the Grille and the Patio offer casual meals. Wild game is often on the menu.

The resort is located in the middle of a forest of hardwoods. While Garland is famous for its golf, its woodlands offer more than thirty miles of hiking and biking trails, three lighted tennis courts, and indoor and outdoor swimming pools. Garland also offers a hunting and shooting program.

Garland's four championship golf courses are the culmination of a life's work. It all began in 1951, when Herman Otto built a nine-hole golf course for friends of his Detroit-based too

LEWISTON, MICHIGAN

GARLAND RESORT

and-die company. Today the Monarch, Swampfire, Reflections, and Fountains courses attract players from all over the world. The courses are meticulously landscaped and groomed. Each has a distinct personality. And they are tough, with water on more holes than one can count.

These resorts are representative of what the Midwest has to offer golfers: exceptional courses of all types, accommodations of every variety, reasonable prices, and great hospitality. Few areas of the country can offer such diversity.

SIGNATURE CUISINE

Local delicacies such as morel mushrooms and pheasant or fresh

salmon, trout, or venison were the inspiration for a menu of

gourmet recipes developed by Garland's renowned chefs.

A GIANT OF A CABIN

Garland enjoys the reputation of being the largest log lodge east of the

Mississippi, but don't be fooled by its rustic appearance. Personal service and

attention to detail combine with northern Michigan ambience to create an

elegant destination. The lodge's designers brought nature's beauty indoors,

too. The natural stone fireplace, stained glass windows, earth tones, and

comfortable rustic furnishings offer a restful haven for Garland's guests.

GOLFING

GARLAND RESORT

Architect: Ron Otto

FOUNTAINS COURSE
Par: 72
Bentgrass fairways and greens
Yardage/Rating/Slope:
Black tees
6,733/73.0/130
Blue tees
6,401/71.5/127
White tees
5,853/68.7, 74.1*/121, 128*
Red tees
4,617/67.3*/115*

MONARCH COURSE
Par: 72
Bluegrass/bentgrass fairways,
bluegrass/bentgrass/
Poa Annua greens
Yardage/Rating/Slope:
Black tees
7,145/75.6/140
Blue tees
6,612/73.0/137
White tees
6,181/71.2/131
Red tees
4,860/69.5*/123*

SWAMPFIRE COURSE
Par: 72
Bluegrass/bentgrass fairways,
bluegrass/bentgrass/
Poa Annua greens
Yardage/Rating/Slope:
Black tees
6,854/73.9/138
Blue tees
6,422/71.7/135
White tees
6,108/70.0/131
Red tees
4,791/68.4*/121*

REFLECTIONS COURSE
Par: 72
Bluegrass/bentgrass fairways,
bluegrass/bentgrass/
Poa Annua greens
Yardage/Rating/Slope:
Blue tees
6,407/70.8/127
White tees
5,967/68.6/124
Red tees
4,714/66.8*/117*
*Women's ratings

RUGGED RESORTS

BY CORI KENICER

ALTHOUGH FAR-FLUNG IN location, spanning seashore to mountaintop, the golf resorts of the Northwest share in common the rich aura of rare gems, inextricably intertwined with an air of fragility. When Rocky Mountain golf courses like Teton Pines and Sun Valley emerge in late spring from under deep blankets of snow, grateful golfers greet opening day with jubilation, knowing full well how fleeting yet glorious the golf season will be.

Hardy mountain men, drawn by wide open spaces and often the lure of golden treasure, fought for their place in the newly civilized towns of the Old West. Today vast areas of untamed wilderness in Montana, Idaho, Wyoming, and other western states have been set aside as parks to preserve the wild lands and natural habitats of vanishing wildlife species. Some of the top golf resorts in the Northwest abut national parks, sharing an appreciation for the priceless treasure of natural beauty. Although in remote locations not easily accessible, these hidden jewels exude a level of sophistication more often found in urban settings.

The pioneer spirit inspired modern-day heroes to carve golf courses out of craggy mountain terrain and along rocky coastlines, to the continuing delight of millions of golfers who come from far and wide to enjoy the exceptional gems of the Northwest.

You couldn't find a more typically "western" environment than Jackson Hole, Wyoming, home to Teton Pines resort. "Jackson Hole" refers to the large valley itself, surrounded by the jagged Teton mountain range, which rises abruptly to heights of ten thousand feet and more. In the town of Jackson, sturdy arches made of hundreds of elk antlers anchor the four corners of the town square, covered wooden sidewalks protect shoppers from the harsh winters, and the Million Dollar Cowboy Bar invites patrons to settle onto barstools topped with western saddles. Jackson Hole Mountain Resort draws skiers to its peaks, but golfers have found their niche at Teton Pines resort and country club.

Teton Pines sits just seven miles west of the town of Jackson and five miles south of the ski mountain and Teton Village, definitely off the beaten path. Private members and resort guests share the golf course, designed by Arnold Palmer and Ed Seay, for a limited golf season that generally runs from early May to mid-October. The two-story, cathedral-ceilinged clubhouse with big leather couches and a stone fireplace is comfortably western, but with country-club cachet. It houses the pro shop, a cozy bar with carved swinging doors, and the gourmet Pines restaurant.

Sixteen spacious suites, which offer luxurious amenities, high ceilings, and balconies, are spread over four buildings overlooking the eighteenth green. Two three-bedroom townhomes are also available.

TETON PINES

Away from the hustle of everyday life, Teton Pines offers an intimate oasis of serenity in a majestic mountain setting.

• Step out your door and tee up on the golf course, or play tennis, swim, or hike in the nearby mountains.

• Learn to tie a fly, read a stream, and cast for prize-winning trout with a nationally recognized fly-fishing expert.

• Enjoy sumptuous meals on the patio terrace overlooking the golf course and trout ponds.

• Take a short trip to Grand Teton or Yellowstone parks, or visit the art galleries, boutiques, and restaurants of Jackson Hole.

DISTRACTIONS

With the spectacular Grand Tetons as a backdrop, players at the Teton Pines Golf Course may find it difficult to focus on the game.

Secluded Teton Pines is small and intimate, with gracious service. Complimentary breakfast is served in the lobby bar, with made-to-order waffles.

The golf course opened in 1987 and, while flat and generally walkable, it plays long and has water hazards on almost every hole. Expect to carry water on most of the par-threes. Trophy homes in the $2 million-plus range are set back from some of the fairways, but close enough to the practice and lesson area that lower-compression golf balls are used to avoid contact. Don't judge your distance by your range shots.

The front nine is more open, while the back is more wooded and tucked away. The high-pitched chirping osprey, swooping eagles, and occasional bugling elk enliven your round. From the golf course and elsewhere, the mountains look near enough to reach out and touch. Willows, aspens, and pines line the fairways, and natural grasses frame the ponds.

The peninsula green on hole 6 is surrounded by water, but hole 7 is the number-one handicap hole, a long par-five with Grand Teton, or "The Grand," as the locals say, soaring in the distance. The four finishing holes all face the Tetons, with hole 15 generally considered the toughest on the course. A giant bunker to the right narrows the fairway as it bends gently to the left toward the green set just beyond a pond. Hole 16 is the signature hole, a short par-three over water to a green that slopes toward the water in front.

TETON PINES

JACKSON, WYOMING

RESORT RATING:	
CHALLENGE	★★★★☆
BEAUTY	★★★★★
LODGING	★★★☆
CUISINE	★★★☆
AMENITIES	★★★★☆

Dinner at the Pines is a welcome respite after a day at the links. It's a sophisticated gourmet restaurant with friendly, professional service and excellent food. Grilled Arctic char, a light pink fish similar to trout, is a menu mainstay. The house-made cinnamon doughnuts sound more like a breakfast item but are yummy served with cappuccino ice cream for dessert. A jazz combo or pianist generally plays during the dinner hour, adding to the ambience.

Teton Pines has a private stocked pond where guests can learn fly-fishing from Jack Dennis, a leading outfitter in Jackson since 1966. Fishing float trips run mostly on the Snake River, which begins in Yellowstone National Park and winds past the Tetons, flowing south through Jackson Hole and defining the valley's landscape. Catching a famous native Snake River cutthroat trout is almost as good as getting a birdie.

In Sun Valley, Idaho, Elkhorn Resort offers an attractive and affordable golfing retreat. Originally built in 1976, the resort has undergone a recent multimillion-dollar renovation that upgraded the main lodge, lobby, restaurants, and the 132 guest rooms. The contemporary-style lodge is done in warm, neutral tones, and the rooms are well equipped. Just off the lodge is a plaza area with a general store, bike and skating rentals, and two restaurants.

SERENITY UNLIMITED

An endless assortment of tranquil settings provides opportunities for reflection and solitude at Teton Pines. The reception area offers soothing, rustic décor, as do the private condos and townhomes.

QUIET PURSUITS

Flowing streams, miles of trails, and a location just minutes from Yellowstone and Grand Teton national parks make Teton Pines an ideal spot for hiking, fly-fishing, tennis, and cross-country skiing.

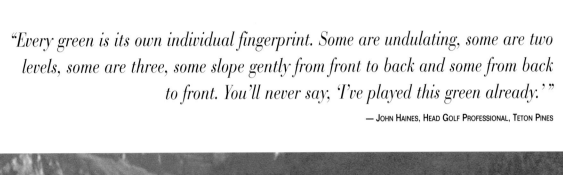

"Every green is its own individual fingerprint. Some are undulating, some are two levels, some are three, some slope gently from front to back and some from back to front. You'll never say, 'I've played this green already.'"

— JOHN HAINES, HEAD GOLF PROFESSIONAL, TETON PINES

GOLFING

TETON PINES

TETON PINES GOLF COURSE
JACKSON, WYOMING

Architects: Arnold Palmer,
Ed Seay

Par: 72

Bluegrass fairways,
bentgrass greens

Yardage/Rating/Slope:

Gold tees
7,412/74.8/137

Blue tees
6,901/71.0/125

White tees
6,330/69.2, 72.5*/122, 125*

Red tees
5,474/70.1*/124*

*Women's ratings

ONE OF A KIND

Wildlife and classic Palmer

features make playing

Teton Pines a memorable

experience.

RESORT RATING:

CHALLENGE	★★★
BEAUTY	★★★★
LODGING	★★★☆
CUISINE	★★★☆
AMENITIES	★★★★

EXPERIENCING

ELKHORN RESORT

Rustic materials, breathtaking surroundings, and a palette of outdoor activities make Elkhorn Resort a dream destination.

• Relax in the newly renovated resort, where warm natural hues, hand-tinted historic photos, and a huge river-rock fireplace recall Idaho's rich mining history.

• Explore the dramatic mountain ranges and abundant rivers in adventurous ways, from kayaking and llama trekking to glider rides and rock climbing.

• From the base of River Run, take the chairlift up and ride a mountain bike down world-famous Bald Mountain.

• After a day of activity, refresh yourself with a dip in an Olympic-sized swimming pool or relax in a natural hot spring.

The dinner-only River Rock Steak House offers indoor and patio seating and features beef, seafood, and wild game. Nearby Joe's Grill, open for breakfast, lunch, and dinner, serves up Tex-Mex fare in a casual, family atmosphere.

The golf course opened in 1974, a joint collaboration between Robert Trent Jones, Sr. and Robert Trent Jones, Jr. While Jones, Sr. is generally credited with influencing the design of the front nine, which is hilly, wide open, and four hundred yards longer than the back nine, the shorter and narrower back nine is attributed to Jones, Jr. Elkhorn plays long, and some days it feels like

SUN VALLEY, IDAHO

ELKHORN RESORT

it goes on forever. Because of its high elevation, Elkhorn is open, windswept, and almost treeless, and the surrounding mountains seem close. The back tees of stunning hole 5, a long par-five, face a soaring mountain view, then the second shot drops downhill and is somewhat difficult to hit. Wind becomes a major factor at Elkhorn, creating hardpan for more roll, and the greens don't always hold well. Range balls are included in the greens fees, but the uphill driving range makes it somewhat hard to judge distances.

Elkhorn's attractive new clubhouse was part of the renovation and sits atop a hill, within walking distance from the lodge. It contains a well-stocked pro shop and indoor and outdoor seating for breakfast and lunch at the Clubhouse Grill, which overlooks the golf course.

A THRILL TO PLAY

Long approaches and well-trapped greens make Elkhorn golf a challenge for any player.

GOLFING

ELKHORN RESORT
ELKHORN GOLF CLUB

Architect: Robert Trent Jones, Sr.,
Robert Trent Jones, Jr.
Par: 72
Kentucky bluegrass fairways,
bentgrass greens
Yardage/Rating/Slope:
Blue tees
7,021/72.2/127
White tees
6,501/69.9/122
Red tees
5,414/69.3/125

WHAT A SETTING

The Sawtooth Mountain Range towers over Elkhorn Resort's golf course, making for a spectacular backdrop to challenging play.

MOUNTAINTOP FERRY

High-speed quad lifts carry wintertime visitors to the top of Bald Mountain

for snow skiing. In the summer, hikers and bikers ride to mountaintop

picnics, breathtaking views, and well-marked trails for the downhill trek.

SUMMER PLEASURES

Although Sun Valley Resort is known most widely as a ski resort,

when the slopes are no longer white, golf reigns supreme.

QUIET RESPITE

The elegantly appointed Sun Room is

just one of many spots to relax, listen

to music, and enjoy the breathtaking

beauty surrounding Sun Valley.

Sun Valley Resort is the indisputable "grande dame" of mountain resorts. At the stately four-story Lodge with its oak-paneled walls and big overstuffed chairs, thick carpets overlay the polished floors and romantic music wafts from the Duchin Lounge, the place to go for a quiet conversation or after-dinner dancing. The rooms are comfortably appointed in traditional style, some with elegant furnishings, and the Lodge Apartments have full kitchens and fireplaces. The opulent Lodge Dining Room evokes an earlier era with its crystal chandeliers and wall sconces, rose-colored swag draperies, and live music, which invites dancing between courses. Snuggle into one of the big booths along the wall and let the

"The course is so tight that if you veer off even slightly you'll be in solid trees. Lay back a bit so you're on the short grass and have more control."

—DOYLE CORBETT, HEAD GOLF PROFESSIONAL, SUN VALLEY

SUN VALLEY RESORT

SUN VALLEY, IDAHO

RESORT RATING:	
CHALLENGE	★★★☆
BEAUTY	★★★★☆
LODGING	★★★★
CUISINE	★★★★
AMENITIES	★★★★

formal waiters pamper you with such classic dishes as oysters Rockefeller or a Caesar salad prepared tableside.

What about the golf? The Sun Valley Golf Course originally opened as nine holes in 1938, expanded to eighteen in 1962, then was renovated in 1978 by Robert Trent Jones, Jr., who lengthened the front nine and added more than one thousand aspen, pine, and river birch trees.

Because of those mature trees, it's wise to stay in the fairway. Sun Valley is not a particularly long course and it looks deceivingly open. But if you go off the fairway, you run the risk of an unplayable lie, such as under the dense branches of the blue spruce that line much of the fairways. The course has a varied layout. Some holes on the front nine go through the woods, then emerge into a clearing, but you always have great views of Baldy and the surrounding mountains. Hole 15 is the undisputed signature hole, a 244-yard par-three from the back tees, all carry over Trail Creek from an elevated tee. The finishing holes are all strong, and more elevated than the front holes.

DINING FOR EVERY MOOD Sun Valley offers restaurants for every taste, from a relaxing pub or an authentic western barbecue to the elegant white-gloved table service of the Lodge Dining Room.

SUN VALLEY RESORT
SUN VALLEY, IDAHO

Architect: Robert Trent Jones, Jr.
Par: 72
Kentucky bluegrass fairways,
Poa Annua greens
Yardage/Rating/Slope:

<u>Blue tees</u>
6,674/71.4/126

<u>White tees</u>
6,083/68.9, 73.7*/120, 135*

<u>Red tees</u>
5,197/68.5*/116*
*Women's ratings

THE BIGGEST OBSTACLE

Water hazards, elevation
changes, and tight fairways
challenge golfers, but not
as much as the temptation
to stop and stare at the
majestic mountains.

"Our floating green is like a mini barge that moves back and forth from the tee box. You've got to get the ball in the air, so play an extra club."

—Bob Nuttelman, Head Golf Professional, Coeur d'Alene

COEUR D'ALENE, IDAHO

THE COEUR D'ALENE

Lake Coeur d'Alene has long been a popular recreational area, even before the Coeur d'Alene resort was built in 1986; its golf course followed in 1991. Vibrant red geraniums spill out of planter boxes and border fairways, in striking contrast to the startling blue water.

The eighteen-story hotel rises over the lake, featuring spectacular water views from the premier rooms, oversized mini-suites in the Lake Tower with balconies and some fireplaces. Take the elevator down to the seventh floor for gourmet dining at Beverly's, the award-winning signature restaurant in a romantic lakefront setting with comfy booths and window tables. The wine list features over eight hundred labels.

But golf is the real highlight at Coeur d'Alene, even though you can't see the course from the hotel—it's around a forested point. Two mahogany water taxis transport golfers around the bend, and a forecaddy greets them at the dock at the end of the short ride. Golf clubs, magically whisked away when golfers check in at the hotel, are waiting on their carts. The uniformed forecaddies speed the pace of play and are like personal golf concierges. They do all the usual caddic things plus provide distances by using laser distance readers and order lunch via a fax machine at the turn, delivering it in a picnic basket.

The course has no members and no houses, and almost every hole has a wonderful lake view. Tall Douglas firs line the fairways. The varied design goes from flat long holes to short, steep holes that are more wooded. Holes 5 and 6 are beautiful back-to-back par-threes with steep elevated tees facing the lake, affording the best views on the course. Several holes run along the lake, the highlight of which is hole 14, the world's only floating green.

The famous green measures 15,000 square feet, twice the size of a normal green, but it still looks awfully small out there. It's anchored to the lake bottom by a series of cables that allow for daily movement, varying the length from 100 to 175 yards. Golfers should use one club more than they would usually hit for the distance to compensate for winds off the lake (and a slight intimidation factor). After successfully driving the green, a foursome will board the "Putter" for a short ride out to the green. Playing hole 14 is the highlight of the round, although the entire golf experience is superb. A photographer stands ready to take golfers' photos, and a certificate of achievement awaits those who make par or better on number 14.

Even golfers who miss out on the massage at the driving range can still be pampered from head to toe at the resort's fancy European-style spa, which offers body wraps, massages, facials, the works—even the trendy Hot Stone Massage.

SAND BORDER

The green on hole 2 of the Coeur d'Alene resort golf course is well protected by bunkers.

LAKEFRONT ACCOMMODATIONS

The Coeur d'Alene resort dominates the tourist trade in Coeur d'Alene, Idaho. A number of slips are available to those who arrive by boat, and the resort's five ferries can be chartered for group or individual excursions.

COEUR D'ALENE
COEUR D'ALENE, IDAHO

Architect: Scott Miller
Par: 71
Penn-Eagle bentgrass fairways,
Penn-Cross bentgrass greens
Yardage/Rating/Slope:
Blue tees
6,309/69.6/121
Tan tees
5,899/68.2/117
Mauve tees
5,428/70.3/118
Copper tees
4,446/64.6/104

FLOATING GREEN

The fourteenth hole features the world's only floating, movable golf green. Weighing nearly five million pounds, the green is anchored to the lake bottom by cables that allow its placement to vary.

GROUSE MOUNTAIN LODGE

EAGLE BEND GOLF CLUB
BIGFORK, MONTANA

CHAMPIONSHIP 18

Architects: William Hull,

Jack Nicklaus, Jr.

Tour stops: 1994 USGA U.S.

Amateur Public Links

Tournament, 1995 Pacific

Northwest PGA Section

Championship

Par: 72

Bentgrass fairways and greens

Yardage/Rating/Slope:

Blue tees

6,724/71.2/121

White tees

6,189/69.1/117

Red tees

5,429/70.1*/119*

LAKE 9

Architects: William Hull,

Andy North

Par: 36

Bentgrass fairways and greens

Blue tees

3,497/71.3/124

White tees

3,125/69.3/119

Red tees

2,574/68.9*/120*

*Women's ratings

ENHANCED BEAUTY

The twelfth hole of Eagle

Bend Golf Club's

championship course

showcases the

combination of stunning

setting and deft

landscaping.

Farther north, in Big Sky Country, the mountain resort community of Whitefish, Montana, manages to maintain small-town livability amid its growing popularity as a golf destination. In fact, northwestern Montana seems to be center stage for controversy, as the wide-open spaces are fast being snapped up by those who come for the climate and the great outdoors, yet bring their own trappings of civilization with them. There's some concern that the verdant hills may become more like Beverly Hills. For now, prices are quite reasonable for what you get in still-unspoiled Whitefish and the surrounding Flathead Valley, so called because of Flathead Lake to the south, the largest freshwater lake west of the Mississippi River.

At the casually elegant Grouse Mountain Lodge in Montana, large picture windows bring in the stunning mountain scenery and panoramas of the adjacent Whitefish Lake Golf Club while a grand fireplace covered with local river rock creates a welcoming atmosphere. Convenient indoor/outdoor Jacuzzis and an indoor swimming pool pamper guests after a day on the links. Rooms in the three-story lodge are comfortable and understated, offering a variety of floor plans including loft rooms. Grouse Mountain Lodge was built with skiers and families in mind. Mounted game and animal skins grace the walls throughout, while stunning sculptures like the huge golden grizzly in the conference center look almost too real. Look up and you might see a crouching cougar atop a tall cabinet. An elk-antler chandelier and stone fireplace lend a warm glow to fine dining in the inviting Logan's Bar & Grill, which serves up contemporary, regional fare like peppercorn-crusted elk carpaccio and grilled meat dishes.

Grouse Mountain Lodge borders the eighteenth fairway of the South Course of Whitefish Lake Golf Club, Montana's only thirty-six-hole complex. The North and South courses have been so carefully tended that you may be surprised to learn this is a city-owned facility. Both courses are walkable for green fees are only $35.

The more traditional North Course is fairly flat, wide, and tree-lined, cut into the thick forest of surrounding pines. Golfers can bring their drivers and swing away; with few bunkers and little water, the worst hazard is missing the fairway. Deer and black bear frequent the course, and from some of the holes one can see the boats and homes along nearby Whitefish Lake.

The newer South Course requires more placement shots, mostly because its creative layout presents more water. Attractive rock work lines some of the water features. Hole 7, the signature hole, is all carry to an island green off of Lost Coon Lake. New, pricey homes border the holes on the course, except for holes 6 through 13, which are tucked away and have a remote feeling. Hole 18 faces the ski runs of Big Mountain and brings golfers back to Grouse Mountain Lodge.

"Northern Pines has a native grass that can grow to eighteen inches. Don't get in it! If you do, use a wedge to get back on the fairway."

—TODD ROBERTS, HEAD PROFESSIONAL, NORTHERN PINES GOLF CLUB

WHITEFISH, MONTANA

GROUSE MOUNTAIN

LODGE

RESORT RATING:

CHALLENGE	★★★⯨
BEAUTY	★★★⯨
LODGING	★★★⯨
CUISINE	★★★⯨
AMENITIES	★★★★

EXPERIENCING

GROUSE MOUNTAIN LODGE

This is genuine Montana, where championship golf meets pristine wilderness.

• Get an aerial view from the "Glacier Chaser" gondola or a hot-air balloon.
• Learn about the topography at a fireside talk or a narrated "jammer" tour along Going-to-the-Sun Highway.
• Spin a rope, hear western lore from a genuine cowboy, or take a dinner ride in a Clydesdale-drawn wagon.
• Take a refreshing dip in a sunny indoor pool or relax in a hot whirlpool overlooking the golf course and surrounding mountains.

GROUSE MOUNTAIN LODGE
WHITEFISH LAKE GOLF CLUB
WHITEFISH, MONTANA

NORTH 18 COURSE

Architect: John Steidel

Par: 72

Bluegrass fairways, bentgrass greens

Yardage/Rating/Slope:

Blue tees
6,556/69.8/118

White tees
6,297/68.7/116

Red tees
5,556/70.1/115

SOUTH 18 COURSE

Par: 71

Bluegrass fairways, bentgrass greens

Yardage/Rating/Slope:

Blue tees
6,551/70.5/122

White tees
6,139/69.0/120

Red tees
5,361/70.3/120

NORTHERN PINES GOLF CLUB
KALISPELL, MONTANA

Architects: Andy North, Roger Packard

Par: 72

Bluegrass/rye fairways, bentgrass greens

Yardage/Rating/Slope:

Green tees
7,015/72.5/121

Blue tees
6,628/70.7/119

White tees
6,180/68.6/115

Red tees
5,421/69.9/118

SIGNATURE HOLE

The sixteenth hole of Northern Pines Golf Club sports an incredible view of the green from the tee box.

"A lot of people take chances and try to blow it past the 150s, but then the fairway narrows. If you can get to the 150 markers on your tee shots, . . .

Both courses share the rustic log clubhouse, which was constructed in 1936 along with the first nine holes and has recently been restored. The thick log walls and crisscrossed beams were cast with handworked lodgepole pine from the surrounding forest. The clubhouse contains the pro shop and the Whitefish Lake Restaurant, which is far more than a golfers' grill. With cheerful flowered curtains at the windows and the big stone fireplace blazing, the Whitefish Lake Restaurant feels like a cozy mountain chalet. The restaurant is well regarded for its warm atmosphere and great meals, including prime rib on weekends and the lamb shank braised in locally made Black Lager.

RESORT RATING:		SUN RIVER, OREGON
CHALLENGE	★★★★☆	
BEAUTY	★★★★☆	
LODGING	★★★☆	
CUISINE	★★★☆	
AMENITIES	★★★★☆	

SUNRIVER RESORT

you have a better chance to score well."

—JON NOACK, HEAD GOLF
PROFESSIONAL, WOODLANDS COURSE

WISE CHOICE

Sunriver Resort's Owl's Nest
Pub serves up northwest
microbrews and light dinner fare.

Sunriver Resort is located in central Oregon at the foot of the Cascade Mountains, whose towering volcanic peaks frame the distant views. It's fifteen miles south of Bend, the nearest town. The moderate high-desert climate means Sunriver has a longer golf season than most mountain resorts, and is usually able to open as early as March. Its private airport can accommodate jets and is located only five hundred yards from the first fairway of the Meadows Course. The resort will send a golf cart over to pick guests up.

Sunriver consists of a 3,500-acre resort

community in a woodsy setting with over two hundred guest rooms and suites plus private homes and condos. The overall feel is one of comfort, more rustic than elegant; Sunriver emphasizes a casual, outdoor lifestyle. Don't expect pricey shops and luxurious spa treatments. The recently renovated main lodge displays a Pacific Northwest style with exposed timber and logs and polished woods, in keeping with the country comfort for which Sunriver is known.

PRIVILEGES

Guests of Sunriver Resort have

access to the Crosswater Course.

QUIET EVENINGS

The Sunriver Lodge sits on the edge of the Sun River, offering

spectacular views of the river and Meadows Course beyond.

FAMILY FUN

There are many non-golf pursuits available

to Sunriver Resort guests, including

mountain biking on local trails.

NORTHWEST LUXURY

Each of the thirty-three River Lodges at

Sunriver Resort are individually decorated

and look out on spectacular vistas.

"The greens are fair, not real large, and always in great shape with good speed. Many are tiered and difficult, so you have to make good putts."

—TONY BLASIUS, HEAD GOLF PROFESSIONAL, MEADOWS COURSE

GOLFING

SUNRIVER RESORT
SUNRIVER, OREGON

CROSSWATER COURSE
Architects: Bob Cupp
and John Fought
Tour stops: 2000 Pacific Amateur
Golf Classic, 2000 NCAA
Division I Women's National
Championship, 2000 Jaguar
CEO Tour Championship, 2001
PGA Club Professional
Championship
Par: 72
Bentgrass fairways and greens
Yardage/Rating/Slope:
Gold tees
7,683/76.9/150
Silver tees
7,273/74.8/144
Blue tees
6,811/74.8/133
White tees
6,185/69.4/126
Red tees
5,359/69.8/125

WOODLANDS COURSE
Architect: Robert Trent Jones, Jr.
Par: 72
Kentucky bluegrass/rye fairways,
Poa Annua greens
Yardage/Rating/Slope:
Blue tees
6,880/73.0/131
White tees
6,068/68.8/124
Red tees
5,446/70.2/127

MEADOWS COURSE
Tour stops: 2002 USGA
Women's Amateur Public Links
Championship
Architect: John Fought
Par: 71
Rye fairways, bentgrass greens
Yardage/Rating/Slope:
Black tees
7,012/72.8/128
Blue tees
6,625/71.0/126
White tees
6,022/68.0, 74.3*/119, 136*
Red tees
5,287/69.8/127
*Women's ratings

AN INCOMPARABLE CLASSIC

For more than three-quarters of a century, the Lodge at Pebble Beach has welcomed guests. From the classic entryway to each tastefully appointed room, an atmosphere of elegance is radiated.

Crosswater is the crown jewel of Sunriver's three golf courses and offers private membership. The course meanders through marshy wetlands and along the Deschutes and Little Deschutes Rivers, which crisscross the fairways. Difficult shots, as on holes 5 and 6, require players to carry the river from the tee, and meadow grasses often intrude as well. Boardwalk-style cart paths cross the wetlands. The Woodlands Course ranges through thick pine woods, which often come into play. Golfers encounter not only trees but lakes and lava outcroppings, remnants of ancient volcanic activity, on this scenic course. Accuracy and proper club selection will improve your score. The Meadows Course starts at the main lodge

THE LODGE AT	RESORT RATING:	
	CHALLENGE	★★★★★
PEBBLE BEACH	BEAUTY	★★★★★
	LODGING	★★★★½
	CUISINE	★★★★½
PEBBLE BEACH, CALIFORNIA	AMENITIES	★★★★

and is more open, with more water than Woodlands. Seven holes border the Sun River, as the course winds through meadows and groves of pines. The whole family can enjoy the nine-hole putting course at the Meadows.

Golf treasures of the West lie not only in the high mountains, but also along its rugged coastline, home of the famed Pebble Beach Golf Links in northern California. Secure in its place in golf history as the site of four U.S. Open tournaments, Pebble Beach is revered for its beautiful setting and unforgettable challenge. But it's not easy to reach golf's "Shangri-la." After pulling on to the famous 17-Mile Drive, it can be confusing to navigate the little streets winding through the Del Monte Forest, especially on a foggy night. Somehow that adds to the sense of achievement once you've arrived.

CHAMPIONS

Pebble Beach has been the site of professional golf's classic wins, both old and new.

"Pebble Beach is difficult, with unpredictable winds and weather. From a scoring standpoint, the course almost always wins. The experience—to appreciate and soak up all that Pebble Beach is, with its history and tradition and championship conditions—is where the player really wins."

—CHUCK DUNBAR, HEAD GOLF
PROFESSIONAL, PEBBLE BEACH GOLF LINKS

WORLD-FAMOUS

The finishing hole at Pebble Beach Golf Links provides the satisfying view and spectacular play that golfers from all over the country seek out.

The luxurious lodge guest rooms extend from either side of the main building, and most have a private balcony and wood-burning fireplace, stacked daily with oak logs. Prime ocean-view rooms and suites with unobstructed views are located near the eighteenth green. Secluded Casa Palmero, adjacent to the lodge, has twenty-four rooms set in an elegant Mediterranean-style villa with private gardens and courtyard fountains. Personal valets tend to each guest. Next door, the 22,000-square-foot Pebble Beach Spa offers its own private-label products and signature body treatments, based on the healing properties of the surrounding forest and sea. Guests can have a massage in one of the fireplace rooms or book the couple's room for shared treatments.

The grand Lodge at Pebble Beach has been pampering guests since it opened its doors in 1919. Just past the registration desk, the large lobby area opens to tall French-pane windows that reveal the spectacular view of the crisp green eighteenth fairway, bright blue Carmel Bay, and the dramatic coastline beyond. One can step outside to the terrace for a closer look and smell the fresh, salty air.

The Stillwater Bar & Grill has the same terrific view and serves breakfast, lunch, and dinner, specializing in seafood and offering an expansive raw bar. Downstairs on the lower level, Club XIX also faces Carmel Bay and the eighteenth hole, and serves lunch and dinner in the glass-and-brick enclosed patio room, warmed by fireplaces, or in the dining room. Jackets are required at dinner, when Club XIX becomes an elegant dining experience well worth the high tab. Chef Hubert Keller of Napa's French

Laundry has created an innovative menu that usually includes two prix-fixe meals, one vegetarian.

The Tap Room is the ideal nineteenth hole, where golfers can have a drink or enjoy a casual lunch or dinner. It resembles a traditional English pub, with dark green walls and wood paneling. The walls are covered with historical photos from the old days of "the Crosby" (precursor to the AT&T) and memorabilia from the various U.S. Open tournaments that have been held at Pebble Beach.

GOURMET OFFERINGS

Club XIX at the Lodge at Pebble Beach serves light

French fare, offering two prix-fixe-meals each evening.

THE LODGE AT PEBBLE BEACH
PEBBLE BEACH, CALIFORNIA

PEBBLE BEACH GOLF LINKS
Architects: Jack Neville,
Douglas Grant
Tour Stops: AT&T Pebble Beach
National Pro-Am, California
State Amateur, Pebble Beach
Invitational, 1999 U.S. Amateur
Championship, 2000 U.S. Open
Championship
Par: 72
Bermuda fairways,
Poa Annua greens
Yardage/Rating/Slope:
Back tees
6,840/74.4/142
Middle tees
6,374/72.1/138
Forward tees
5,217/71.9/130

SPYGLASS HILL
Architect: Robert Trent Jones, Sr.
Tour stops: AT&T Pebble Beach
National Pro-Am, Pebble Beach
Invitational, 1999 U.S. Amateur
Par: 72
Rye fairways, Poa Annua greens
Yardage/Rating/Slope:
Back tees
6,859/75.9/144
Middle tees
6,346/73.0/138
Forward tees
5,642/73.7/133

NEIGHBORS

With its golf shop and first tee directly across from

the Lodge, Pebble Beach Golf Links is the closest

of the four courses guests can utilize.

OUTDOOR PARADISE

In addition to world-class golf, the

grounds around the Lodge at Pebble

Beach contain an impressive array of

equestrian, tennis, and fitness facilities.

It's seven miles along the coast from the Lodge at Pebble Beach to the Inn at Spanish Bay. Set on the wild dunes along the 17-Mile Drive, both the Inn at Spanish Bay and its golf course have a sprawling, open feeling. Built in 1987, in a blending of old Monterey and Spanish California styles, it has a contemporary feel, with earth tones and oversized furniture in the spacious rooms, all 270 of which are in the main building with ocean or forest views.

Spanish Bay is the best place among the Pebble Beach locations to watch the sunset. A lone bagpiper plays his soulful tunes each evening at dusk from the big outdoor terrace.

You can also watch the sunset from inside Roy's, where every table has a view of the ocean,

RESORT RATING:	
CHALLENGE	★★★★★
BEAUTY	★★★★★
LODGING	★★★★½
CUISINE	★★★★½
AMENITIES	★★★★

THE INN AT
SPANISH BAY

PEBBLE BEACH, CALIFORNIA

beach, and golf course. The window-walled, two-level restaurant features the Euro-Asian cuisine Roy Yamaguchi made famous in his Hawaii "Roy's" restaurants. Expect complex, unusual dishes like teriyaki grilled scallops over wasabi garlic mashed potatoes. In contrast, the newer Peppoli offers authentic Tuscan cuisine with an open rotisserie and hearty menu.

Guests at either hotel have preference at the four golf courses of the Pebble Beach resorts. Being a resort guest is about the only way to get on Pebble Beach itself. Non-resort guests may call twenty-four hours in advance and hope for an opening, which usually works best for singles.

No one ever rushes the day at Pebble Beach—the tee time is too hard to come by and the experience so special it's worth savoring, even commemorating with a photo or two.

A LINK TO THE PAST

Th Inn at Spanish Bay cherishes its association with Scottish culture, hiring a bagpiper to play nightly at sunset.

SHELTER FROM BLUSTERY WEATHER

When the wind off the Pacific gets too much,

guests at the Inn at Spanish Bay have cozy, well-

appointed rooms to which they can retreat.

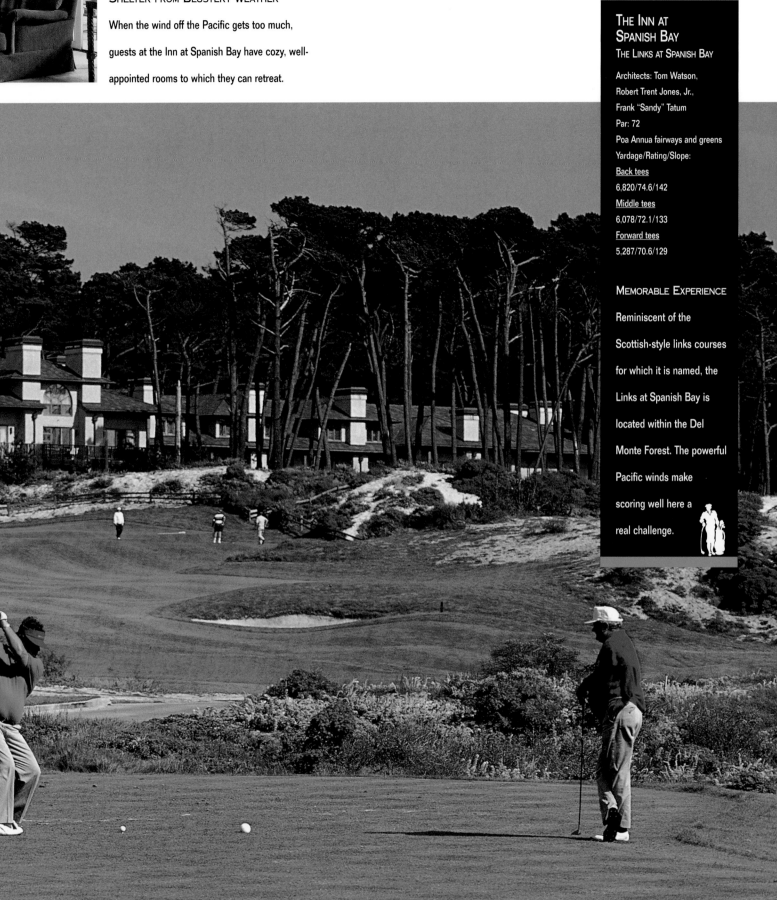

GOLFING

THE INN AT
SPANISH BAY
THE LINKS AT SPANISH BAY

Architects: Tom Watson,
Robert Trent Jones, Jr.,
Frank "Sandy" Tatum
Par: 72
Poa Annua fairways and greens
Yardage/Rating/Slope:
Back tees
6,820/74.6/142
Middle tees
6,078/72.1/133
Forward tees
5,287/70.6/129

MEMORABLE EXPERIENCE

Reminiscent of the

Scottish-style links courses

for which it is named, the

Links at Spanish Bay is

located within the Del

Monte Forest. The powerful

Pacific winds make

scoring well here a

real challenge.

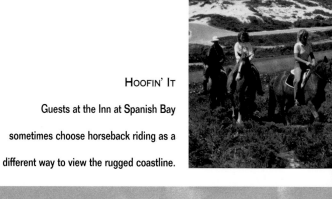

EXPERIENCING

THE INN AT SPANISH BAY

PEBBLE BEACH, CALIFORNIA

Within the Del Monte Forest and accessible from the famed 17-Mile Drive, the Inn at Spanish Bay is a paradise to naturalists and golfers alike.

• Your day begins among cozy overstuffed furnishings, plush comforters, your own fireplace, and a private patio or balcony with magnificent views.

• Take advantage of the many recreational opportunities, including jogging or hiking on sandy beach trails, horseback riding through the Del Monte Forest, browsing through a promenade of shops and boutiques, or visiting Carmel-by-the-Sea.

• Blend culinary delights with spectacular views at the exhibition kitchen of Roy's at Pebble Beach, or treat yourself to an evening at Traps with their wide selection of cigars and Scotch whiskey.

• Be sure to return before dark for a favorite tradition: the lone bagpiper walking the links and saluting the setting sun.

• For the last indulgence of the day, order a bedtime snack—freshly baked cookies and a pitcher of milk!

17-MILE DRIVE

Cyclists thread their way along two-lane 17-Mile Drive, one of only nine private toll roads in the country and the only one west of the Mississippi. It provides incredible views of the Pacific coastline.

The stunning setting of emerald fairways along rugged cliffs that slops to the sea is enough to distract the most dedicated player. Enthusiasm notwithstanding, players may find themselves undone by the unexpected difficulty of the course, especially when the fog and mist roar in from the sea, drastically altering club selection.

The golf holes along the ocean attract special attention, most notably hole 7, just over one hundred yards from an elevated tee to a cliffside green where there's little margin for error. By hole 8, players are used to the tiny greens, but this approach over a deep ocean chasm is one of the most difficult. The dramatic eighteenth hole hugs the rocky shoreline all along the left side of the fairway.

Pebble Beach is tough but Spyglass Hill is tougher. Its golf holes are named in honor of one-time resident Robert Louis Stevenson. In hole 1, called "Treasure Island," the long par-five heads downhill to a small green that is like an island surrounded by bunkers.

The Links at Spanish Bay is as close as you're likely to get to an authentic Scottish-links course on this side of the Atlantic. Most holes run along the ocean with outstanding views and little protection from the wind. Spanish Bay is a placement course. Environmental restrictions mandated that sensitive areas be protected, so there are many forced carries, and ball retrieval tends to be maddeningly disallowed.

The kinder, gentler Del Monte Golf Course is the oldest course in continuous operation west of the Mississippi. Del Monte began as a nine-hole layout in 1897. Greens fees are less than half those of the other Pebble Beach courses, and the fairly flat layout makes the course very walkable. Some of the thick, twisted oak trees are as old as the course itself. Although the holes are mostly straight, avoiding the trees can mean playing to a dogleg, as in the finishing hole.

"The greens are small and pitched forward so the best way to play Del Monte is not to go long. There's definitely trouble if you go long; you're always chipping or putting downhill."

—NEIL ALLEN, HEAD GOLF PROFESSIONAL, DEL MONTE GOLF COURSE

A GLIMPSE

Deer can be seen in the misty wild land that edges the famed 17-Mile Drive.

THE INN AT SPANISH BAY
DEL MONTE GOLF COURSE
PEBBLE BEACH, CALIFORNIA

Architect: Charles Maud

Tour stops: Pebble Beach
Invitational

Par: 72 (Women 74)

Rye fairways, Poa Annua greens

Yardage/Rating/Slope

<u>Back tees</u>
6,339/71.0/125

<u>Middle tees</u>
6,069/70.3/123

<u>Forward tees</u>
5,526/71.6/120

GREAT ALTERNATIVE

The Del Norte Golf Course

is a more accessible

course in the Pebble Beach

area. It's also a

pleasure to play.

RESORT RATING:

CHALLENGE	★★★★
BEAUTY	★★★★
LODGING	★★★★⯪
CUISINE	★★★★
AMENITIES	★★★★

CARMEL, CALIFORNIA

QUAIL LODGE

RESORT AND GOLF CLUB

INVITING WATERS

At Quail Lodge, swans glide over tranquil ponds, great blue herons and stately egrets patrol the shores of sparkling lakes, and dramatic landscaping beckons visitors to ramble outdoors.

Del Monte is actually on the grounds of the Monterey Hyatt, but transportation can be arranged from Pebble Beach. Del Monte is usually in great condition, and it's easier to get a tee time.

While wispy tendrils of fog drift in and out of the trees of Del Monte Forest, just twenty minutes away, Quail Lodge Resort and Golf Club is bathed in sunshine. It is three and a half miles inland from Highway 1, in Carmel Valley, well past the coastal fog belt, and covers more than eight hundred acres of countryside, much of which is designated as a nature preserve. Quail Lodge is known for its beautiful landscaping in a tranquil setting of mature trees with rolling hills all around. Quail's recent acquisition by Peninsula Hotel Groups of Hong Kong brought international recognition to this parklike country retreat of only one hundred rooms.

The main building of wood and glass houses the Covey, which offers everything from complimentary continental breakfast to lunch on the lakeside Deck and fine dining in a casually elegant setting. The "wine-country cuisine" pairs local organic produce and innovative dishes with Carmel Valley wines, which are becoming recognized for their excellence. Paintings by area artists featuring local scenes grace the walls. The Covey overlooks Mallard Lake, accented by a lighted fountain and arched footbridge. For a change of pace, walk cross the road to Baja Cantina for casual Mexican food in a colorful, funky setting.

Walkways lined with lush bushes and plants conveniently connect the one- and two-story dark brown shingled buildings where guest rooms are located. The best rooms are the new suites, with private entrances, state-of-the-art music systems, and luxurious bathrooms, or those facing Mallard Lake and the soothing sounds of the cascading fountain. Some of the mallards may waddle up to say hello as you're reaching for the morning paper at your door.

The golf course is only a short way from the lodge. It's flat and well laid out, ideal for walking. Fairways are lined with lush willows and oaks, the ten lakes attract ducks, geese, and even swans, and the Carmel River winds through the layout. Meticulously landscaped grounds are accented by clumps of vibrant wildflowers.

Pricey homes border many of the fairways on the front nine, with some too close for comfort. One should hope the pin placement is not up front on hole 4, because any approach attempts that fall short risk rolling back down the severe slope in front of the elevated green. Hole 10, a narrow fairway bordered by the Carmel River on the left and a densely wooded hillside on the right, sets the tone for the serene back nine, which has few houses and more wildlife.

The Northwest region is as diverse as it is rich in recreational opportunities. From fine wines to cowboy bars, fly-fishing to floating greens, the wide open spaces of the Northwest provide an ideal environment for those seeking to tee it up not far from where the deer and the antelope play.

QUAIL LODGE RESORT AND GOLF CLUB

Quail Lodge's pristine natural setting provides an inspiring backdrop for refreshing the mind and rejuvenating the soul.

• Start off with a continental breakfast, join a morning fitness walk, or spend a quiet moment in Quail Lodge's gardens, where wildlife and wildflowers abound.

• Shop in the boutiques at Carmel-by-the-Sea or explore Big Sur's dramatic coastline on your way to Cannery Row, the Monterey Bay Aquarium, the many local wineries, or the famous 17-Mile Drive.

• Dine in the Covey restaurant, where "wine country cuisine" features fresh seafood, locally grown ingredients, and fragrant herbs from the resort's own gardens.

• Indulge yourself with a "Quail Touch" mini-adventure, featuring wine tasting, scenic excursions, romantic getaways, or spa treatments.

• Quail Lodge even pampers pets, so bring yours along and treat them to a soft pet bed with sheets, their own special menu, treats to take home, and a walker or sitter.

RUGGED COASTLINE

Big Sur's dramatic coastline offers a splendid counterpoint to Quail Lodge's manicured grounds.

CARMEL-BY-THE-SEA

The picturesque village known for its delightful shops, upscale boutiques, and elegant restaurants is near Quail Lodge.

EXECUTIVE PRIVILEGE

A variety of guest rooms and suites are available, including Executive Villas. Each of these one- and two-bedroom suites boasts its own living room, hot tub, fireplace, and wet bar.

QUAIL LODGE RESORT AND GOLF CLUB
CARMEL, CALIFORNIA

Architect: Robert Muir Graves
Tour stops: California Women's
Amateur Championship, 2000
USGA Women's Amateur
Regional Qualifier
Par: 71
Bentgrass/Poa Annua fairways
and greens
Yardage/Rating/Slope:
Blue tees
6,516 /72.1/129
Gold tees
6,140/70.4/125
Red tees
5,451/71.8*/124*
*Women's ratings

FUN BUT CHALLENGING
The par-seventy-one course
is fairly straightforward, but
prevailing winds blowing
from the ocean, a series of
well-bunkered greens, and
a few tight fairways add a
challenging aspect.

SUNWASHED ESCAPES

BY WILLIAM TOMICKI

THE SOUTHWEST IS truly a golfer's Oz, where magical lakes, pools, fountains, and streams blend with snowcapped mountains, azure ocean, dense forests, and searing desert to form the backdrop for some of America's most compelling golf resorts. The ways in which nature has been tamed here, combined with the benevolent climate, easygoing lifestyle, and sunny hospitality, make this region a unique magnet for year-round visits.

Golf resorts continue to be created in the Southwest at a dizzying pace. Never before has there been such a stunning variety of terrific places to experience. The creation of a great golf resort has been likened to the task a chef faces when presented with many ingredients to create a grand meal. It requires special knowledge and total dedication to orchestrate so many elements of resort hospitality—cuisine, wines, comfort, lodging, atmosphere, and amenities—to meet the needs and desires of a discriminating visitor. Whether you are looking for challenge, history, superb condition, fine hotel-keeping, raw natural beauty, or gourmet dining and world-class shopping (after all, not even the most avid golfer can golf all the time), it's all to be found in the Southwest.

The Southwest may not have the grande dame elegance of the South or the pedigree of the Northeast, but there is an undeniable allure here that results from forward thinking and openness to new ideas. Expect cutting-edge cuisine, soothing indulgences, a relaxed ambience, top-notch spa services, and state-of-the-art technology in this part of the world.

Southwestern resorts do not ooze tradition; they vibrate with innovation. Where else but here would you find e-mail terminals on the tees and separate dining room menus for your pets? Where else are massages given to the accompaniment of Indian tom-toms? This is, after all, the part of our country where your very own personal goldfish can be rented for your resort stay.

The cachet of the southwestern golf resort lies in an energy that is as boundless as the landscape. Add to that a devotion to the game and a commitment to maintaining the highest standards of excellence, and you have the magic of this memorable region.

Magic and energy abound at the Lodge and Spa at Cordillera. Majestically nestled in a high alpine setting, it feels more like a private château than the luxury retreat it is. Perhaps it is the 6,500 very private acres of mountains, forests, and meadows that surround the resort. Some say the enchantment of the Vail Valley and the awe-inspiring Sawatch Range cast their spell. Certainly, the sweet cry of magpies and hawks and the rustle of aspens and blue spruce have their impact. Whatever the reasons, a sense of tranquility steals over guests the moment they settle in here.

GOLFING

THE LODGE AND SPA AT CORDILLERA

MOUNTAIN COURSE
Architect: Hale Irwin
Tour stops: 1997 Shell's
Wonderful World of Golf
Par: 72
Bluegrass fairways,
bentgrass greens
Yardage/Rating/Slope:
Gold tees
7,444/73.6/141
Silver tees
6,788/70.8/137
Blue tees
6,186/68.0/130
Red tees
5,226/68.6/128

VALLEY COURSE
Architect: Tom Fazio
Par: 71
Bluegrass fairways,
bentgrass greens
Yardage/Rating/Slope:
Gold tees
7,005/72.2/130
Silver tees
6,569/69.8/128
Blue tees
6,033/67.2/121
Red tees
5,162/69.4/128

10-HOLE SHORT COURSE
Architect: Dave Pelz
Par: 27
Bluegrass fairways,
bentgrass greens
Yardage:
Gold tees
1,252
Blue tees
1,050
Red tees
592

ROCKY MOUNTAIN VIEWS

Golfers who play the 10-Hole Short Course are

treated to great golf and spectacular views of

the Colorado Rockies in the distance.

VINTAGE IRWIN

The Mountain Course utilizes the seemingly endless, rolling slopes

of the Cordillera terrain. Hole 12 is a perfect example.

EUROPEAN STYLINGS

With the look and feel of a Belgian

estate, the Lodge and Spa rests on a

6,500-acre private wilderness.

Cordillera is just twenty-five minutes from the slopes of Vail, and part of its appeal is surely that the same happy families come back here to enjoy themselves year after year, whether it be fall or winter, summer or spring. An intimate place of just fifty-six rooms, it is easy to quickly get on a first-name basis not only with the eager-to-please, fresh-faced staff, but with the other low-key guests as well.

After a day of golf or walking in the wilderness of the back country, it is bliss to sink into the soft couches of the lodge and gaze, cool drink in hand, at the spectacular mountain views. Wide, welcoming patios are perfect for quiet conversations. There are details every-

THE LODGE AND	RESORT RATING:	
	CHALLENGE	★★★★⯪
	BEAUTY	★★★★★
SPA AT CORDILLERA	LODGING	★★★★⯪
	CUISINE	★★★★⯪
	AMENITIES	★★★★
EDWARDS, COLORADO		

where that remind so many of a very hospitable Belgian country estate: hand-troweled plaster walls, native stone, Chinese slate roofs, hand-forged ironwork, beautifully crafted furniture, tiled bathrooms, and high ceilings. On cool misty mornings, the fragrance of burning oak from the resort's many fireplaces fills the air.

In the award-winning Restaurant Picasso, guests are embraced by a world of dark wood beams, original Picasso lithographs, and over-stuffed armchairs. After enjoying a deceptively rich meal (Chef Fabrice Beaudoin achieves intense tastes through juices, purees, fresh

HEALTH AND FITNESS

With an endless array of indoor and outdoor activities, it's no wonder the Spa at Cordillera is often called an "adventure spa." Along with invigorating spa treatments, there's hiking, mountain biking, swimming, and more.

fruits, and vegetables), one can wander out to the grounds to enjoy the brilliant night skies that have become lost to most city dwellers. If a more boisterous evening is anticipated, the resort's authentic Irish Pub is full of laughter and spirited fun.

The lower level of the lodge is devoted to a sybaritic spa. Moments after arriving, it is not unusual to feel better, even before the talented team starts their work. There is nothing quite like Cordillera's Thai Massage, an

"The elevations of our various courses range from seventy-two hundred feet at the Valley Course to approximately nine thousand feet at the Summit Course. Because of the thin air at these elevations, the ball flies farther and straighter, and club selection has to be made accordingly."

— PENTTI TOFFERI, DIRECTOR OF GOLF, THE CLUB AT CORDILLERA

ATTENTION TO DETAIL

Every room at the Lodge and Spa at Cordillera contains beautifully crafted furniture, tiled bathrooms, and high ceilings. Most include fireplaces and decks with breathtaking views.

acupressure and stretching session on a padded floor, or their LaStone Therapy, 110 minutes of smooth basalt rocks placed at strategic body points. And who wouldn't be totally refreshed by the unique Apricot Exfoliation, a body peel using crushed, rounded apricot kernels, ending with a nutritional "vitamin cocktail massage?" Those searching for more exotic delights can find enhancing mud, seaweed, salt, and even champagne treatments for body and face.

Cordillera has long been thought of as the premier golf community in the Rocky Mountains. Three courses, each different in character and playability, captivate golfers for different reasons beyond their breathtaking scenery. The Hale Irwin–designed Mountain Course is a showcase for the great outdoors. Golfers swear that the high elevations give their ball an extra zip. Cordillera's Valley Course plays through a mountain desert terrain of natural ravines dotted with sage and junipers. Even if your game isn't on, you can take pleasure in watching the scurrying rabbits and foxes or the soaring eagles. The Dave Pelz–designed Short Course is a fourteen-acre gem perfect for tuning up the short game.

Any stay at Cordillera is an adventure, with tennis, fishing, jeep touring, rafting, hiking, horseback trekking, and mountain biking close at hand. Many guests test their limits, but many more prefer to simply relax. The rewards are many for those who choose this exhilarating, dramatic, and romantic getaway in the full splendor of the Rockies.

The Rockies also nicely set the grand stage for the Sheraton Tamarron. At the base of thousand-foot cliffs in the deep Colorado forest

lies the Cliffs, the resort's championship course. Here the only drive required is that of a proper swing and the only traffic comes from the occasional curious elk.

With the course at a staggering 7,600 feet above sea level, lowland golfers delight to discover how much farther their ball sails in the rarefied air. The rugged Wild West spirit of the jagged mountains and the unique topography (the area was once home to volcanoes and continental glaciers) contribute to the remarkable course.

A QUIET EVENING

The Lodge and Spa at Cordillera is known for its fabulous dining at Restaurant Picasso.

FOUR COURSES, FOUR DESIGNERS

With dramatic views of the New York and Sawatch Mountain ranges, the championship golf courses showcase Cordillera's compelling scenery.

HIDDEN COURSES

Lined with aspen trees and pine groves, hole 13 of the Mountain Course winds gracefully through the wilderness, preserving Colorado's natural beauty and its wildlife. Golf at this elevation is an uplifting experience.

"The greens are quick, undulated, and extremely hard to putt. Ninety percent of the time they'll break away from the nearest mountain."

—LAURA SCRIVNER, DIRECTOR OF GOLF, THE CLIFFS

RESORT RATING:

CHALLENGE	★★★★
BEAUTY	★★★★½
LODGING	★★★½
CUISINE	★★★★
AMENITIES	★★★★

DURANGO, COLORADO

SHERATON TAMARRON

RESORT

FIRST-CLASS AMENITIES

With its on-site health club, fine dining facilities, and classic mountain golf, a stay at Sheraton Tamarron can be a tranquil retreat or an active adventure.

But golfers beware: one of the most nefarious pitfalls is not the narrow fairways or the eight water hazards, but the yellow-bellied marmots—beaver-sized burrowing mammals who have an inexplicable penchant for golf balls. Fear not, the scariest thing on this course is the monster eleventh hole, a par-five at 555 yards from the blues where accuracy triumphs over power.

The area's history centers on its geological riches. Miners from every corner were lured to the region for its gold and silver. The Durango Narrow Gauge Railroad, which winds along steep mountain passages and dangles over breathtaking valleys and sheer rock faces, revealing ghost towns, is the only physical remnant of this bygone era. The nearby Native American dwellings of Mesa Verde National Park and lists of adventure tours mesmerize tourists.

All that fresh air helps build up an appetite quickly, easily satisfied with a pastrami sandwich at the Kokopelli Deli or a casual meal at the Antlers Grille, where the glow from the fireplace flickers off the dark beams of the wood ceiling. Handsome leather chairs meld with homey stone walls and Navajo-style rugs, evoking the feel of a cozy cabin. Views from every room in the resort look out onto stately ponderosas, ancient eroded cliffs, and, typically, some sort of inquisitive wildlife. The rustic, Old West mood is complete when you hear the whistle and feel the rumble of the train as it rolls by.

There is little of this rusticity at the Broadmoor. Return guests love to call it a "grande dame" and they are right; the Broadmoor has a grand reputation and is aging beautifully. Here is a place secure in history, where time-honored traditions are being upheld just as they were when the doors first swung open in 1918.

When Philadelphia entrepreneur Spencer Rose planned his Italianate pink showpiece on the site of a nineteenth-century gambling casino in the Rockies, it was the flawless blue skies and clear Colorado air that attracted him. Guests still revel in the moderate climate, usually sunny days, and clear nights.

The impressive stucco buildings of the Broadmoor are Mediterranean in motif, and many of the adornments were imported from art centers in Europe and beyond. Some of the Oriental art dates back to the Ming and T'sing dynasties. Toulouse-Lautrec lithographs line the walls of the Tavern. A huge carved African mahogany bar dominates the Golden Bee Pub. Handworked frescos, bas reliefs, wall hangings, and priceless old paintings are captivating. Rooms and suites seem to have historic personalities and are continually being refurbished around existing antiques and works of art.

There is a mood and moment for every taste bud at the Broadmoor. No fewer than eleven restaurants dish out specials from the opulent to the casual, from haute cuisine to hamburgers, from dinners followed by swing dancing to poolside western buffets.

SHERATON TAMARRON RESORT

THE CLIFFS
DURANGO, COLORADO

Architect: Arthur Hills

Par: 72

Bluegrass/rye fairways, bentgrass greens

Yardage/Rating/Slope:

<u>Gold tees</u>

6,885/73.0/142

<u>Silver tees</u>

6,355/70.5/135

<u>Jade tees</u>

5,330/70.6/124

.

MOUNTAIN ADVENTURES

Both adventurous and not-so-adventurous types can find a variety of ways to explore the surrounding San Juan Mountains. Jeep tours, hiking trails, horseback rides, and white-water rafting are just a few.

MOVING ALONG

Golf at Tamarron promises to move quickly. The Cliffs frequently rates high in speed-of-play rankings.

SHAPING UP

The Sheraton Tamarron Resort has a fully equipped health spa and fitness professionals who can offer guests individual workout plans.

A DESIGN MASTERPIECE

The East Course, surrounded by walls of pines, maples, oaks, and elms, offers challenges fit for handicappers of every level.

EXPERIENCING

THE BROADMOOR

Built in 1918, the Broadmoor offers a legacy of elegance, impeccable service, and exquisite cuisine in the scenic foothills of the Rocky Mountains.

• Enjoy world-class tennis and golf, miles of hiking trails, horseback riding, swimming, and even hot-air ballooning.

• For sophisticated pampering and unique personal treatments, visit the Spa at the Broadmoor with its rich baths, mellow whirlpools, and cascading waters from a pure mountain spring.

• Ride the Cog Railway to the top of Pikes Peak or tour the U.S. Air Force Academy or the nearby U.S. Olympic Training Center.

• After a day of sightseeing or recreation, enjoy an evening of cocktails and dancing or knee-slapping sing-alongs at the Golden Bee.

THE RESORT

The Broadmoor spans three hundred acres and is located at the foot of Cheyenne Mountain, just five miles from Colorado Springs. In addition to three championship golf courses, the property boasts twelve tennis courts, riding stables, and even a fly-fishing school.

UNDERSTATED ELEGANCE

The spacious grandeur of the lobby is typical of the entire Broadmoor complex, where guest rooms feature comfortable period furnishings and subtle handwork by European artisans.

All this makes social life more than just interesting. Happily, gentlemen are still expected to wear a coat in the Penrose Room, a tribute to the gracious standards the Broadmoor continues to uphold.

The Broadmoor doesn't offer just one golf course. Nor does it have only two. There is a trio of immaculate places to play, sculpted from the foothills of the Rockies. Master architect Donald Ross designed the original East Course in 1918. Robert Trent Jones, Jr. did the West Course, and Ed Seay and Arnold Palmer created the Mountain Course. Pick one and weave your way through cathedrals of white pine, Douglas fir, blue spruce, Siberian elm, maple, and oak.

The Broadmoor's spa seems to extend the

"The greens are smooth, fast, and somewhat undulated. Ball placement on the green is crucial in scoring."

—RUSS MILLER, DIRECTOR OF GOLF OPERATIONS, THE BROADMOOR

THE BROADMOOR

COLORADO SPRINGS, COLORADO

RESORT RATING:

CHALLENGE	★★★★
BEAUTY	★★★★½
LODGING	★★★★½
CUISINE	★★★★
AMENITIES	★★★★½

resort's eighty-two-year tradition of warmth into another dimension, that of renewal of the body, mind, and spirit. Sure, there are pampering and unbounded exercise options at this delightful spot, but what makes things different at the Broadmoor is a prevailing notion of moderation, not deprivation. Health conscious "Cuisine Vivante," an approach full of life and energy, exceeds expectations.

Everything is top drawer here. Recreation options at the Broadmoor feature tennis on twelve all-weather courts under the direction of Dennis Ralston, U.S. Davis Cup Captain and Hall of Famer. There's paddle boating, horseback riding in the rugged Cheyenne Mountains, biking, and nearby river rafting, fishing, and hot-air ballooning. Corporate bigwigs can often be seen sweating it out at the Action Learning Center, a program for personal, team, and organizational development. If less strenuous pursuits might better suit, there are always wine tastings to try, the zoo to visit, and Pikes Peak to gawk at. The Broadmoor even has a "Fifth Avenue" of quality shops selling high fashion and goodies from an old-fashioned soda fountain.

FUN IN THE SUN

Guests at the Broadmoor can relax by the pool or enjoy a wide variety of recreational opportunities, including horseback riding, hiking, and fitness training.

THE BROADMOOR
COLORADO SPRINGS, COLORADO

EAST COURSE
Architects: Donald Ross,
Robert Trent Jones, Jr.
Par: 72
Rye fairways, bentgrass greens
Yardage/Rating/Slope:

<u>Blue tees</u>
7,119/73.0/127

<u>White tees</u>
6,562/70.5/122

<u>Red tees</u>
5,921/72.7/139

WEST COURSE
Architects: Donald Ross,
Robert Trent Jones, Jr.
Par: 72
Rye fairways, bentgrass greens
Yardage/Rating/Slope:

<u>Blue tees</u>
7,190/73.3/132

<u>White tees</u>
6,493/70.0/130

<u>Red tees</u>
5,573/70.5/127

MOUNTAIN COURSE
Architects: Arnold Palmer,
Ed Seay
Par: 72
Rye fairways, bentgrass greens
Yardage/Rating/Slope:

<u>Blue tees</u>
6,781/72.1/133

<u>White tees</u>
6,108/69.1/120

<u>Red tees</u>
5,609/71.5/126

<u>Yellow tees</u>
4,834/67.3/117

MASTERPIECE

The three golf courses at
the Broadmoor offer beauty
and challenge from golf's
most legendary
designers.

SHERATON STEAMBOAT RESORT

Quiet elegance, Old West charm, and plenty of exciting activities make this a popular destination for outdoor enthusiasts.

• Experience the thrill of a hot-air balloon ride, the comfort of a rooftop hot tub, or the invigoration of a workout at the fitness center.

• Sample spectacular water activities, from white-water rafting or world-class fly-fishing to tubing, canoeing, or kayaking on the Yampa River.

• Experience a wild western rodeo or explore the countryside on horseback.

• After an adventurous day, relax with a drink in front of the fireplace, then enjoy spectacular views and a variety of entertainment choices in one of the three fine restaurants.

MOUNTAIN GOLF

The ruggedly beautiful course at Sheraton Steamboat Resort offers visitors classic mountain golf play.

Guests should come here prepared to be enchanted. They can restore, replenish, and revitalize naturally at the Broadmoor, where a brilliant combination of raw beauty and diverting recreational amenities set the stage. It was, after all, in these very same parts that Catherine Lee Bates was inspired to write "America the Beautiful" in 1893.

Who knows how much more music Miss Bates might have written had she spent some time at the Sheraton Steamboat in Steamboat Springs? At nearly 6,700 feet above sea level, guests claim that the lively ambience is created by the invigoratingly crisp air. The small, unpretentious village town boasts extensive adventure sports for the hardy. No stay ever seems long enough. Folks can fill their "need for speed" with white-water rafting, mountain biking, kayaking, hot-air ballooning, and tubing down the rushing Yampa River. For the faint of heart, the town lures shoppers with antique and boutique bargains. Gondola rides up the mountain, and the pro rodeo series and outdoor summer concerts fill the nighttime hours.

When a wave of tired satisfaction sweeps over, a soak in one of the private rooftop spas soothes most aches and pains. In the resort's 3 Saddles Bar and Grill, a spectacular panoramic view of the mountains provides the backdrop for cocktails and conversation. For a more elegant evening, Sevens' delectable choices range from juicy filet mignon and crab cakes to the more exotic margarita bread pudding.

Considered the "mountain jewel," Sheraton Steamboat's popular eighteen-hole course, designed by Robert Trent Jones, Jr., continues to garner top awards, and with good reason. This course covers over 150 acres and is shaped by aging aspens, noble evergreens, and the babbling Fish Creek. Among the most attractive alternatives, appealing to all skill levels, are the generous turf-covered landing areas and rolling bentgrass greens. At the end of a game, golfers enjoy lunch and a full bar under the shade on one of the decks at the Fish Creek Grille.

Some say Steamboat is something of a journey in itself. Its personality is warm and vibrant. Its carefree attitude is without pretension and its natural attributes are awe-inspiring. This is a place to hit the trail with abandon or collapse and read a good book.

Colorado's Keystone stands proud as a resort for all four seasons. Ever protective of its stunning assets, Keystone is a certified pioneer in eco-friendly resort planning, striving to minimize its impact on native wildlife and vegetation. In winter, one is impacted immediately by the brisk Rocky Mountain air as it whispers through glades of stately trees. Summer meadows, laced with wildflowers and crisscrossed with clear streams, beckon guests to discover the endless bounty.

Award-winning environmentalist Michael Hurdzan designed Keystone's second golf course, the River Run, which moseys along the Snake River.

STEAMBOAT SPRINGS, COLORADO

SHERATON STEAMBOAT

RESORT

RESORT RATING:

CHALLENGE	★★★⯪
BEAUTY	★★★★⯪
LODGING	★★★★
CUISINE	★★★⯪
AMENITIES	★★★★

"This is the kind of course you can ease into. The front nine is fairly forgiving but the back nine turns into more of a shot-makers course. The greens are very undulating . . .

and in most instances you have to fly the ball to the hole, but the greens hold well so you can shoot right at the pin."

—GARY CRAWFORD, DIRECTOR OF GOLF/HEAD PROFESSIONAL, SHERATON STEAMBOAT GOLF CLUB

AWE-INSPIRING BEAUTY

It's hard to tell which view is more spectacular: the one outside of the Yampa Valley or the one that greets you when you enter your room. Both are filled with Old West charm.

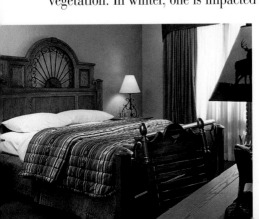

RUSTIC ELEGANCE

The Sheraton Steamboat boasts a
warm western environment where
guests feel comfortable in jeans,
a ski suit, or a tux.

OUT OF THE TRAP

Robert Trent Jones, Jr. cooked
up all sorts of hazards to
frustrate golfers at the
Steamboat Golf Club.

SHERATON STEAMBOAT RESORT

STEAMBOAT GOLF CLUB
STEAMBOAT SPRINGS,
COLORADO

Architect: Robert Trent Jones, Jr.
Tour stops: Ski Town USA Golf
Classic
Par: 72
Bluegrass/rye fairways,
bentgrass/Poa greens
Yardage/Rating/Slope:
Championship tees
6,902/72.0/138
Middle tees
6,293/70.2/131
Forward tees
5,536/72.6/123

WHITE-WATER HAZARD

From mid-May to late
October, golfers can enjoy
the sound of rushing water
as they play the course
at Steamboat
Golf Club.

GOLFING

KEYSTONE RESORT
KEYSTONE, COLORADO

KEYSTONE RANCH COURSE
Architect: Robert Trent Jones, Jr.
Par: 72
Bluegrass/rye fairways,
bentgrass greens
Yardage/Rating/Slope:
Blue tees
7,090/71.4/130
White tees
6,521/68.9/120
Gold tees
5,842/66.6/112
Red tees
5,582/70.7/129

RIVER COURSE
Architect: Dana Fry,
Michael Hurdzan
Par: 71
Bluegrass fairways,
bentgrass greens
Yardage/Rating/Slope:
Black tees
6,886/70.3/131
Blue tees
6,507/68.8/121
White tees
6,003/67.0/114
Gold tees
5,359/64.4/105
Red tees
4,762/64.5/113

ENVIRONMENTAL COMMITMENT

At Keystone, guests are encouraged to play in nature while helping to preserve it. Nearly all of Keystone's lodging units are involved in an environmental program that enables guests to recycle and conserve energy.

ROLLING HILLS AND ALPINE LAKES

With a traditional Scottish linksland front nine and a traditional mountain valley back nine, the Ranch Course challenges golfers and offers spectacular views.

VIEW FROM THE TOP

The mountains near Keystone are a year-round playground, perfect for skiing, hiking, mountain biking, horseback riding, and more.

Lake Dillon serves as a backdrop for the eighteenth hole and it isn't unusual to catch a glimpse of a snowshoe hare between holes. Native flowers and grasses have been lovingly planted everywhere.

Keystone tempts one year-round with a culinary school, sailing, ecology walks, and horseback riding in the spring and summer. The Alpine Institute combines recreation with education, allowing guests to learn new skills and hobbies and to take home more than just a vacation experience. There is no spa per se, but plenty of rafting and sailing, and yoga is on the menu at sunrise. The nearby White River National Forest is just waiting to be explored. And when the weather turns, guests

KEYSTONE, COLORADO	RESORT RATING:	
	CHALLENGE	★★★★
KEYSTONE RESORT	BEAUTY	★★★★
	LODGING	★★★½
	CUISINE	★★★★
	AMENITIES	★★★★½

warm up the credit cards at the boutiques, galleries, and bistros.

Entertainment at Keystone ranges from clogging to cooking classes to bluegrass. Or one can simply take the chill out of the evening with a glass of wine in front of the lodge's limestone fireplace. A quick tram ride to an awesome 11,444 feet brings guests to the doors of the Alpenglow Stube, where treetop perspectives, wooden beams, candlelight, and gourmet cuisine make dinner a treat. For grilled buffalo, curious diners flock to the Ski Tip Lodge, once a stagecoach stop. Keystone produces tasty six-course gourmet dinners, but is also willing to pack a lunch for guests who want to take part in the llama lunch hike.

Literature is a perfect companion for a happy visit to the Hyatt Regency Beaver Creek Resort and Spa. Pearching atop its own beautiful mountain, the resort is reminiscent of an alpine European village. Against a backdrop of snow-capped Rocky Mountains, which seem to stretch endlessly toward powder blue skies, it is far from the cares of the world and full of captivating charms.

HIGH DESIGN

The attention to detail at the River Run complex at Keystone Resort rivals the golf offerings.

BARN DANCE AND BBQ

Two favorite activities at Keystone are horsedrawn wagon rides to a western barbecue and weekly barn dances.

LUNCH IS SERVED

Keystone Resort offers a llama lunch hike during the summer months as an interesting alternative to dining at the resort.

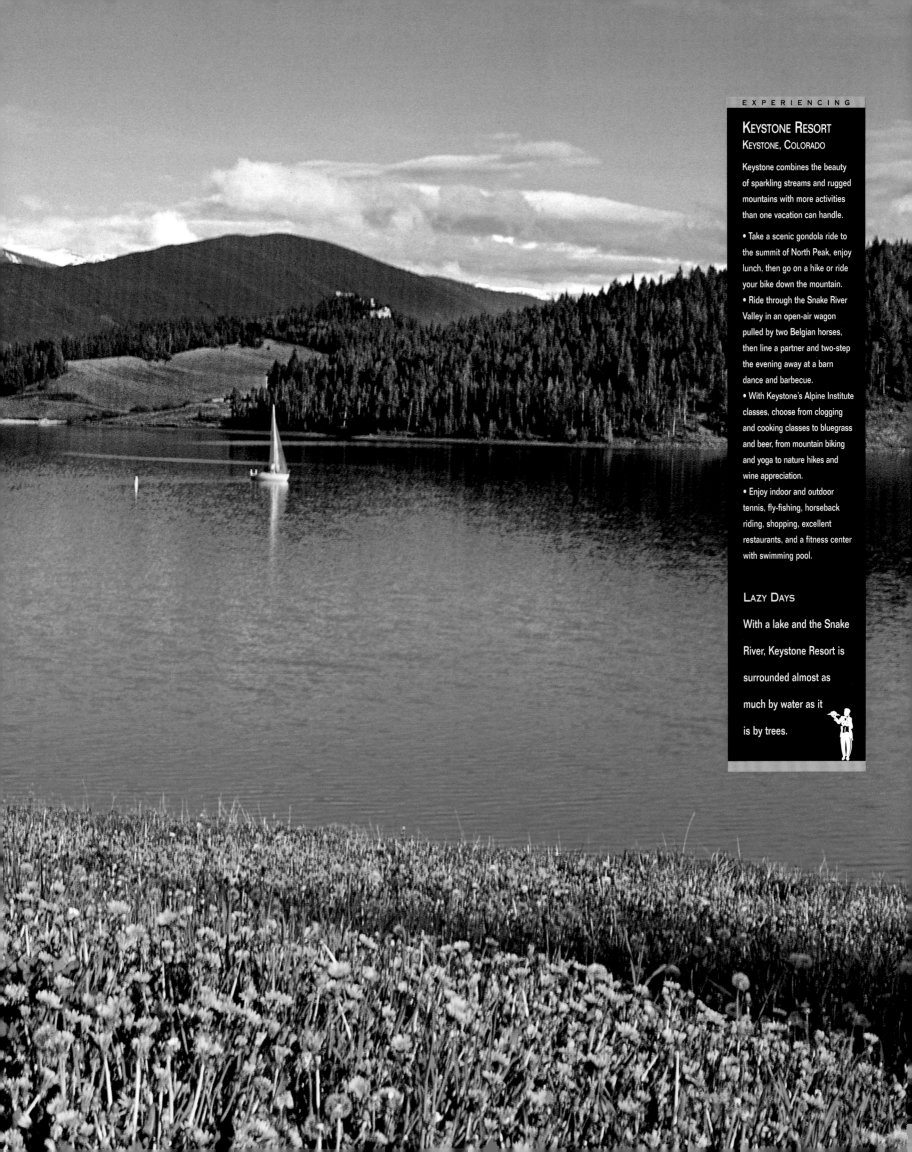

"Beaver Creek requires careful placement of shots as you wind through numerous trees, bunkers, and the roaring Beaver Creek."

—JEFF HANSON, HEAD GOLF
PROFESSIONAL, BEAVER CREEK GOLF CLUB

RESORT RATING:		VAIL, COLORADO
CHALLENGE	★★★★	
BEAUTY	★★★★	
LODGING	★★★★	
CUISINE	★★★★	
AMENITIES	★★★★⯨	

HYATT REGENCY BEAVER CREEK

RESORT AND SPA

GARDEN FRESH

Executive chef John Benson uses fresh ingredients and herbs from Beaver Creek's gardens. The Crooked Hearth Tavern, a casual fireside venue, is one of four enticing restaurants at the resort.

The hotel is modeled after the great castles, monasteries, and convents near Innsbruck, Austria. Native stone offset with stucco and rough timbers, peaked roofs and copper flashing, pine ceilings and walls, and wrought iron accents by talented artisans seem more like St. Moritz than Colorado.

A stream weaves its way through the Robert Trent Jones, Jr.–designed, 6,400-yard championship course, set in the Beaver Creek Valley and surrounded by the White River National Forest. Several of the resort's majestic private homes line the seasoned fairways.

For visitors who want to take a break from the greens, there is a wealth of choices, including tennis, fishing, hiking, shooting, rock climbing, horseback riding, llama trekking, white-water rafting, mountain biking, and all-terrain vehicle touring.

There are also dining options galore, but none compare with an evening sleigh ride to Beano's Cabin on Beaver Creek Mountain for carefully prepared game, fowl, beef, and fish entrees. Beautiful Belgian horses carry guests to the restaurant, while a van purrs close by for the less adventurous.

Seasonal pleasures abound at the Phoenician in Scottsdale. Fine touches, to-die-for décor, unsurpassed amenities, and white-glove service make every stay an unforgettable one. Italian marble shines all around. The exquisite stone was imported from Carrara, where Michelangelo procured his marble for sculpting. Prior to its installation, each piece was numbered so that the sequencing of color and veining could be matched, a painstaking attention to detail seldom seen. The quantity of marble on the property would equal two quarries the size of nearby Camelback Mountain.

HARD TO IMAGINE

What could be nicer than a soothing whirlpool and

softly falling water? Five equally charming whirlpools

are scattered throughout the resort grounds.

EXPERIENCING

HYATT REGENCY BEAVER CREEK RESORT AND SPA

In the breathtaking setting of secluded Beaver Creek Valley, the Hyatt Regency has everything for your perfect western vacation.

• Take a stroll or drive through nearby Avon, with its numerous art galleries and magnificent bronze sculptures placed in a variety of areas throughout the town.

• Plan an action-packed day of mountain biking, a leisurely hike along scenic Beaver Creek, or a horseback ride to an authentic western dinner.

• Choose the perfect spot to watch the majestic mountain sunsets—in one of the five whirlpools, beside the indoor/outdoor pool, or in a lounge chair in front of the huge fire pit.

• Try the balance experience, where two therapists work in harmony using balancing herbs, aromatherapy, and a blend of essential oils, at the feng shui–inspired Allegria spa.

PARADISE OUT BACK

The swimming pool and outdoor fire

pit are two perfect spots for relaxing

on lounge chairs and watching the sun

set over the mountains.

A SHOT-MAKER'S COURSE

Robert Trent Jones, Jr. included a number of difficult

bunkers when he designed the Beaver Creek course.

Combined with the tree-lined fairways and nearby creek,

it becomes a tight, exciting place to play.

HYATT REGENCY BEAVER CREEK RESORT AND SPA

BEAVER CREEK GOLF CLUB
VAIL, COLORADO

Architect: Robert Trent Jones, Jr.

Par: 70

Bentgrass/rye fairways, bentgrass greens

Yardage/Rating/Slope:

<u>Gold tees</u>
 6,784/71.0/140

<u>Blue tees</u>
 6,478/69.6/138

<u>White tees</u>
 5,973/67.7/134

<u>Red tees</u>
 5,088/70.3/124

WHAT A VIEW!

Tracing the winding Beaver Creek, the par-seventy golf course requires good shot selection and careful club choice to negotiate the trees, bunkers, and challenging terrain.

THE PHOENICIAN

Architect: Homer Flint,
redesigned by Ted Robinson

OASIS COURSE
Par: 35
Bermuda fairways,
TifEagle greens
Yardage/Rating/Slope:
Championship tees
3,250/70.3/130
Phoenician tees
2,995/69.0/122
Ladies' tees
2,559/65.2/109

DESERT COURSE
Par: 35
Bermuda fairways,
TifEagle greens
Yardage/Rating/Slope:
Championship tees
3,060/69.4/131
Phoenician tees
2,847/67.8/124
Ladies' tees
2,465/63.5/111

CANYON COURSE
Par: 35
Bermuda fairways,
TifEagle greens
Yardage/Rating/Slope:
Championship tees
3,008/70.1/130
Phoenician tees
2,844/68.1/127
Ladies' tees
2,312/63.7/107

VALLEY OF THE SUN

At the base of Camelback
Mountain, the Phoenician
lies amid lush desert
terrain in the Valley of the
Sun. Fountains, lakes,
rolling gardens, and a
spectacular golf course
have a soothing effect
on all who visit.

The Phoenician is so much more than a world-class luxury resort. But what exactly makes life here so special? A dazzling, multimillion-dollar art collection, for starters. Life-size bronze sculptures, photorealist waterscapes by David Kessler, and rare European paintings and antiques are prominently displayed throughout.

The parklike, two-acre Cactus Garden stretches along the northern edge of the resort's grounds. This scenic spot showcases over 350 varieties of cacti and succulents from Arizona, Texas, Mexico, and other areas around the world.

Grand pianos galore grace the Phoenician. Eleven majestic Steinways are situated here and there. Guests can test their talents on the ivories in the Terrace Dining Room, Mary Elaine's restaurant, the main lobby, and each of the four Presidential suites.

Personal butlers stand at attention. All presidential suites feature this signature, twenty-four-hour service, with amenities such as limousine transportation; unpacking and pressing service; choice of cotton or satin linens and foam, feather, or down pillows; a reserved poolside cabana; daily selections of fruit, snacks, and nuts, plus a full bar with liquor, wines, and beers.

Endless water flows and flows for the pleasure of the guests. The Canyon Building offers an "edgeless" oval swimming pool covering more than 2,800 square feet and filled with nearly 74,000 gallons of water. The graduated meeting of water and deck create a pool that gently brims over. Canyon Pool Cabanas measure 200 square feet and feature ceiling fans, bathrooms with shower and amenities, phones with cordless handsets, and computer ports.

Oenophiles take note: At Mary Elaine's restaurant, a $3.6-million wine collection offers over 1,800 wine labels with multiple vintages. The restaurant also employs Arizona's only master sommelier. The

THE PHOENICIAN

SCOTTSDALE, ARIZONA

RESORT RATING:

CHALLENGE	★★★★
BEAUTY	★★★★☆
LODGING	★★★★☆
CUISINE	★★★★☆
AMENITIES	★★★★☆

SCOTTSDALE, ARIZONA

resort's oh-so-refined daily afternoon tea service features "Rothschild Bird" patterned Hungarian Herend china. This unique bird pattern was designed especially for the Rothschild family of Vienna in the 1860s.

Nothing is left to chance. Room service delivers a toaster to each room (instead of toasting breads beforehand) to ensure warmth. The Praying Monk dining salon was built around an Italian solid wood table, which is surrounded by sixteen French tapestry-covered chairs. The resort's pasta and bake shop prepares decadent pasta, pastries and candies, breads and rolls, and ice cream daily.

The desert has its own special drama and allure, forged by the inexorable forces of time. Spectacular rock outcroppings. Ancient saguaros. Rambling foothills. Prehistoric boulders. Long ago, the Hohokam people worshiped a sacred site in Carefree, Arizona, that is today the Boulders. The Hohokam reverence for nature and balance has truly come to life.

NO TROUBLES

Those who visit the Phoenician year after year describe its ambiance in a single word: freedom. The spacious lobbies, tranquil guest rooms, and even the Arizona sky liberate visitors from their usual day-to-day concerns.

Heavy Hitter

The championship Golf Oasis features three separate nine-hole

courses, each with its own distinctive flavor and panoramic views. *Golf*

magazine calls it one of the best resort courses in the country.

"It doesn't pay to try to cut corners here: you either hit in the water or in the desert. Straight is better than long and crooked."

—JOHN JACKSON, DIRECTOR OF GOLF, THE PHOENICIAN

EXPERIENCING

THE PHOENICIAN
SCOTTSDALE, ARIZONA

Enjoy the blue skies, warm days, and rich colors and textures of the great American Southwest in a place with unparalleled elegance.

• Indulge in soothing massage, facials and fitness, as well as meditation and southwestern body treatments, at the luxurious Centre for Well-Being spa.
• Relax by any one of the nine magnificent swimming pools, including one completely inlaid with mother-of-pearl tiles, and ringed by lounges, umbrellas, and private cabanas.
• Enjoy a variety of dining options from southwestern, Italian, and French to the Phoenician's heart-healthy Choices spa cuisine.
• Perfect your game at the Tennis Garden's twelve courts, including a fully automated practice court and a Wimbledon championship grass court.

A PEARL OF A POOL

The Phoenician's

painstaking attention to

detail is present at

each of its nine

shimmering pools.

"Our golf courses are not terribly long, so accuracy off the tee boxes is important. The majority of golfers here don't use their three woods, five woods, or longer irons enough. . . .

RESORT RATING:

CHALLENGE	★★★★⯪
BEAUTY	★★★★★
LODGING	★★★★★
CUISINE	★★★★⯪
AMENITIES	★★★★⯪

Leave your drivers in your bag on most holds and find the center of the fairways."

—ROB TURNER, HEAD GOLF
PROFESSIONAL, THE BOULDERS

HISTORIC REMINDERS

El Pedregal, an adobe
marketplace in the Boulders,
calls to mind the simple lifestyle
of the Hohokam Indians who
once lived around Carefree.

CAREFREE, ARIZONA

THE BOULDERS

The name of the town alone, Carefree, signals the sort of stay one can expect to indulge in. What most praise about the Boulders is the way in which it blends so easily with the environment. It is obvious that even the local wildlife hardly notices man is on the scene. There seem to be daily breakfast appearances by quail and deer on the resort's lawns, much to the delight of parents and children alike. One endangered species appears to get special Boulders' attention: the Gila monster. Hardly a monster, this colorful lizard flourishes here, proof that man and nature can happily coexist in unison.

Impeccable attention to detail? Guests are given keyholders containing a letter of welcome, general information, a map, and descriptions of the fauna and flora that might eventually be happened upon. At check-in, in fact, no guest stands in front of a counter but rather sits before a desk and easily converses with the gracious receptionists.

Everyone seems to like the fact that tipping is done only on food and beverages, that staff almost always call everyone by name without automatically assuming a first-name basis, and that towels are deftly spread out at poolside.

There is a consistent endeavor to restore guests' spirit and energy at the Boulders. The rooms reinforce this goal and invite lounging on large, soft leather chairs and ottomans. And oh, those soft Egyptian combed cotton sheets! Each accommodation is unique, with colorful Native American artifacts. Casitas are sculpted into the natural terrain, and the cool desert night is best enjoyed before the warmth of their wood-burning fireplaces. Families and groups of friends wanting a more spacious setting seem to gravitate to the Pueblo Villas with their full kitchens, dining and living rooms, laundry facilities, and garages.

Golf, too, has been carefully thought out at the Boulders. Course designer Jay Morrish recently enlarged the greens and made the two championship courses more user-friendly and enjoyable, yet he has carefully preserved their integrity. There is seldom any problem for guests to get right on to play. However, once golfers are in a cart and off to the first tee, it isn't difficult for them to forget the game and focus on what beauty Mother Nature has wrought here.

And when hunger strikes, there is the Latilla. Latilla wood has been used for centuries in this part of the world, and it forms the dark hand-sculpted ceiling. Executive Chef Mary Nearn's forte is regional American cuisine. Mary is fond of saying, "Like a good book, good cooking has to hold your attention." And hold it she does with entreés from rack of lamb to prime beef to lobster (shipped overnight from the East Coast).

CHAMPAGNE SUNSETS

Two of the Boulders' most stunning features are the

giant saguaro cacti and hot-air balloon rides, which

carry guests to view gorgeous Arizona sunsets.

THE BOULDERS
CAREFREE, ARIZONA

NORTH COURSE

Architect: Jay Morrish

Par: 72

Bermuda/rye fairways, bentgrass greens

Yardage/Rating/Slope:

<u>Black tees</u>

6,950/73.4/144

<u>Blue tees</u>

6,717/72.3/135

<u>White tees</u>

6,277/70.2/130

<u>Gold tees</u>

5,449/70.6/120

<u>Red tees</u>

4,893/68.2/111

SOUTH COURSE

Architect: Jay Morrish

Par: 72

Bermuda/rye fairways, bentgrass greens

Yardage/Rating/Slope:

<u>Black tees</u>

7,007/73.3/146

<u>Blue tees</u>

6,589/71.4/137

<u>White tees</u>

6,073/69.2/127

<u>Gold tees</u>

5,141/70.8/118

<u>Red tees</u>

4,715/68.1/114

TWISTS AND TURNS

With thirty-six holes offering some of the most challenging golf in the Southwest, the Boulders receives much recognition, including *Golf* magazine's Gold Medal and *Golf Digest's* "America's 25 Best Resort Courses" awards.

SOUTHWESTERN COMFORT

Each of the 160 guest casitas has its own distinct character, a fireplace, private patio, and southwestern furnishings.

PINS AND NEEDLES

The Boulders offers a rare golf experience where guests can, among other things, tee off from the tops of giant boulders, look out over the Sonoran Desert, walk among ancient cacti along the course, and play on unique local grasses chosen for the fairways.

THE FAIRMONT SCOTTSDALE PRINCESS
TOURNAMENT PLAYERS CLUB OF SCOTTSDALE

STADIUM COURSE
Architects: Tom Weiskopf, Jay Morrish
Tour stops: PGA Tour's Phoenix Open
Par: 71
Bermuda/rye fairways and greens
Yardage/Rating/Slope:
TPC tees
7,089/74.5/135
Championship tees
6,508/71.0/124
Regular tees
6,049/68.9/120
Forward tees
5,567/71.6/122

DESERT COURSE
Architects: Tom Weiskopf, Jay Morrish
Par: 71
Bermuda/rye fairways and greens
Yardage/Rating/Slope:
TPC tees
6,369/71.4/112
Championship tees
5,738/67.4/109
Regular tees
5,174/64.8/103
Forward tees
4,554/65.9/105

DAYS AND NIGHTS

The Spanish colonial architecture provides a romantic setting for honeymoons, anniversaries, and weekend escapes. Outdoor enthusiasts enjoy the variety of sporting pursuits, from golf and tennis to splashing in the pool and exploring the mountains.

WIDE-OPEN SPACES

Each of the Fairmont Scottsdale Princess's oversized guest rooms captures the charm and grace of the Southwest, with scenic mountain or golf course views from a private terrace or balcony.

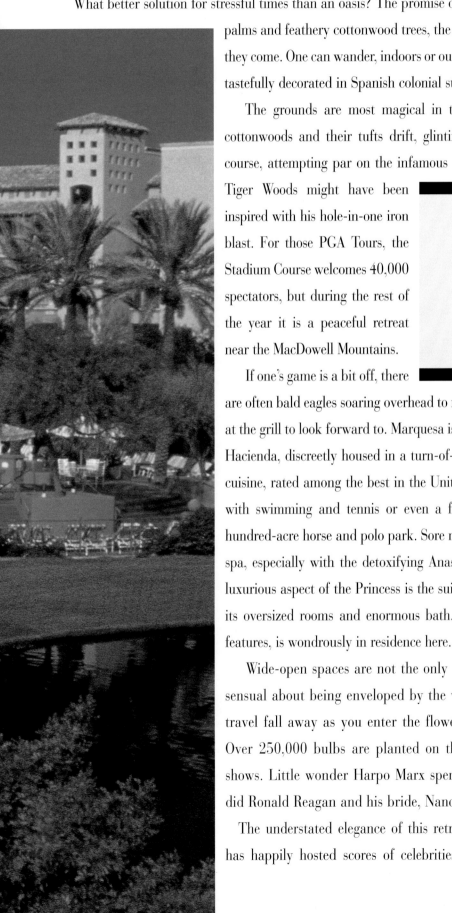

Unspoiled is a cliché today, for so few places can live up to the word. The Boulders is among those few. Life here allows a person to bask in the stark landscape under a peaceful golden light and drift toward a greater discovery of the desert and its wily inhabitants, rare in this hurly-burly twenty-first-century world.

What better solution for stressful times than an oasis? The promise of one is often a mirage, but with its regal palms and feathery cottonwood trees, the Fairmont Scottsdale Princess is as real as they come. One can wander, indoors or out, and find intimate nooks in the shadows, tastefully decorated in Spanish colonial style.

The grounds are most magical in the fall, when warm breezes nudge the cottonwoods and their tufts drift, glinting in the lengthening light. Out on the course, attempting par on the infamous sixteenth hole, it is easy to imagine how Tiger Woods might have been inspired with his hole-in-one iron blast. For those PGA Tours, the Stadium Course welcomes 40,000 spectators, but during the rest of the year it is a peaceful retreat near the MacDowell Mountains.

If one's game is a bit off, there are often bald eagles soaring overhead to revel in, dry-aged steaks and a microbrew at the grill to look forward to. Marquesa is home to Mediterranean savories, and La Hacienda, discreetly housed in a turn-of-the-century adobe, delivers fine Mexican cuisine, rated among the best in the United States. Longer stays can be sprinkled with swimming and tennis or even a foray to Westworld, a neighboring four-hundred-acre horse and polo park. Sore muscles and spirits are well soothed at the spa, especially with the detoxifying Anasazi Herbal Wrap. But perhaps the most luxurious aspect of the Princess is the suite that awaits at the end of the day, with its oversized rooms and enormous bath. Space, one of the West's most alluring features, is wondrously in residence here.

Wide-open spaces are not the only draw of the desert. There is something sensual about being enveloped by the warmth it radiates, and the logistics of travel fall away as you enter the flowering grounds of the Arizona Biltmore. Over 250,000 bulbs are planted on these thirty-nine acres annually, and it shows. Little wonder Harpo Marx spent his honeymoon here; so did Ronald Reagan and his bride, Nancy.

The understated elegance of this retreat, an establishment that has happily hosted scores of celebrities and dignitaries over the

THE FAIRMONT
SCOTTSDALE PRINCESS
SCOTTSDALE, ARIZONA

RESORT RATING:	
CHALLENGE	★★★★
BEAUTY	★★★★
LODGING	★★★★
CUISINE	★★★½
AMENITIES	★★★½

EXPERIENCING

THE FAIRMONT SCOTTSDALE PRINCESS

An impressive array of amenities and award-winning restaurants welcome visitors to this magnificent oasis.

• Enjoy an invigorating workout in the fitness center, participate in a yoga or box-aerobics class, then indulge yourself in a mind-relaxing and body-pampering spa treatment.

• Tour an underground gold mine, visit a ghost town, or explore the desert and its spectacular colors.

• When the sun goes down, lounge on a colorful float and enjoy your favorite theater snack at the poolside "dive-in movies," or dine in luxury at the resort's elegant restaurants.

years, is calming and soothing. Designed by Frank Lloyd Wright, the Biltmore is an architectural treasure, built of uniquely molded concrete blocks. Surrounding canals were built along those originally dug by the Hohokam tribe.

Rooms and villas are dressed in beige, sand, and ivory; 1930s-style lamps lend a Deco air. Marble baths and expansive views of Squaw Peak or the Paradise Pool complete the modern yet graceful accommodations.

When soft sunlight awakens guests, they look forward to a day at the spa. No fewer than eighty treatments are the enticements, and many of the restorative therapies are derived from the Native American tribes who once inhabited Phoenix. Dreamcatcher therapy is the

RESORT RATING:

CHALLENGE	★★★★
BEAUTY	★★★★
LODGING	★★★★⯪
CUISINE	★★★★
AMENITIES	★★★⯪

• PHOENIX, ARIZONA

ARIZONA BILTMORE

RESORT AND SPA

latest enlightening treatment. Using eight essential oils blended for each guest, a massage promises a "dream like" state of relaxation.

For sports lovers, there are seven lighted tennis courts and two adjacent golf courses (Clark Gable lost his wedding ring on one—it was dutifully returned by an employee). Some folks just hide themselves away in a cabana, dreaming of Marilyn Monroe, who regularly frolicked in the Catalina Pool. The Paradise Pool has an entertaining ninety-two-foot water slide.

Desert light spills through the tall windows at Wright's, the hotel's signature restaurant. Service is impeccable. This hot spot boasts a wine cellar containing the most extensive list in the Southwest and turns out innovative cuisine, such as pan-seared John Dory with caramelized leek, fennel, and red pepper. Satisfied guests wander into the night and warm air greets them again, this time along with the stars.

Wright himself said, "Give me the luxuries of life and I will willingly do without the necessities." The Arizona Biltmore delivers on both with ease.

ENCHANTING ACCENTS

Original artwork creates a feeling of timelessness.

INSPIRED BY WRIGHT

The distinctive influence of Frank Lloyd Wright,

consulting architect on the original hotel, has made it

an Arizona landmark since its 1929 opening.

GOLFING

ARIZONA BILTMORE RESORT AND SPA
ARIZONA BILTMORE COUNTRY CLUB

ADOBE COURSE
Architect: William Bell
Tour stops: 1992 Senior U.S. Open Qualifier
Par: 72
Bermuda/rye fairways and greens
Yardage/Rating/Slope:
Champion tees
6,449/70.1/119
Regular tees
6,122/68.4/115
Ladies' tees
5,796/72.2/118

LINKS COURSE
Architect: Bill Johnston
Par: 72
Bermuda/rye fairways and greens
Yardage/Rating/Slope:
Champion tees
6,300/69.7/126
Regular tees
5,726/67.4/118
Ladies' tees
4,747/66.5/106

AN OASIS

The Arizona Biltmore Country Club offers two spectacular

championship courses for members and guests of the resort.

A HOST OF LUMINARIES

The resort has hosted scores of celebrities

and entertainers. During a 1978 visit,

Frank Sinatra, Sammy Davis, Jr., and Liza

Minnelli offered an impromptu concert in

the hotel's lobby.

EXPERIENCING

ARIZONA BILTMORE RESORT AND SPA

Set in the foothills of Squaw Peak, the resort is renowned for its magnificent grounds and Frank Lloyd Wright–inspired design.

• Choose from exclusive guest villas, classic private cottages, and luxurious resort suites with views of sparkling pools and the majestic Phoenix Mountain Preserve.

• Enjoy a wide variety of dining venues, from afternoon tea to a romantic supper in the resort's signature restaurant, or a casual snack beside the pool or at its swim-up bar.

• Experience the beauty of the desert on a guided jeep tour or mountain hike, or relax by the Paradise Pool, complete with a water slide and private cabanas.

• For pure pampering, visit the spa and enjoy your body, facial, or salon services in a private outdoor garden setting.

THE NEWER COURSE

The Links at the Arizona Biltmore demands well-placed shots from those who play it.

"The Adobe, with its lush green fairways and impeccable course condition, is fairly long but has a traditional and forgiving layout. The Links Course has narrow fairways, water hazards, and tactically placed bunkers, making accuracy far more important than distance."

—RANDY BEAUPRE, HEAD GOLF PROFESSIONAL, ARIZONA BILTMORE COUNTRY CLUB

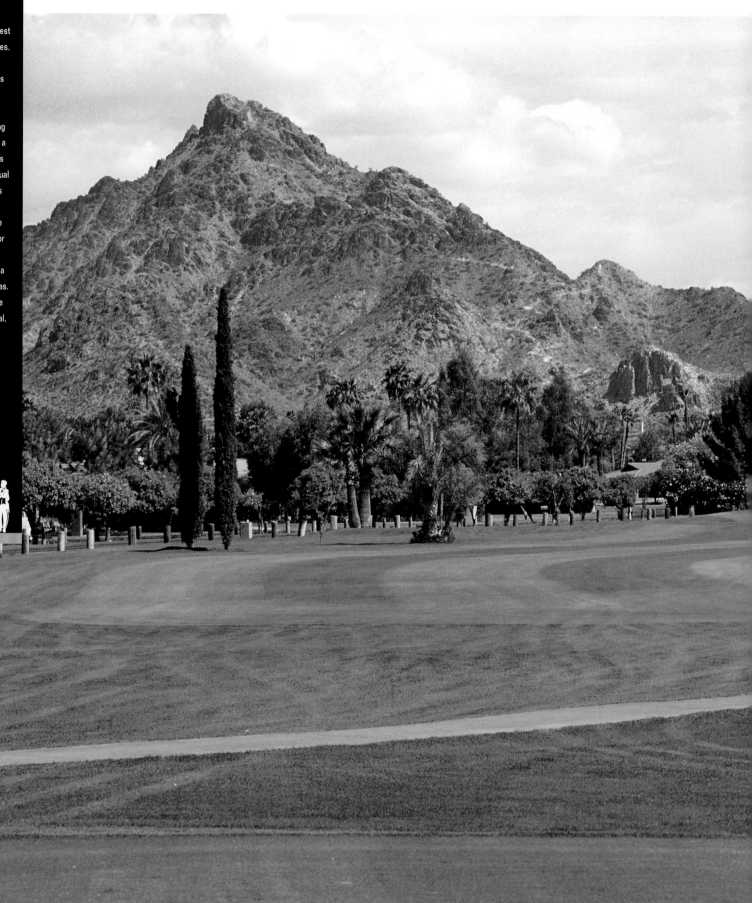

A Classic

The fifty-year-old Adobe Course offers an elegantly simple design that appeals to many Arizona Biltmore guests.

MOUNTAIN PRESERVE

The Pointe Hilton Tapatio Cliffs

Resort is built into the terrain, near a

mountain preserve area.

EXPERIENCING

POINTE HILTON TAPATIO CLIFFS RESORT

A neighboring mountain preserve provides a spectacular backdrop for this world-class, all-suites resort.

• Unwind at The Falls, a dramatic oasis of shimmering pools and cascading waterfalls surrounded by luxurious private cabanas and a poolside café.

• Leave your cares behind and enter a world of pampering at Tocaloma Spa and Salon, offering a complete array of amenities and services.

• Enjoy a workout at the mountainside fitness center, or choose from a wide range of activities including golf, tennis, horseback riding, and hiking.

• Discover an array of dining choices, from mesquite-grilled barbecue to modern bistro and classic cuisine.

THE FALLS

Just steps from each suite, magnificent waterfalls cascade down the cliffs to a myriad of areas that vie for attention. There are meandering walkways, secluded oases, shimmering pools with private cabanas, and a variety of spots for romantic dining.

TAPATIO CLIFFS

Dramatic scenery forms a perfect setting for golf at the Pointe Hilton Golf Club on Lookout Mountain. Players of every level are intrigued by the towering cliffs and challenging golf.

Attention to luxury is also a cherished hallmark of life at Pointe Hilton Tapatio Cliffs Resort. Snug against a mountain preserve, the resort offers some of the most theatrical golf in Phoenix. Speckled with craggy ravines and washes, the course on Lookout Mountain follows the undulations of the land, especially on the tenth hole. Teeing off 175 feet above the fairway, one can only hope that the prevailing breeze is kindly and that the traps won't gobble the ball. Not demanding enough? One can stay for a month and play a different course in the area each day.

It is the elevation that separates this resort from the others in the greater Phoenix area. At eighteen hundred feet above the city, the air is fresher and crisper, and the topography is respectfully incorporated into the architecture. Rocky outcroppings that long ago tumbled down the hillside are now the anchor for white walls and turquoise pools, cascading one into another. Tennis is close at hand, but the hiking and horseback riding are the most seductive distractions for taking off those spikes. One can wander over eight thousand acres of unspoiled Sonoran beauty.

Nights are bedazzling with the twinkling lights of the city below. A Different Pointe of View, Tapatio Cliff's restaurant of note, offers an award-winning cellar and fresh regional foods, some gathered from the chef's own garden. Perhaps fresh is the word for this resort. And it's that freshness that brings the discerning back.

Loews Ventana Canyon Resort is no stranger to devoted returning guests. Overlooking Tucson on a high plateau, the ninety-three acres that make up the property appear to reach into the very secrets of the Sonoran Desert. A waterfall cascades eighty feet down from the Catalina Mountains to feed a shimmering lake. Discreet paths and terraces are laced through virgin mesquite, squawbush, and blue paloverde. Nearby, elusive wildlife moves undisturbed. It is a superb and sensitive symphony, where it is said, "Nature is the entertainer."

The resort's design is bold and modern, merging gracefully with the landscape. Step into the lobby and behold muted colors of mauve, sage green, and bleached-pine whites. The furnishings are plushly residential, the accents of native copper. Stunning displays of desert amethyst and commissioned works by Arizona artists are set off by the light of verdigris chandeliers that dim automatically in deference to the approaching sunset. A two-story glass wall overlooks the pool and mountains, bringing the outdoors in.

Beyond the lobby lie 398 serene rooms and suites with comfortable washed-oak furniture and subtle sunset tones, original works of art, and private balconies. Bathrooms feature tubs for two. Many rooms have fireplaces and Jacuzzis.

"Score early. The first six holes are straightforward, with a couple of par fives that offer the best chance to make good scores."

—MITCH ROSS, HEAD GOLF PROFESSIONAL, POINTE GOLF CLUB ON LOOKOUT MOUNTAIN

POINTE HILTON

TAPATIO CLIFFS RESORT

PHOENIX, ARIZONA

RESORT RATING:	
CHALLENGE	★★★★
BEAUTY	★★★★
LODGING	★★★★
CUISINE	★★★★
AMENITIES	★★★★

DIFFERENT POINTE OF VIEW
This restaurant lives up to its name, with spectacular views of the valley, innovative regional American cuisine, extraordinary service, and an internationally acclaimed wine cellar.

SUITE RETREATS

Two-room suites are the standard here, with spacious living rooms for privacy or entertaining.

STARTLING CONTRAST

The Lookout Mountain Golf Club features lush, intensely green fairways placed in rugged Sonoran Desert terrain.

POINTE HILTON TAPATIO CLIFFS RESORT
POINTE GOLF CLUB ON LOOKOUT MOUNTAIN
PHOENIX, ARIZONA

Architect: Bill Johnston

Tour stops: 1989 Arizona Senior Classic, 1993–1996 Skills Challenge

Par: 72

Bermuda/rye fairways and greens

Yardage/Rating/Slope:

Farthest Pointe tees
6.617/71.2/135

Middle Pointe tees
6,002/68.4/128

Forward Pointe tees
4,557/65.3/113

PLUSH

Well-manicured greens, challenging play, and incredible weather make the Pointe Golf Club a prized golf destination.

LOEWS VENTANA CANYON RESORT

Championship golf, award-winning architecture, and Tucson's Catalina Mountains provide the perfect backdrop for a memorable vacation.

• Enjoy an afternoon of mountain biking, hiking, or rock climbing, then relax with a dip in the pool or a drink by the Jacuzzi.

• Learn about the flora and fauna of the desert on a naturalist-guided hike through the canyons, where an eighty-foot waterfall cascades into a shimmering lake.

• Shop for the perfect Native American gift in Tucson's historical district, followed by afternoon tea at the hotel.

• Enjoy southwestern-style cuisine at the resort's top-floor Ventana restaurant, where every table faces a wall of glass and looks out over panoramic views of the city below.

CONTRASTS

Water is used to strong effect at Loews Ventana Canyon, contrasting with the cactus-lined hills that surround the resort.

The Ventana Room is the resort's flagship restaurant under the leadership of chef Jeffrey Russell, whose new American cuisine has earned Zagat's number one rating for all of Tucson. Guests often debate which is more beautiful and inspiring: the glittering skyline views or Russell's artfully composed plates, such as Dover sole with coconut basmati rice and truffle beurre blanc. While a harpist strums quietly in a corner, over four hundred varieties of wine slumber in the cellar, waiting for an entrée.

Simpler mesquite-grilled items can be had at Bill's Grill. The Canyon Cafe serves breakfast, Sunday brunch, lunch, and dinner, while the Flying V Bar & Grill combines southwestern and Latin American flair. Afternoon tea is a must at the Cascade Lounge.

As compelling as all of this is, in a land of perpetual sunshine one naturally is drawn outside to play tennis or indoors to visit the spa. Two Tom Fazio–designed PGA championship golf courses begin just steps from the resort's lobby and ramble dramatically into the desert through gullies and over ridges alive with ocotillo, hackberry, and blue paloverde. Further activities (in what was once the Cochise stronghold) include mountain biking, croquet, jogging on fitness trails, hiking, horseback riding into the 1.8-million-acre Coronado National Forest, or simply stargazing. Nearby Tucson also beckons with its culture, sports, dining, and shopping.

Smiles and laughter are evident in every corner of Loews Ventana Canyon Resort, and part of this comes from the lighthearted staff. But it also emanates from the many children who vacation here as a result of Loews' year-round "Generation G" packages, which promote bonding among the junior and senior generations, a refreshing idea that makes "grandtravel" fun and educational.

Loews Ventana Canyon Resort was created with the idea of partnering luxury with the striking environment. The goal was to design an escape of solitude and adventure that appears as if it were dropped into the desert from above. Its designers have succeeded admirably.

It is this same sense of escape and excitement that distinguishes the Sheraton El Conquistador. Some consider it the premier sports resort in southern Arizona. Midway between Tucson and the Santa Catalina Mountains, it attracts active adults beguiled by civilized activities such as golf, tennis (it boasts the largest resort facility in the West), and equestrian pursuits among animal spectators that are more than a little wild.

Javelina, bobcats, and mountain lions often can be seen, albeit from a distance, on the early morning links, drinking from the water hazards. Blue heron seem to favor the moated green on the Pusch Ridge's (nine holes, par-thirty-five) fifth hole, a true beauty.

TUCSON, ARIZONA

LOEWS VENTANA CANYON

RESORT

RESORT RATING:	
CHALLENGE	★★★★
BEAUTY	★★★★½
LODGING	★★★★½
CUISINE	★★★★
AMENITIES	★★★★

"The Canyon Course is a traditional desert-style course with relatively wide fairways. What makes it challenging is the greens. They're very fast . . .

and there's a lot of undulation. To avoid a three-putt on every hole, you've got to be in the right position when you approach from the fairway."

—WARREN WEBSTER, HEAD GOLF PROFESSIONAL, THE LODGE AT VENTANA CANYON

LOEWS VENTANA CANYON RESORT
TUCSON, ARIZONA

CANYON COURSE
Architect: Tom Fazio
Par: 72
Rye/Bermuda fairways,
bentgrass greens
Yardage/Rating/Slope:
Black tees
6,819/73.0/147
Gold tees
6,235/70.5/139
Silver tees
5,778/67.5, 72.4*/134, 128*
Copper tees
4,919/66.9/112
*Women's ratings

SUITABLE NAMESAKES

The Mountain Course and
the Canyon Course at
Ventana Canyon are
appropriately named for the
terrain and views
unique to each.

SO MUCH TO DO

As if golf, tennis, and mountain exploring weren't enough, the resort also includes two complete fitness centers with spas and saunas, regulation basketball and volleyball courts, and four outdoor swimming pools, one of which is an NCAA six-lane lap pool.

SHERATON EL CONQUISTADOR RESORT AND COUNTRY CLUB

PUSCH RIDGE 9-HOLE RESORT COURSE
Architects: Greg Nash, Jeff Harden
Par: 35
Bermuda/rye fairways and greens
Yardage/Rating/Slope:
Blue tees
2,788/65.6/110
White tees
2,579/63.7/106
Red tees
2,322/63.8/106

CONQUISTADOR COURSE
Architects: Greg Nash, Jeff Harden, renovated by Greg Nash
Par: 71
Tiffway Bermuda 419 fairways, TifEagle greens
Yardage/Rating/Slope:
Coronado tees
6,801/72.7/126
Deanza tees
6,331/70.5/124
Cortez tees
5,656/67.0, 73.7*/119, 131*
Balboa tees
4,821/69.0*/121*

CAÑADA COURSE
Architects: Greg Nash, Jeff Harden, renovated by Greg Nash
Par: 72
Bermuda 328/rye fairways, Tifdwarf Bermuda/rye greens
Yardage:
Back tees
6,800
Forward tees
5,300
*Women's ratings

LAID-BACK LIFESTYLE

The Sheraton El Conquistador delights visitors with sensational views and the brilliant colors of an Arizona Sunset.

However, the owls can be distracting and may become endangered when they perch on the two towering cacti that loom in front of the tee on the Sunrise Course's (6,819 yards) eighth hole, perhaps the toughest par-three in all of Tucson. The third course, Conquistador, has devilish, short par-fives and long par-fours.

The U.S. Tennis Association often holds championships or meetings here, and energetic locals keep things thriving. Hiking is highly encouraged, particularly with the hidden pools of the Catalinas nearby. Many on staff can offer advice as naturalists, a genuine response to the flora and fauna surrounding the resort. Even the Sundance Cafe has adapted the indigenous ways,

TUCSON, ARIZONA

SHERATON EL CONQUISTADOR

RESORT AND COUNTRY CLUB

RESORT RATING:

CHALLENGE	★★★✫
BEAUTY	★★★★
LODGING	★★★✫
CUISINE	★★★✫
AMENITIES	★★★★

baking fish on cedar planks or making sandwiches from Indian fry bread.

Riding offers an enticing array of adventures. In the early morning, one can saddle up, English or western, and dreamily saunter along the trail, the smell of cowboy coffee and griddle cakes beckoning up ahead. And then there is the enchantment of a moonlit ride, the landscape fragrant and mysterious in the night. This is when the desert replenishes itself, and one gratefully indulges in the process.

Wherever one settles into the desert, the first day is simply an overture to the fulfillment to come. Against the breathtaking backdrop of the Santa Catalina Mountains, centuries-old cacti lift their arms to the sky. Cottontail rabbits and coveys of quail scurry in the underbrush. Coyotes call to each other, their

EXPERIENCING

SHERATON EL CONQUISTADOR RESORT AND COUNTRY CLUB

Sensational views and abundant year-round activities offer plenty of fun at this high-desert resort.

• Explore the southwestern desert along miles of hiking, jogging, and biking trails.

• Relax by the pool, or enjoy a game of basketball, racquetball, or volleyball.

• Saddle up at the resort's riding stable, or work out at one of the two fitness centers, complete with spas, saunas, and massage therapy.

• Mosey on over to the steak house for saloon-style entertainment or enjoy fine wine and world-renowned cuisine at the country club restaurant.

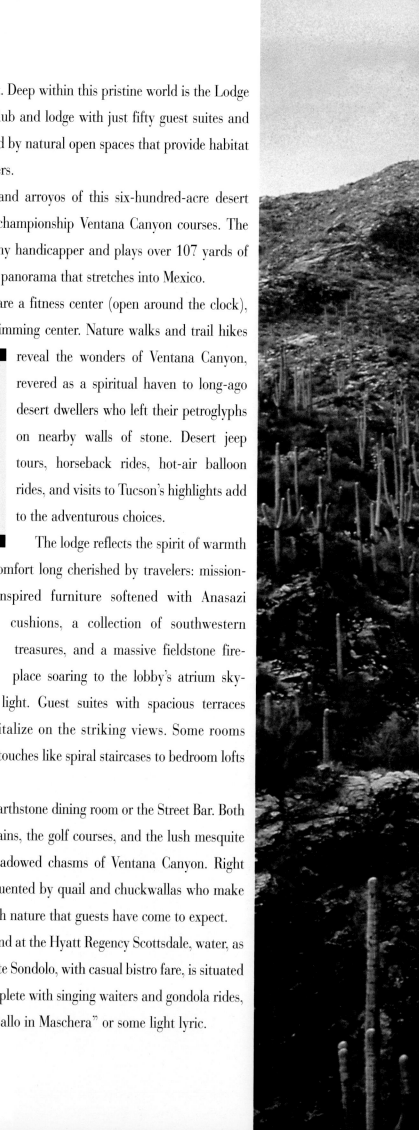

voices echoing across the high Sonoran Desert. Deep within this pristine world is the Lodge at Ventana Canyon, a very private country club and lodge with just fifty guest suites and thirty-six holes of spectacular golf, surrounded by natural open spaces that provide habitat for deer, redtail hawks, and other desert critters.

Winging through the mystical canyons and arroyos of this six-hundred-acre desert preserve are Tom Fazio's two eighteen-hole championship Ventana Canyon courses. The Mountain Course's hole 3 is a challenge to any handicapper and plays over 107 yards of cactus and canyons from a tee that looks to a panorama that stretches into Mexico.

Among the other pleasures of the lodge are a fitness center (open around the clock), twelve lighted tennis courts, and a sports swimming center. Nature walks and trail hikes reveal the wonders of Ventana Canyon, revered as a spiritual haven to long-ago desert dwellers who left their petroglyphs on nearby walls of stone. Desert jeep tours, horseback rides, hot-air balloon rides, and visits to Tucson's highlights add to the adventurous choices.

RESORT RATING:	
CHALLENGE	★★★★½
BEAUTY	★★★★½
LODGING	★★★★½
CUISINE	★★★★
AMENITIES	★★★★

THE LODGE AT
VENTANA CANYON

TUCSON, ARIZONA

The lodge reflects the spirit of warmth and comfort long cherished by travelers: mission-inspired furniture softened with Anasazi cushions, a collection of southwestern treasures, and a massive fieldstone fireplace soaring to the lobby's atrium skylight. Guest suites with spacious terraces capitalize on the striking views. Some rooms have special touches like spiral staircases to bedroom lofts and old-fashioned iron-footed bathtubs.

The cuisine is not the only draw at the Hearthstone dining room or the Street Bar. Both command vistas of the Santa Catalina Mountains, the golf courses, and the lush mesquite trees, paloverdes, and saguaros lining the shadowed chasms of Ventana Canyon. Right outside, the Sabino terrace dining area is frequented by quail and chuckwallas who make themselves at home, just the kind of union with nature that guests have come to expect.

All creatures gravitate to precious water. And at the Hyatt Regency Scottsdale, water, as in Venice, is the prominent attraction. Ristorante Sondolo, with casual bistro fare, is situated on a two-and-a-half-acre water playground, replete with singing waiters and gondola rides, where the gondoliers are prone to croon "Un Ballo in Maschera" or some light lyric.

DESERT PARADISE

An intimate setting with just fifty guest suites, mission-style furnishings, and some of the most spectacular desert views west of the Mississippi make the Lodge at Ventana Canyon a sought-after destination.

SOFT AND SUBTLE

A soft-color palette rich in texture, along with

bleached oak, brass, and marble accents,

enhances the comfort of every room.

GOLFING

HYATT REGENCY SCOTTSDALE AT GAINEY RANCH

GAINEY RANCH GOLF CLUB

Architects: Brad Benz,
Michael Poellot

ARROYO/LAKES COURSE

Par: 72

Common Bermuda/rye fairways,
Bermuda 328 greens

Yardage/Rating/Slope:

Gold tees
6,800/71.9/128

Green tees
6,252/69.2/123

White tees
5,790/75.3*/130*

Magenta tees
5,312/69.9*/120*

LAKES/DUNES COURSE

Par: 72

Common Bermuda/rye fairways,
Bermuda 328 greens

Yardage/Rating/Slope:

Gold tees
6,614/71.1/126

Green tees
6,019/67.7/118

White tees
5,529/74.3*/128*

Magenta tees
4,993/68.3*/117*

DUNES/ARROYO COURSE

Par: 72

Common Bermuda/rye fairways,
Bermuda 328 greens

Yardage/Rating/Slope:

Gold tees
6.662/70.7/124

Regular tees
6,133/68.2/120

White tees
5,681/74.7*/132*

Magenta tees
5,151/69.5*/121*

*Women's ratings

PASTORAL SETTING

Open vistas and undulating

fairways make the course

at Gainey Ranch a

feast for the eyes.

This fantasyland is also very American. One can swirl down a three-story water slide, sit under the "thunderfall" waterfall, or just watch the forty-six other waterfalls. Ten swimming pools, four cold plunges, and one white sand beach help to keep loved ones, who are not enthusiasts of the links, blissfully occupied.

And while others are busy floating, a tee time might be in order for the Arroyo Course, the longest of the three on site. It is mildly challenging, ideal for a gentler game where the focus is relaxation rather than breaking par. Of course, for a bit of solidarity with those in the pool, one can dabble on the Lakes Course, which has integrated a variety of streams and ponds and, yes, more waterfalls.

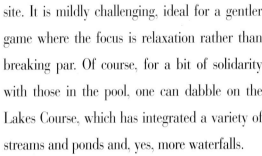

SCOTTSDALE, ARIZONA	RESORT RATING:	
	CHALLENGE	★★★★
HYATT REGENCY SCOTTSDALE	BEAUTY	★★★★
	LODGING	★★★★
	CUISINE	★★★½
	AMENITIES	★★★★
AT GAINEY RANCH		

The Hyatt Regency Scottsdale might try to be all things to all people—pre-Columbian artifacts and Thai puppet masks are decorating elements, and there is a flamenco guitarist in residence. But southwestern gems like Squash Blossom Restaurant, Camp Hyatt Cachina, and the Native American Learning Center are what grounds the resort. Certainly, desert culture dominates the architecture. At the Gainey Ranch entrance, guests are drawn inside and then greeted by an 820-square-foot sliding glass wall, framing the crisp creases of the McDowell Mountains. The ultimate in southwestern décor.

Speaking of entrancing décor, the old floors, dating from 1928, gently creak beneath guests' feet as they enter the Wigwam Resort, welcoming both regulars and first-time visitors. This is authentic Arizona.

EXPERIENCING

HYATT REGENCY SCOTTSDALE AT GAINEY RANCH

Experience the natural wonders of the Sonoran Desert at a spectacular oasis where waterfalls cascade into magnificent pools.

• Explore the adventures of the Southwest with horseback riding, off-road adventures, hot-air ballooning, and world-class golf and tennis.

• Play to your heart's content in a two-and-a-half-acre water playground of ten swimming pools, including pools for two, a volleyball pool, and a quiet pool just for adults.

• Discover a state of renewed balance at Sonwai Spa, featuring everything from soothing massages and body treatments to workout rooms and spa cuisine.

"The three courses at the Wigwam are classic designs. Although the greens are large, elevated, and well-bunkered, they play rather small and getting up and down is difficult. . . .

One is instantly taken by the casual elegance of the resort, a long-time favorite of those looking for a sun-filled escape. A stone fireplace and antique leather furniture grace the lobby, and rows of flowers and fruit trees lead to the casitas.

Pueblo-style cottages that form a small village are filled with luxuries like Berber carpeting, whitewashed wood floors, Mexican ceramic tiling, and all the amenities first-class travelers know to look for: thick terry robes, data port telephones, and treats like chocolate-dipped strawberries at turndown.

Golf on at least one of the three championship courses is a must. Robert Trent Jones, Sr. created the Gold Course (eight ponds and one hundred traps), and he redid the Blue Course in 1938. The modern Red Course, with its gigantic greens, was designed by Robert "Red" Lawrence. Guests may choose to rise above the desert in a hot air balloon, head into the afternoon atop a horse, or unwind at the spa, but most pursue the quality golf that *Golf* magazine acknowledged with its Silver Medal.

RESORT RATING:

CHALLENGE	★★★⯨
BEAUTY	★★★★
LODGING	★★★★
CUISINE	★★★★
AMENITIES	★★★★⯨

LITCHFIELD PARK, ARIZONA

THE WIGWAM RESORT

The Wigwam offers activities for the very sportive, as well as for those seeking only to relax. The faint aroma of mesquite wafts by the pool, signaling dinnertime. One can linger over cocktails next to the outdoor fire pit at the Kachina Bar, or simply enjoy the plush accommodations and order room service. Traditional southwestern cuisine prevails, complementing the "authentic Arizona" experience the resort favors.

In the company of distant silhouettes of purple mountains and breezes that tickle the leaves on massive trees, the Wigwam is a fortuitous reflection of a very different time, ideal for those wanting rugged beauty and historical intrigue.

There are few resorts in Arizona that evoke such a feeling of times past more than does Marriott's historic Camelback Inn in Scottsdale. Indeed, its motto is "Where Time Stands Still." The general air is of the old Southwest, especially with kiva-beamed ceilings and flagstones, although the twenty-first century is clearly in evidence with in-room microwaves. Even the resort's courses, although recently renovated, have a parkland feel, reminiscent of the early days of development, when cold-climate landscapes were first imported to the desert.

If you're going to miss the green, you have to decide which side you want to miss it to."

—KEITH KALNY, DIRECTOR OF GOLF, WIGWAM GOLF CLUB

QUITE A RANGE

The Wigwam Resort offers a range of activities for visitors, those active or looking to relax. Whether lounging poolside or driving off the tees, resort guests can find what they're looking for.

This is a grand home for old ghosts, the many Golden Age celebrities who used to winter here. One can almost hear Kate Hepburn and Cary Grant having a laugh on the practice range, or catch oneself wondering if the bunker burying your ball also held Barry Goldwater in a quandary. Camelback was one of the senator's favorite spots, as it was for Hopalong Cassidy. In his honor, Hopalong College still offers playful programs to young guests.

THE WIGWAM RESORT

Amid lush gardens, cozy casitas, and breathtaking southwestern scenery, the Wigwam Resort offers a myriad of activities and adventures.

• Enjoy the luxury of your own adobe casita with its private patio, walk-in closets, and maid service three times a day.

• Soak up the Arizona sunshine as you relax beside the pool, play water volleyball, or have lunch at the poolside cabana.

• Sample award-winning cuisine made from unique local ingredients and recipes from ancient southwestern cultures.

• Ride off into the sunset on horseback, or fly high above in a hot-air balloon.

• Plan a trip through the rugged desert to fascinating Indian ruins, historical attractions, and the Grand Canyon.

COZY CASITAS

Walkways lead to the Wigwam Resort's charming collection of guest casitas, which has its own design and décor.

THE WIGWAM RESORT
WIGWAM GOLF CLUB
LITCHFIELD PARK, ARIZONA

Tour stops: Arizona Tour

GOLD COURSE
Architect: Robert Trent Jones, Sr.
Par: 72
Bermuda/rye fairways and greens
Yardage/Rating/Slope:
<u>Gold tees</u>
7,074/74.1/133
<u>White tees</u>
6,504/71.2/128
<u>Red tees</u>
5,663/72.8/126

BLUE COURSE
Architect: Robert Trent Jones, Sr.
Par: 70
Bermuda/rye fairways and greens
Yardage/Rating/Slope:
<u>Blue tees</u>
6,85/69.1/122
<u>White tees</u>
5,724/67.8/119
<u>Red tees</u>
5,178/69.3/115

RED COURSE
Architect: Robert "Red" Lawrence
Par: 72
Bermuda/rye fairways and greens
Yardage/Rating/Slope:
<u>Blue tees</u>
6,865/72.4/126
<u>White tees</u>
6,306/69.4/118
<u>Red tees</u>
5,808/72.4/118

FORE AND AFTER

After golfing on Wigwam's

open, airy fairways and

large greens, guests can

head back to the clubhouse

for a sauna, steam,

spa, and massage.

MARRIOTT'S CAMELBACK INN
CAMELBACK GOLF CLUB

RESORT COURSE

Architect: Arthur Hills

Par: 72

Bermuda/rye fairways and greens

Yardage/Rating/Slope:

Back tees

6,903/72.8/132

Burgundy tees

6,456/70.7/121

Copper tees

6,014/67.3/116

Silver tees

5,069/68.6/114

CLUB COURSE

Architect: Jack Snyder

Par: 72

Bermuda/rye fairways and greens

Yardage/Rating/Slope:

Burgundy tees

7,014/72.6/122

Beige tees

6,486/69.6/119

Teal tees

5,808/71.5/118

KILLER VIEWS

The recently unveiled Resort Course, which features stunning panoramic view corridors.

QUICK TO PLEASE

Marriott's Camelback Inn's Jackrabbit Pool complex spoils guests with tiered sundecks, whirlpools, and a child's sand and water playground.

Sadly, the most smitten golfer cannot play golf all day long. Diversions include swimming to underwater music or sand volleyball, and five tennis courts are lit for night games. At the spa, the Desert Nectar Herbal Wrap is worth the fatigue that required it.

Camelback Mountain looms large from most places, especially from Chaparral, the best restaurant and vantage point on the property. One can relish Black Angus beef or divine seafood, all the while savoring the blue sky as it deepens from orange to magenta. Shadows disappear from the saguaro cacti that stand stiffly at attention, a contrast to the warm and inviting

> *"Keeping the ball in play off the tee and executing precise iron shots to relatively small greens are key to scoring well."*
>
> —MIKE RYAN, DIRECTOR OF GOLF, CAMELBACK GOLF CLUB

MARRIOTT'S CAMELBACK INN

SCOTTSDALE, ARIZONA

RESORT RATING:	
CHALLENGE	★★★⯪
BEAUTY	★★★⯪
LODGING	★★★★
CUISINE	★★★⯪
AMENITIES	★★★★

staff who deftly place liqueurs at the table. And then, sinking into the chair, it is easy to imagine that the dapper fellow across the room looks a lot like Tyrone Power.

Tyrone Power would have felt equally at home at the Westin La Paloma in Tucson. An incomparable playground for the rich and famous, it offers guests all they really need to feel terribly spoiled and pampered. Snuggled high in the foothills of the Santa Catalina Mountains, the grand lobby's thirty-foot-high arched windows look out onto rugged mountains and the kaleidoscopic Sonoran Desert. Guests can stand on one of the expansive terraces and sip a beverage from the lobby's Desert Garden Lounge while watching the sun sink behind behemoth succulents and blooming posies.

EXPERIENCING

MARRIOTT'S CAMELBACK INN

Thirty-six holes of championship golf, eight tennis courts, and a European health spa are just a few of the facilities at Marriott's Camelback Inn.

• From the patio or balcony of your own pueblo-style casita or suite, enjoy breathtaking views of the desert and a complete array of luxuries.

• Experience a variety of fitness facilities, treatments, and salon services at the hacienda-inspired spa.

• Sample the fare at a diverse selection of restaurants and lounges, from heart-healthy spa cuisine or lunch by the pool to a gourmet coffeehouse and bakery.

"La Paloma Country Club is a typical Nicklaus signature course. Nicklaus was forgiving off the tee but placed a premium on shot-making into the greens. . . .

RESORT RATING:

CHALLENGE	★★★★
BEAUTY	★★★★✰
LODGING	★★★★✰
CUISINE	★★★★
AMENITIES	★★★★

TUCSON, ARIZONA

THE WESTIN LA PALOMA

Thus, the greens are well guarded with deep bunkers, mounds, and drop-offs, all strategically placed to penalize errant shots."

— ALBERT L. LAROSE, HEAD GOLF PROFESSIONAL, LA PALOMA COUNTRY CLUB

La Paloma is home to a spectacular twenty-seven-hole Jack Nicklaus signature golf course. It is not uncommon to overhear golfers, who have just finished a round, talking about the challenge and exuding about the originality of the course. One can even play golf in the morning and later ski 9,100-foot Mount Lemmon in the afternoon.

Some finish the day with a swim in one of the resort's three pools (kids delight in the Slidewinder, a 177-foot water slide). Others catch a quick game of tennis or racquetball. Beyond the resort, Tucson offers visitors all the history of the American West, like the picturesque Mission San Xavier del Bac. Guests can hike or saunter on horseback through the desert wilderness. The more adventurous cross the border for a day trip down to Nogales, Mexico.

Since having fun is such hard work, a visit to the Personal Services Center is an apt reward. A surefire response to ennui is the self-heating Oxygenating French Seaweed mask or the unique Paraffin Body Wrap, which combines an herbal sloughing cream, an essential oil massage, and a thermal wrap in warm paraffin.

La Paloma gleams with absolutely everything under the sun to amuse and delight. Naturally, it is an elysian setting, promising fulfilling days and nights.

For golfing travelers, it's no gamble to head northwest to the state of Nevada for winning fun and games. The recent trend of upmarket hotels on and off the Las Vegas Strip paved the way for the Regent Las Vegas.

THE BEST OF EVERYTHING

Nestled in the foothills of the Santa Catalina

Mountains, The Westin La Paloma offers guests the

height of resort luxury and golf challenge.

EXPERIENCING

THE WESTIN LA PALOMA

Nestled in the foothills and surrounded by desert gardens, a waterfall, and natural rock formations, this extraordinary environment is a natural catalyst to wonderful vacations.

• Visit the Tennis and Health Center for tennis, indoor racquetball, ongoing aerobics classes, the latest cardiovascular equipment, and personalized spa services.
• Shoot down the Southwest's longest resort water slide, swim up to the bar, or relax in a therapeutic spa.
• Venture beyond the resort to a nearby mission or desert museum, the famous movie sets of Old Tucson, the Saguaro National Monument, or Kitt Peak National Observatory.

VILLAGE SETTING

Village-style guest buildings surround the pool, swim-up bar, water slide, and spas. The resort offers a full range of activities plus access to health and tennis facilities at La Paloma Country Club.

THE WESTIN LA PALOMA
LA PALOMA COUNTRY CLUB
TUCSON, ARIZONA

Architect: Jack Nicklaus

HILL/RIDGE COURSE

Par: 72

Bermuda/rye fairways, bentgrass greens

Yardage/Rating/Slope:

Black tees
7,017/74.6/155

Gold tees
6,464/72.0/150

Silver tees
5,984/69.9/140

Copper tees
5,714/68.7, 73.2*/138, 137*

Jade tees
4,878/68.5/123

RIDGE/CANYON COURSE

Par: 72

Bermuda/rye fairways, bentgrass greens

Yardage/Rating/Slope:

Black tees
7,088/75.4/155

Gold tees
6,635/72.3/149

Silver tees
6,011/69.9/138

Copper tees
5,731/68.8, 73.9*/136, 134*

Jade tees
5,075/70.1/123

CANYON/HILL COURSE

Par: 72

Bermuda/rye fairways, bentgrass greens

Yardage/Rating/Slope:

Black tees
6,997/75.4/155

Gold tees
6,453/72.2/152

Silver tees
5,955/69.0/140

Copper tees
5,505/67.7, 73.0*/135, 134*

Jade tees
5,057/70.6/126

*Women's ratings

SAGUARO PRESERVE

The Jack Nicklaus–designed golf course preserves the Saguaro cactus population, some of which are over 150 years old.

A PLACE TO MEET

Elegant public spaces provide guests with comfortable surroundings outside of their private rooms.

THE REGENT
LAS VEGAS

Combining the excitement of
Las Vegas with global luxury
standards, the Regent creates
a genuine, personalized
hospitality experience.

• For an exhilarating, refreshing
afternoon, visit the Aquae Sulis
spa, founded on the purifying
power of water and the ancient
traditions of ritual bathing and
body treatments.

• Sample a wide variety of dining
options, from classic seafood
and continental dishes
overlooking the garden and
waterfalls, to the ambience and
charm of Ireland's finest pubs.

• Try your luck at the resort's
own casino or visit the high-limit,
high-action Salon Privé,
featuring all the amenities a
high-end player desires.

PEACEFUL OASIS

Located just eleven miles
from the famed Strip at Las
Vegas, the Regent offers
unforgettable golf, casino,
dining, and spa facilities in
a tranquil setting accessible
to, but removed
from, the city.

Here is a jewel in the Mojave Desert, a resort that seduces with canopies of palms, waterfalls, and secluded pools. While it is in the sights of the neon explosion of the Strip, the Regent offers quiet elegance and style that is worlds apart.

The quiet Red Rock Canyon area of Summerlin, twenty-five minutes from the airport, is home to the Regent. Bordered by three championship golf courses including the Tournament Players Club (home of the Las Vegas Senior Classic), there is plenty for golfers to do. Courtesy vans shuttle players to and from a total of ten local courses, where guests have preferred access to prime tee times. The resort controls fifty percent of the tee times at the Tournament Players Club alone. A tavern and putting green sit adjacent to the resort.

Two six-story towers are home to 541 guest rooms and suites. Every room has a view of either the Red Rock Canyon National Conservation Area, the gardens, the lights of Las Vegas, or the golf courses.

The Aquae Sulis ("water of the sun") spa is another attraction and is centered around the healing powers of H_2O. The spa's signature treatment—the Aquae Sulis ritual—is modeled on ancient Roman ritual bathing traditions. Utilizing aromatics like lavender plus Dead Sea salt, virgin olive oil, and flowers, this indulgence is designed to take the body through a series of water stimuli, including cold and hot plunges, a soak in the warm whirlpool and outdoor hydrotherapy pool, steam, sauna, and waterfall showers.

THE REGENT LAS VEGAS

LAS VEGAS, NEVADA

RESORT RATING:	
CHALLENGE	★★★★
BEAUTY	★★★⯪
LODGING	★★★★★
CUISINE	★★★★⯪
AMENITIES	★★★★⯪

Regent has a proud reputation for fine dining, and at this property they have reason to crow. Restaurant Parian serves new American cuisine, Ceres prepares the freshest seafood, and Nevada Nick's is a bastion for carnivores. Lest peckish guests get bored, other restaurant options include Hamada of Japan, Chez Napoleon, Cafe de Paris, Spiedini Ristorante, and Gustav Mahler's Cigar Bar. And consider this: an authentic Irish Pub, J. C. Woolougham, was built in Dublin and air shipped to Las Vegas just for the Regent. The Upstairs Market Buffet, an open-market-style eatery, takes guests on a world culinary tour, the best spread in town.

Of course, the Regent has gambling—a casino with fifty thousand square feet worth of it—including 1,200 slot machines. Las Vegas may be the resort's lifeline, but it will never be its soul.

Plenty of soul awaits at the Hyatt Regency Lake Las Vegas. Seventeen miles and half a world away from the glitzy, overcrowded Vegas action, on the shores of Lake Las Vegas, rises a resort that looks and feels like a Moroccan palace.

Sunlight spills through the Hyatt Regency Lake Las Vegas's two-story windows framed by vaulted arches. Deep loggias decorated in rich hues of reds, golds, and siennas, are accented by ornamental ironwork, conjuring up an exotic charm all its own.

THE HIGH LIFE

The Regent Las Vegas offers an escape from the sound and fury of the Strip, but still offers some Vegas delights. The Regent boasts a full casino, including 1,200 slot machines.

UNCOMMON BUFFET

The Upstairs Market Buffet

features cuisine from Italy, Asia,

Mexico, and America.

FUN, SUN, AND WATER

The resort's elaborate gardens

include a grass-edged pool with

waterfall, as well as four swimming

lanes and two giant spa pools

equipped with handicap lifts.

THE REGENT LAS VEGAS

TOURNAMENT PLAYERS CLUB
AT THE CANYONS
LAS VEGAS, NEVADA

Architects: Bobby Weed,
Raymond Floyd
Tour stops: Las Vegas Senior
Classic
Par: 71
Tifdwarf Bermuda/rye fairways,
bentgrass greens
Yardage/Rating/Slope:
TPC tees
7,063/73.0/131
Blue tees
6,772/70.9/128
White tees
6,110/67.7/118
Red tees
5,039/67.0*/109*
*Women's ratings

DESERT GOLF

The Tournament Players
Club's Championship
Course at the Canyons is
the site of the annual Las
Vegas Senior Classic. A
par-71 course, it features
canyon fairways flanked by
rugged desert terrain.
World-class golf at nine
other area courses
is also available.

"We usually tell players to locate the Stratosphere Tower on the Las Vegas Strip, and generally their putts will tend to break in that direction. Conversely, if they're putting toward the mountains, their putts will be a lot slower going in that direction."

—Dan Hammell, Head Golf Professional, TPC at the Canyons

A MEMORABLE STAY

Like all Regent hotels, the Regent Las Vegas is committed to fulfilling guests' needs through luxurious amenities, exceptional service, and the attentive attitudes of each staff member.

HYATT REGENCY LAKE LAS VEGAS RESORT
REFLECTION BAY GOLF CLUB

Architect: Jack Nicklaus

Tour stops: Wendy's Three-Tour Challenge

Par: 72

Bermuda/rye fairways, Crenshaw bentgrass greens

Yardage/Rating/Slope:

Black tees
7,261/74.8/138

Blue tees
6,862/73.2/135

White tees
6,391/70.3/128

Gold tees
5,891/68.1*/124*

Red tees
5,166/70.0*/127*

*Women's ratings

TRANQUIL HAVENS

Every spacious guest room, suite, and casbah features Moroccan décor and sweeping views of Lake Las Vegas and palm-lined fairways.

A TRUE OASIS

On the private shores of Lake Las Vegas, guests enjoy a variety of water sports or just the warm desert sun and beautiful beach.

ENCIRCLED BY GREEN

The Jack Nicklaus–designed Reflection Bay Golf Club surrounds the Hyatt Regency Lake Las Vegas.

A stroll around the grounds makes guests wonder if they have stepped into another world. And indeed they have. After a perfect day spent on the greens at the Reflection Bay Golf Club or enjoying some water sports and fishing on the lake, an evening in the European-style casino overlooking the lake makes relaxation come easily.

Jack Nicklaus designed the course here and it represents his first effort in Nevada. It follows the lakefront shoreline over five holes, so if you're shanking, there are always bobbing boats and hopeful fishermen to gawk at.

The Hyatt Regency Lake Las Vegas seems to cast a spell over its guests. The resort's Spa Moulay is keen on nontraditional treatments,

such as the Limu Body Masque (think heated seaweed and an essential oil massage) and Tandem Massages. At the restaurant Japengo, guests can sample exotic Pacific Rim–inspired creations complemented by a noble wine list.

All this combines to feel anything but like Las Vegas. It is far beyond the blackjack tables, beyond the crowds, beyond the imagination.

California is the undisputed land of imagination. "Queen of the Desert" is the moniker La Quinta has earned since its debut in 1926. It all started with John S. Morgan, the wealthy owner of the Morgan Oyster Company, who purchased 1,400 acres of "Happy Hollow" land named by the Cahuilla Indians. It was here that Morgan envisioned a small, self-contained resort where guests would be coddled in total privacy.

The excellence of La Quinta was apparent from the beginning as stars arrived in style. Garbo, Hepburn, Joan Crawford, Bette Davis, Errol Flynn, and Ginger Rogers all made the journey, joining business moguls such as the Du Ponts and Vanderbilts.

"The course is generous off the tee then demanding on the approach shots to the greens, which are guarded by bunkers and water, requiring accuracy."
—BRIAN JENSEN, HEAD GOLF PROFESSIONAL, REFLECTION BAY GOLF CLUB

HYATT REGENCY

LAKE LAS VEGAS RESORT

HENDERSON, NEVADA

RESORT RATING:	
CHALLENGE	★★★★
BEAUTY	★★★★½
LODGING	★★★★
CUISINE	★★★★
AMENITIES	★★★★

WATER ABOUNDS
A 320-acre lake is the centerpiece of the Hyatt Regency Lake Las Vegas Resort. The ten miles of shoreline make for spectacular views and thrilling water hazards.

FOCUS

With so many Las Vegas–style distractions, it's a wonder that golfers are able to concentrate on their games.

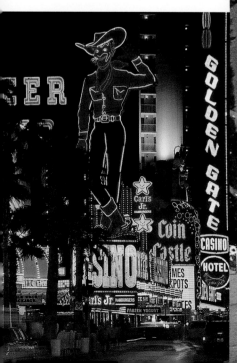

ACCESSIBLE EXCITEMENT

Set in a world all its own, with no crowds or busy streets, the Hyatt Regency at Lake Las Vegas seems far removed from the Las Vegas glitter. But the resort is a mere seventeen miles from the downtown casinos.

HYATT REGENCY LAKE LAS VEGAS RESORT
HENDERSON, NEVADA

Set on a terraced hillside overlooking the shores of Lake Las Vegas, this resort, casino, and spa offers sun-drenched relaxation just minutes from the Las Vegas Strip.

• Choose from water sports galore, including yacht cruises, boat rentals, sailing, kayaking, and fishing.

• Plunge into the water slide, bask in the warm desert sun on a white-sand beach, or take a dip in either of the two sparkling pools with their palm-shaded terraces.

• When you've had enough excitement, recuperate with a visit to the Spa Moulay, featuring luxurious spa treatments and a fully equipped fitness center. When night falls, treat yourself to sparkling entertainment, world-class cuisine, and a European-style casino.

DESERT FUN

Diving into one of the two Hyatt signature pools, relaxing beneath the palm trees, and lunching in the sun are just a few of the ways to enjoy the day.

Today, stars and tycoons still come, joined on the fairways by families and Gen Xers. La Quinta draws an enthusiastic crowd to its oasis set among orange and lemon trees at the base of the Santa Rosa Mountains.

But things have changed since Morgan's days. He brought a legacy of golf to the area, creating a nine-hole course that was open to the public for one dollar. Though the original course no longer exists, La Quinta Resort has become a golf mecca with five eighteen-hole championship courses available to guests, both at the resort and at PGA West. Jack Nicklaus, Pete Dye, and Greg Norman all had a hand in designing the local golf courses.

RESORT RATING:

CHALLENGE	★★★★¼
BEAUTY	★★★★¼
LODGING	★★★★¼
CUISINE	★★★★
AMENITIES	★★★★

LA QUINTA, CALIFORNIA

LA QUINTA RESORT

AND CLUB

EXPERIENCING

LA QUINTA RESORT AND CLUB

Visitors to this breathtaking desert oasis find endless choices, timeless charm, and world-class golf and tennis.

• Enjoy accommodations that promise comfort and privacy for every guest and range from cozy casitas to spacious suites.

• Refresh yourself in one of the twenty-five sparkling secluded pools, or play a game of tennis on your choice of surfaces.

• Enjoy shopping in the resort's collection of intriguing boutiques or dining in a variety of restaurants that appeal to every palate.

• Indulge yourself at Spa La Quinta, where nature's majesty is reflected in signature treatments like open-air showers, stone therapy, and massage.

The resort offers a complete retreat, Spa La Quinta, dedicated to the concept of overall wellness by combining today's knowledge with the treatments of the indigenous Mexican and Native American cultures. One popular approach is the Cahuilla Sage Wrap, an application of desert sage concentrate on targeted areas. Then there's Bindi, based on the five-thousand-year-old Indian healing science, ayurveda, which uses personally selected therapeutic herbs and essential oils to restore balance.

Digging into mole poblano or fiery chicken empanadas at La Quinta's Adobe Grill, where handmade glassware from Guadalajara holds frosty margaritas, one is transported into old Mexico. This is especially true on the patio, which overlooks flower gardens, waterfalls, and the shops of the resort's central plaza. But foodies are most attracted to Azur by Le Bernardin, an offshoot of New York's critically acclaimed gourmet seafood restaurant. Morgans has all-day dining that captures the essence of California cuisine.

SOMETHING FOR EVERYONE

Since 1926, La Quinta has welcomed Hollywood celebrities, noted industrialists, and discerning vacationers in search of elegant amenities and outstanding recreation.

GOLFING

PGA WEST

TPC STADIUM COURSE
Architect: Pete Dye
Par: 72
Bermuda/rye fairways and greens
Yardage/Rating/Slope:
Tournament tees
7,266/75.9/150
Championship tees
6,739/73.0/142
Regular tees
6,166/69.9/132
Gold tees
5,700/74.5*/137*
Red tees
5,092/70.0*/124*

JACK NICKLAUS
TOURNAMENT COURSE
Architect: Jack Nicklaus
Tour stops: 2000 Qualifying
School
Par: 72
Bermuda/rye fairways and greens
Yardage/Rating/Slope:
Tournament tees
7,204/74.7/139
Championship tees
6,522/71.9/131
Regular tees
6,061/69.0/124
Gold tees
5,627/72.9*/127*
Red tees
5,023/69.9*/121*

GREG NORMAN COURSE
Architect: Greg Norman
Par: 72
Bermuda 419/rye fairways.
Tifdwarf Bermuda greens
Yardage/Rating/Slope:
Black tees
7,156/74.0/134
Blue tees
6,671/71.8/128
White tees
6,227/69.7/121
Gold tees
5,737/73.1*/121*
Red tees
5,281/71.0*/122*
*Women's ratings

MOUNTAIN RETREAT

Nestled among the Santa Rosa foothills, La Quinta has long been the hideaway of choice for some of the world's most discriminating travelers.

PATHWAYS TO PARADISE

Beautifully landscaped pathways wind from one venue to the next.

WORTH THE EFFORT

The Mountain Course tests every skill

level with elevated greens, pot-bunker

design, and mountain terrain.

"The Stadium Course has extremely deep pot bunkers, railroad ties, jagged-edged rocks, and an island green called Alcatraz. Take lots of golf balls and your sense of humor."

—GREG RALEIGH, HEAD GOLF PROFESSIONAL, PGA WEST STADIUM CLUBHOUSE

GOLFING

LA QUINTA RESORT AND CLUB
LA QUINTA, CALIFORNIA

MOUNTAIN COURSE

Architect: Pete Dye

Par: 72

Bermuda/rye fairways and greens

Yardage/Rating/Slope:

Tournament tees

6,756/74.1/140

Championship tees

6,320/71.5/130

Middle tees

5,405/67.0, 71.4*/113, 127*

Forward tees

5,005/71.0/123

DUNES COURSE

Architect: Pete Dye

Tour stops: 1998 PGA Tour

Qualifying Final Stage

Par: 72

Bermuda/rye fairways

and greens

Yardage/Rating/Slope:

Tournament tees

6,747/73.1/137

Championship tees

6,230/70.1/124

Middle tees

5,748/67.1, 73.9*/114, 133*

Forward tees

4,997/69.1/125

*Women's ratings

LOTS OF CHOICES

La Quinta Resort and Club

and PGA West resort

share five highly

regarded courses

for resort guests.

*"At the Resort
Course, the ability
to hit a high, soft,
lob shot will pay
dividends on these
elevated greens."*

—RANDY DUNCAN, HEAD GOLF
PROFESSIONAL, WESTIN MISSION HILLS
RESORT, PETE DYE COURSE

RESORT RATING:		RANCHO MIRAGE, CALIFORNIA
CHALLENGE	★★★★	
BEAUTY	★★★★	
LODGING	★★★★	
CUISINE	★★★⯪	
AMENITIES	★★★★	

THE WESTIN MISSION HILLS

RESORT

ENCHANTING

Spectacular settings provide
the backdrop for a variety of
outdoor activities. Whether
guests want to play in the pool
or enjoy a candlelit dinner,
Mission Hills resort can
accommodate their needs.

To say nothing has changed here over the years would not be true. But it is fair to say that the same magic that attracted Hollywood's luminaries of yesteryear has hardly waned. The resort no longer provides chauffeurs and footmen, but the discriminating keep coming from Tinsel Town and from the rest of the world, young and old, to discover the timeless charm that has always been La Quinta.

Time has been very kind to the Westin Mission Hills Resort in Rancho Mirage, and the public has responded accordingly. Known as the "Playground of Presidents," it easily lives up to all expectations of a first-class resort. The beauty of painted canyons and blooming cacti against the backdrop of snowcapped mountains greets guests at most turns.

The casual refinement of the hotel is clearly evident: Spanish-Moorish architecture is highlighted by polished blue domes and detailed wrought-iron balconies. Sumptuous, all-white, signature Heavenly Beds accented by Ultrasuede pillows make for deep sleeps.

Executive chef Joel Delmond rides the ranges at two restaurants, Bella Vista and La Concha, with expertise. La Concha's creative menu features contemporary American, focusing on seafood and Angus beef dishes, while Bella Vista offers a lighter, California cuisine. The hotel also has several bars, one at each of the three pools placed between pavilions.

At a glance, it becomes clear that the hotel's two superior courses are a golfer's paradise. The Gary Player signature course was conceived to blend in with and enhance the desert environment. It is a serious test, with many tee placements and small greens. But it also gives the less expert player an advantage, with wide fairways and flat putting surfaces. The par-seventy Pete Dye course has a more Scottish links look. Players try to hit their shots anywhere but near his trademark railroad ties and deep pot bunkers. Both courses demand skill and concentration, and a visit to the Troon Golf Institute on the grounds can prove most beneficial.

The newly opened Spa at Mission Hills extends this sense of relaxed grace with its innovative collection of treatments, many of which emphasize therapeutic techniques specifically for golfers and the healing therapies of the Native Americans. True to local culture, the outdoors is a key element to well-being, so it is not uncommon to receive a massage under the sun or the stars.

It is to the heavens that great golf owes its very existence. With the abundance of courses in the American Southwest, it is easy to forget that the sport was founded in rain-soaked Scotland. How healthy the courses are here, with only fifteen to twenty days of rainfall each year. Hyatt Grand Champions resort in Indian Wells is no exception. And with all that sunshine, it is more than surreal to tee off facing a glacier. Such is the breadth and grandeur of this locale.

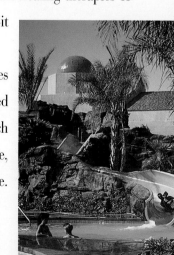

THE WESTIN MISSION HILLS RESORT

Enjoy all the desert has to offer in the midst of luxurious accommodations.

• Visit the full-service luxury spa for a soothing massage, exotic herbal wraps, and refreshing facials.

• Stay fit at the health club, complete with workout room, aerobics, yoga, and personal trainers.

• Sample California cuisine indoors in a lovely atrium setting or on the patio, with its magnificent views of the surrounding mountains.

BELLS AND WHISTLES

The Pete Dye–designed Resort Course at the Westin Mission Hills Resort has it all: target fairways, elevated greens, pot bunkers, and lakes.

THE WESTIN MISSION HILLS RESORT

RANCHO MIRAGE, CALIFORNIA

RESORT COURSE

Architects: Pete Dye, David Pfaff

Tour stops: 1997–1999 Frank Sinatra Celebrity Tournament

Par: 70

Common Bermuda/ perennial rye fairways, Tifdwarf Bermuda greens

Yardage/Rating/Slope:

Championship tees

6,706/73.5/137

Men's tees

6,158/70.3/126

Resort tees

5,587/67.5, 75.0*/117, 121*

Women's tees

4,841/67.4*/107*

NORTH COURSE

Architects: Gary Player Design Company, Jeff Meyers, Joe Duco, Mark Stallone

Tour stops: 1997–1999 Frank Sinatra Celebrity Tournament

Par: 72

Hybrid Bermuda 328/perennial rye fairways, Creeping Penncross bentgrass greens

Yardage/Rating/Slope:

Championship tees

7,062/73.9/134

Men's tees

6,643/71.3/124

Resort tees

6,044/68.0, 75.7*/114, 130*

Women's tees

4,907/68.0*/118*

*Women's ratings

SKILLS TEST

The North Course challenges players of all levels. The twelfth hole is fronted by water and backed up by three sand bunkers.

FINAL DESTINATION
After a day of treatments at
Westin Mission Hills' luxury spa,
guests can return to their rooms
in a state of deep relaxation.

PROMENADE
The Westin Mission Hills was
designed in the Spanish-Moorish
style and evokes the refined
aspects of early California.

A PERFECT FIT

Interior décor at Hyatt Grand Champions

is subtle, with soft desert hues and

Carrara marble throughout.

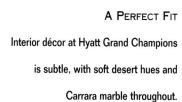

GOLFING

HYATT GRAND CHAMPIONS
GOLF RESORT AT INDIAN WELLS

Architect: Ted Robinson

Tour stops: 1993 Senior Tour, 1994–97 California State Open Championship

WEST COURSE
Par: 72
Bermuda fairways,
TifEagle greens
Yardage/Rating/Slope:
Back tees
6,500/70.7/120
Middle tees
6,157/69.0/115
Forward tees
5,408/71.0/127

EAST COURSE
Par: 72
Bermuda fairways,
TifEagle greens
Yardage/Rating/Slope:
Back tees
6,631/71.7/122
Middle tees
6,232/69.5/117
Forward tees
5,516/71.5/118

DESERT BLOOM

In the heart of the California desert, just minutes from Palm Springs, the Hyatt Grand Champions resort blends seamlessly into the surrounding mountains, and offers two championship golf courses.

The stillness of the desert rarely fails to astonish. It can prove the ideal antidote to the stresses of daily life. Here, sometimes, fantasy becomes reality, as in the case of the two Ted Robinson–designed golf courses that spring from the mountains. Nine lakes bring water into play on sixteen of the holes, and some tee elevations reach sixty feet.

One is drawn to Hyatt Grand Champions not only for the golf, but also for major tennis events. Courts come in all surfaces and are lit at night, so players can serve to the rhythm of chirping crickets. How does one decide whether to slip into a private Jacuzzi or drive to the natural one that gave nearby Palm Springs its name? No need to worry; either choice lets the peace of the Mojave

"The greens are generally fast, so it's wise to keep the ball positioned below the pin when approaching most greens"

— JON DARRAH, HEAD GOLF PROFESSIONAL, INDIAN WELLS

HYATT GRAND CHAMPIONS

INDIAN WELLS, CALIFORNIA

RESORT RATING:	
CHALLENGE	★★★⯪
BEAUTY	★★★★
LODGING	★★★★
CUISINE	★★★⯪
AMENITIES	★★★⯪

settle deep within.

And when it's time to rest, 338 European-inspired suites, rooms, and villas overlook manicured gardens. In serious demand are the Garden Villas, which come with private butlers. The cooking varies from southwestern to California classic to Mediterranean, and the health spa gives Indian clay facials and enzyme peels that set guests aglow.

There are excursions to nearby polo matches, art and history museums, amusement parks, galleries, wildlife reserves, stables, ice-skating rinks, Indian canyons, wineries, shopping centers. But most notably, an aerial tramway takes visitors from the desert floor to the very top of Mount San Jacinto—8,500 feet in twenty minutes. It is breathtaking, like Hyatt Grand Champions resort.

EXPERIENCING

HYATT GRAND CHAMPIONS

In the heart of the California desert, this resort is known for its pampering service.

• Survey the magnificent mountains, manicured gardens, and sparkling pools from your European-inspired parlor suite, garden villa, or penthouse suite.

• Savor everything from southwestern cuisine to California classics in two superb restaurants and a poolside café.

• Take an aerial tram ride, visit botanical gardens or a wildlife park, or sample some of El Paseo Drive's legendary shopping.

• Bask by the pool or pamper yourself at the fully equipped health spa and fitness club.

RESORT RATING:

CHALLENGE	★★★★⯪
BEAUTY	★★★★
LODGING	★★★★
CUISINE	★★★★
AMENITIES	★★★★

MARRIOTT

RANCHO LAS PALMAS RESORT

RANCHO MIRAGE, CALIFORNIA

EXPERIENCING

MARRIOTT RANCHO LAS PALMAS RESORT

Marriott's Rancho Las Palmas Resort distinctively blends the sophistication of Palm Springs with the hospitality and charm of early California.

• Stay in elegantly appointed suites or casitas with their own balconies and patios, ringed by tranquil lakes, gardens, and distinctive architecture reminiscent of the Spanish missions.

• Enjoy desert activities like hot-air ballooning, hiking, jeep tours, and horseback riding, or slip into Palm Springs to ride the Aerial Tramway, shop on El Paseo, or tour celebrity homes.

It is wise to save some breath for Marriott Rancho Las Palmas Resort and Spa in Rancho Mirage. Pathways littered with fragrant desert flowers and lined by blooming oleanders and majestic palms lead the way to early-California-style casitas. Mosaic tiled stairways spiral up towards rooms that peep over a still lake or terra-cotta fountain in a diminutive courtyard. This is most definitely an ideal environment to follow Rancho Las Palmas' only rule: Let go. Have fun.

Rancho Las Palmas Resort combines the calming sensation of a secluded spa with the vaunted sophistication of Palm Springs. Over two hundred acres of resort property hold a tweny-five-court tennis complex, two swimming pools with the stunning Santa Rosa Mountains as their backdrop, and the revitalizing Spa Las Palmas. The spa offers therapeutic treatments collected from some of the most revered spas in the world. The Desert Clay Spirulina Ritual is a classic, as is the skin-renewing Turkish Salt Scrub. The spa pool even has underwater music for fluid ballet moves.

Twenty-seven holes of championship golf designed by respected golf architect Ted Robinson lie in wait for resort guests, as do tennis courts and a scenic jogging trail. Restaurants within Rancho Las Palmas Resort range from the classic Mediterranean-inspired cooking and ambience of Madeira restaurant to Pablo's Restaurant and Tapas Bar, which serves American cuisine with a decidedly Spanish accent.

WHEN THE SUN GOES DOWN

The kiva-style fireplace in the courtyard of

Pablo's Restaurant sets the stage for

romantic moonlight dinners.

COACHELLA VISTAS

The elegant Presidential suite offers multilevel four-bedroom accommodations with a full kitchen, marble bar, private elevator, and spectacular views of the Coachella Valley.

INDIAN WELLS RESORT HOTEL

Friendly staff, the elegance you expect from a full-service resort, and a spectacular location make Indian Wells "the gem of the desert."

• Relax next to the spectacular heated pool, or slide into the hot therapy pool for some deep relaxation.

• Warm up at a state-of-the-art fitness center, then enjoy a brisk game of tennis, all without ever leaving the resort.

• See a play at the McCallum Theatre for the Performing Arts or visit nearby Palm Springs for fine shopping and dining, spectacular views from the Aerial Tramway, or a tour of the Living Desert.

• For a deluxe continental breakfast or an evening of fine dining, visit Loren restaurant, where one of the desert's largest wine cellars complements fantastic service and delectable food.

WORLD CLASS

The Indian Wells Resort offers two championship courses. Resort guests also have privileges at the famed Indian Wells Country Club.

POOLSIDE PARADISE

After working out or playing tennis, a lounge chair is the perfect spot for enjoying tropical cocktails, grilled sandwiches, and a variety of salads from the Palm Terrace poolside bar.

The Tortuga Island Bar and Grille, overlooking the fifth fairway, is a handy spot to meet for burgers and tropical drinks, and the Casa Lounge's casual atmosphere is ideal for sipping an aperitif or nightcap. Rancho Las Palmas is surely one of the desert's most relaxing resorts and a treasure to behold.

The Indian Wells Resort Hotel calls itself "the gem of the desert," and it is indeed a treasure. This resort in the Coachella Valley spreads out on carefully manicured emerald lawns. Palm trees sway gently in the breeze, and an elegant demeanor is apparent from the moment of arrival.

Aside from the two highly regarded golf facilities that are available to hotel guests (the

INDIAN WELLS, CALIFORNIA	RESORT RATING:	
	CHALLENGE	★★★★☆
# INDIAN WELLS RESORT HOTEL	BEAUTY	★★★★
	LODGING	★★★★
	CUISINE	★★★★
	AMENITIES	★★★★

eighteen-hole Indian Wells Golf Resort and the Indian Wells Country Club, which is home to the Bob Hope Chrysler Classic), the resort has a hot therapy pool, an oversized swimming pool, tennis courts, and a fitness center.

Quaint Jake's Lounge is the place to round out the evening with a cold drink. On weekends, the lounge becomes a local hot spot with live entertainment and dancing. But just flopping near the pool at the Palm Terrace is the best way to enjoy the weather, while sipping on tropical libations and munching on a variety of sandwiches and salads. Loren, where one of the largest and most varied wine cellars in the desert assiduously keeps bottles cool, serves exquisite American-Continental cuisine in a Mediterranean-style setting. The level of personal service goes unrivaled by most standards.

Stylishly furnished rooms blend warm desert hues with striking artwork. The marble bathtub, when piled high with fragranced suds, is an ideal end to any day. And the stunning views of a fiery desert sunset can be seen every day from private balconies. It is easy to see why this resort stands above so many others.

THE GEM OF THE DESERT
Off-site desert-focused activities include jeep tours of desert flora and hot-air balloon rides.

LUXURIOUS LOBBY

Indian Wells' elegant lobby offers a pleasant space for guest to mingle.

A BREAK FROM BUSINESS

Indian Wells is a popular spot for meetings, so its golf course is often humming with players taking time out from work.

INDIAN WELLS
RESORT HOTEL
INDIAN WELLS, CALIFORNIA

Architect: Eddie Sussalla
Tour stops: Bob Hope
Chrysler Classic
Par: 72
Rye/Bermuda fairways,
rye greens
Yardage/Rating/Slope:
<u>Black tees</u>
6,598/71.9/125
<u>White tees</u>
6,208/69.9/119
<u>Red tees</u>
5,755/74.1/133

CLASSIC GOLF

The resort offers golf at

two world-class facilities:

the Indian Wells Golf

Resort and the nearby

Indian Wells

Country Club.

"Make sure you get your tee shots into play. Position will reward the golfer. On our multitiered greens, try to be below the hole for best results."

—DREW HUDGENS, HEAD GOLF PROFESSIONAL, MARRIOTT'S DESERT SPRINGS RESORT AND SPA

RESORT RATING:

CHALLENGE	★★★☆
BEAUTY	★★★★
LODGING	★★★★
CUISINE	★★★★
AMENITIES	★★★★

PALM DESERT, CALIFORNIA

MARRIOTT DESERT SPRINGS

RESORT AND SPA

EXPERIENCING

MARRIOTT DESERT SPRINGS RESORT AND SPA

With championship golf and tennis, thirteen restaurants, nine swimming and whirlpools, and acres of lush gardens, guests find no reason to leave the property.

• Sample classes for every fitness level, and one of the largest resort gyms in the country, at the spectacular European-style spa.

• From the breathtaking atrium lobby where waterfalls tumble into the lagoon, take a romantic gondola ride to your dining destination.

• Spend an afternoon hot-air ballooning, shopping, hiking, touring the desert by jeep, or taking a celebrity sightseeing tour.

• Follow the sound of steel drums to the Oasis Pool, where the resort's popular band entertains regularly.

Marriott's Desert Springs Resort and Spa in Palm Desert is another clear-cut winner, wrapped around a wonderland of waterways. The resort has a couple of very respectable options for golfers of all levels. The Valley Course features palm-tree-framed fairways, plenty of effective water hazards, and multitiered greens. There is a great eighteen-hole putting course that's perfect for beginners, families, and seasoned players looking for a warm-up. The Palms Course is Desert Springs' premier championship course. Built in 1987, the Palms earned a best new resort course nomination by *Golf Digest*. Its signature holes, numbers 5 and 18, are renowned for their challenge as well as their beauty. As the Palms Course meanders about the perimeter with a fairly challenging set of back tees, one is eventually drawn back to center, to the hip and lively hub of the resort itself.

Ignore, if you can, the fact that there are nine hundred rooms here, in tall buildings. The massive white complex creates as good a playground as one gets. At poolside, where the lilting rhythms of a steel drum band float deliciously from the Oasis Bar and Grille, one can be transported a world away from the bustle.

Shaded gondolas patiently invite guests to glide along the canals as they contemplate which of the many activities to sample next. Clay, grass, or hard court tennis? Perhaps sand volleyball or croquet. Some time by the pool side be nice. It's all here. Warm days can be followed by hot, hot nights at the high-voltage Costas dance club. Or romantic evenings can linger with a starry-eyed swim in a secluded pool.

Guests can also take the resort's gondolas to many of the restaurants that reside on the property. Lobster-stuffed ravioli and a classic minestrone warm the soul at Ristorante Tuscany, where the wine list has been honored by *Wine Spectator* magazine. Fabulously entertaining chefs joke and juggle—literally—their way through the preparation of Teppan-yaki steak, seafood, chicken, and vegetables at Mikado Japanese Steak House. And don't miss the braised lamb shanks at LakeView, Marriott Desert Springs' cozy, casual establishment that evokes classic California wine country style.

An entire vacation could be spent exploring the marvels of the spa and fitness center, one of the largest in the nation. Morning bouts of kick boxing or yoga can be followed by pampering of almost every genre, from Thai massage to European mud masks to ayurvedic healing. These diversions could be the reason why the resort's mascot is a rainbow-hued hummingbird. Like these sweet little speedsters, one cannot help but dart from this to that, sampling all that is there to be explored.

Inner exploration is one of the central themes of the Ojai Valley Inn and Spa. No wonder Ojai was chosen to be draped as Shangri-la for the classic film *Lost Horizon*.

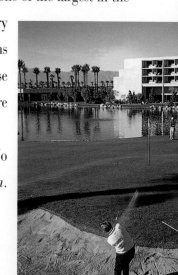

Marriott Desert Springs Resort and Spa

Palms Course
Architect: Ted Robinson
Par: 72
Common Bermuda fairways,
Tifdwarf greens
Yardage/Rating/Slope:
Black tees
6,761/72.1/130
Blue tees
6,381/70.3/126
White tees
6,143/69.2/123
Red tees
5,492/70.8/116

Valley Course
Architect: Ted Robinson
Par: 72
Common Bermuda fairways,
Tifdwarf greens
Yardage/Rating/Slope:
Black tees
6,627/71.5/127
Blue tees
6,323/70.1/125
White tees
6,023/68.7/122
Red tees
5,262/69.6/110

Hardly Parched

Golf at the Marriott Desert

Springs is anything but dry.

The architect of both

championship courses,

Ted Robinson, is known

as the "King of

Waterscapes."

OJAI VALLEY INN AND SPA

Architects: George Thomas, Billy Bell, renovated by Jay Morrish

Tour stops: 1989–1996 Senior PGA Tour, 1997–1998 EMC Skills Challenge

Par: 70

Kikuya/rye fairways, Poa Annua/rye greens

Yardage/Rating/Slope:

<u>Blue tees</u>
6,305/70.7/125

<u>White tees</u>
5,962/69.0/120

<u>Red tees</u>
5,244/71.2/129

PROMISED REWARDS

Golfers pass the spa building as they play the ninth hole at Ojai Valley Inn and Spa.

This charming mountain valley village has long been a sanctuary for spiritual enthusiasts worldwide, and since 1923, the Ojai Valley Inn has stood as its beacon of refinement and serenity.

Padding through the Inn's Spa Village in terry-cloth slippers, one naturally continues the deep breathing of the resort's signature treatment, the Kuyam (Chumash for "a place to rest together"), an inhalation therapy of dry heat and meditation. Hurrying is not on the agenda here. If it were, it would be easy to fill the day with tennis and golf and a guided hike or ride, hoping to get it all in before the "pink moment" infuses the Topa Topa Mountains with sunset's magenta and rose.

But Ojai is meant to be savored, which is a very sensible reason for an extended stay. Certainly the fabulous dining would prompt guests to do so. With an enlightened version of Provençal traditions, Maravilla showcases the local farmers and ranchers.

OJAI VALLEY INN AND SPA

OJAI, CALIFORNIA

RESORT RATING:	
CHALLENGE	★★★★
BEAUTY	★★★★
LODGING	★★★★
CUISINE	★★★★
AMENITIES	★★★★

In the early 1920s, George C. Thomas, Jr., the architect who created the Los Angeles Country Club, among other respected clubs, maximized the contours of the Inn's 220 acres of softly rolling hills to make a course praised then and now.

Vitality is what draws prominent figures from the worlds of entertainment, sports, and arts to La Costa Resort and Spa. Located in Carlsbad just north of sparkling San Diego, La Costa is a sleek refuge for travelers who want to perfect their game, be it tennis, golf, or even diet. The Racquet Club has an admirable twenty-one courts, in all surfaces. With the largest full-service spa in America, La Costa is almost fanatical about fitness. Not only can one indulge in Shiatsu and Aromatherapy treatments, but health counseling is also a popular option, where registered dieticians and physiologists teach healthy eating and exercise habits, customizing plans for guests. Perhaps the most wondrous feature at La Costa Resort and Spa is the spa maternity program, which offers delights like the Warm Sea Foam Treatment. In this treatment, sea mud radiates out from the spine until one resembles a tawny starfish, head to toe.

UNIQUE SPA VILLAGE

Curving outdoor staircases, trickling fountains, and a bell tower rising over the courtyard welcome guests to Spa Ojai, a Mediterranean village housing a bevy of spa facilities and a process-oriented approach to exercise.

OJAI VALLEY INN AND SPA
OJAI, CALIFORNIA

Serene beauty, a multitude of outdoor activities, and the feeling of a Spanish estate await visitors to the Ojai Valley Inn and Spa.

• Enjoy a relaxing fireside massage or try a class in spinning, water aerobics, or tai chi, all in Spa Ojai's charming Mediterranean village-style setting.

• Kick up your heels at a western-style hoedown or saddle up for a trail ride at the Inn's own ranch and stables.

• Hike or bike to the historic Spanish-style village of Ojai or explore the trails of Los Padres National Forest.

• Sample the Inn's California-French cuisine, an imaginative cuisine using locally grown produce and herbs from the Inn's own garden.

SCULPTING IN NATURE

Disturbing as little as possible, designer George Thomas gently carved his golf course from the Ojai Valley, utilizing the natural contours and softly rolling foothills of the surrounding mountains.

"Ojai Valley is a classic type of golf course with eighteen unique holes that don't favor any one type of golfer. It has well-guarded pin placements that require really good shots to get the ball close to the hole."

— MARK GREENSLIT, HEAD GOLF PROFESSIONAL, OJAI VALLEY INN AND SPA

TRANQUIL BEAUTY

Ten buildings at Ojai Valley Inn contain its spacious rooms and suites.
The historic Hacienda building features 1920s-style handmade furniture,
including Morris chairs, mission armoires, and four-poster beds.

DISTINCTIVE DINING

Each of La Costa's restaurants offers spa cuisine and its own specialties: seafood at Pisces, Italian cuisine at Ristorante Figaro, and a champagne brunch at Brasserie La Costa.

LA COSTA RESORT AND SPA

In the foothills of southern California, La Costa offers elegant accommodations, a world-class spa, and championship golf and tennis.

• Enjoy the amenities of a total tennis resort, featuring twenty-one hard court, grass, and clay tennis surfaces.

• Lounge beside a koi-filled lagoon and cascading waterfall or cool off with a refreshing dip in one of the heated pools conveniently scattered throughout the grounds.

• For a relaxing massage or the latest in therapeutic body treatments, visit the spa with its saunas, whirlpool baths, rock steam rooms, and Roman pools.

• Experience a variety of distinctive dining choices, with La Costa's renowned spa cuisine available in each of five restaurants.

MATCH PLAY

Boasting two exceptional eighteen-hole championship courses, La Costa has hosted some legendary matches, including the 1992 Infiniti Tournament of Champions.

LUSH SPLENDOR

Perfect weather and a variety of activities take place on the lawns, fairways, and flower-bedecked grounds at the mouth of the Pacific Lagoon.

La Costa Resort and Spa has been a PGA tour stop for over thirty years, so golfers will recognize the grounds from televised matches. La Costa offers two challenging championship courses, the North Course and South Course. The Both courses are flat, easy-to-walk routes (though caddies are required for walkers) that wind through a valley in the scenic, rolling inland hills. On both courses the fairways are fairly open, although mature trees dot them. Houses closely line some of the fairways, but La Costa generally has a pastoral feel to it.

On the North Course, wind is a constant factor. On many of the North Course's holes water comes into play, but nowhere is the liquid hazard more intimidating than on the par-three eighth hole, where a huge lake protects the green. The North Course's finishing hole is daunting for anyone feeling weak—in the knees or generally. Golfers have to hit uphill, into the wind, clearing water and avoiding the six bunkers that line the left side of the fairway.

The South Course is the La Costa Resort and Spa's slightly more well-regarded course, though both courses are similar in design. It also uses water and wind to challenge players, and its finishing course often has players scratching their heads. Although the 18 starts off reasonably on the tee, the elevated green and ball magnet of a bunker to the right of the green often racks up a higher score than expected.

After a day of golf or spa treatments, visitors relish time in their guestrooms. Soothing shades of salmon accentuate the rooms' interiors, which often have gracefully arched windows opening to the koi-filled lagoon. Hand-carved mahogany tables and armoires fill amply-sized rooms. But even though the accommodations are grand, one must decline in-room dining and experience the dramatics at Pisces instead.

CARLSBAD, CALIFORNIA

LA COSTA RESORT

AND SPA

RESORT RATING:	
CHALLENGE	★★★★
BEAUTY	★★★★
LODGING	★★★★
CUISINE	★★★★
AMENITIES	★★★★

FOOD WITH A FLAIR

La Costa's spa cuisine is artfully prepared, with a menu that changes daily to incorporate the freshest ingredients available.

COURSES OF CHAMPIONS

For thirty years, the PGA Tournament of Champions played here.

In 1999, the resort became home to the World Golf

Championships-Andersen Consulting Match Play Championship.

"Classic design and creative bunkering make our courses challenging yet fair. The hazards are always visible to forewarn you of the decision at hand, and our historic caddie program, one of the few still available in southern California, provides additional insight to playing."

—GARY GLASER, DIRECTOR OF GOLF, LA COSTA RESORT AND SPA

GOLFING

LA COSTA RESORT AND SPA
CARLSBAD, CALIFORNIA

Architects: Dick Wilson, Joe Lee
Tour stops: 1968–1998
Tournament of Champions;
1999, 2000, 2002 World Golf
Championships–Andersen
Consulting Match Play
Championship

NORTH COURSE
Par: 72
Bermuda/rye fairways,
bentgrass greens
Yardage/Rating/Slope:
Gold tees
7,021/74.8/137
Blue tees
6,608/72.1/128
White tees
6,269/69.9/121
Red tees
5,939/76.3*/137*

SOUTH COURSE
Par: 72
Bermuda/rye fairways,
bentgrass greens
Yardage/Rating/Slope:
Gold tees
7,004/74.4/138
Blue tees
6,524/72.0./129
White tees
6,198/69.8/121
Red tees
5,612/74.2*/134*
*Women's ratings

FINE TUNE YOUR GAME

La Costa Golf School's
comprehensive facilities
include chipping, putting,
and driving areas, as well
as high-tech video and
personal instruction geared
toward improving every
golfer's technique
and scoring.

"It's a fair course, but you can get some big numbers if you get into the hazards. Stay below the hole and be patient."

—JIM HILL, HEAD GOLF PROFESSIONAL, RANCHO BERNARDO INN WEST COURSE

RESORT RATING:

CHALLENGE	★★★⯪
BEAUTY	★★★★
LODGING	★★★★
CUISINE	★★★★
AMENITIES	★★★★

EXPERIENCING

RANCHO BERNARDO INN

Escape to a gracious California resort with the warmth, taste, and style of a fine country home.

• Enjoy a full range of activities, from tennis, biking, or volleyball to a workout at the fitness center and a massage at the spa.

• Relax over updated classical French fare in a warm atmosphere, or casual dining with California grill cuisine and sweeping views of the eighteenth hole.

• Lose yourself among the winding pathways, melodic fountains, and beautiful statuary that grace the resort's tranquil gardens.

RANCHO BERNARDO INN

SAN DIEGO, CALIFORNIA

With perfect Dover sole and Maine lobster as enticements, the wait staff has the flair to primp many of its courses tableside. One need not follow suit, as all is relaxed here. With the way a person feels after a week's stay here, most guests exude a decided joie de vivre, the best treatment of all.

Another kind of fabulous treatment happens when resort staff greet one and all as if old friends have returned home. This is most assuredly the welcome at the Rancho Bernardo Inn, thirty miles northeast of San Diego. It hums with the sublime confidence of a family-run estate. And so it is. Soon, intimate pathways encourage one to unwind, settling into a chair in a tranquil garden, listening to a trickling fountain.

It's the peace, not the pace, that draws the faithful here. Only one golf course is needed (however, four others are affiliated with the inn). Tennis and swimming are the other lures, as well as a children's camp. Stands of olive and eucalyptus trees wind their way through the property, while oodles of potted plants are found in every nook and cranny. Draperies and fabrics were loomed and dyed to give a feeling of early California.

For a dozen years, El Bizcocho (French fare) has been awarded the Wine Spectator Award of Excellence. With over 550 labels on the list, it can be a challenge to find just the right pinot noir for a grilled pheasant breast and arugula fettucine. Thankfully, the sommelier has insightful suggestions.

SECLUDED NOOKS

Reminiscent of a California estate, the Rancho Bernardo

Inn is filled with welcoming spaces for intimate

conversation or quiet contemplation before a crackling fire.

GOLFING

RANCHO BERNARDO INN

WEST COURSE
Architect: William Bell, Jr.
Par: 72
Bermuda/rye fairways,
bentgrass greens
Yardage/Rating/Slope:
<u>Black tees</u>
6,631/72.3/133
<u>Blue tees</u>
6,243/70.4/129
<u>White tees</u>
5,780/68.0/124
<u>Gold tees</u>
4,945/68.5/119

OAKS NORTH EXECUTIVE COURSE
Architect: Ted Robinson
Par: 60
Bermuda/kikuya fairways,
bentgrass greens
Yardage/Rating/Slope:
NORTH/EAST
<u>White tees</u>
3,414/55.6, /86
<u>Red tees</u>
3,041/57.0*/86*
East/South
<u>White tees</u>
3,524/56.4/87
<u>Red tees</u>
3,220/57.6*/85*
SOUTH/NORTH
<u>White tees</u>
3,608/56.8/88
<u>Red tees</u>
3,253/57.8*/87*
*Women's ratings

EFFORTLESS ACCESS

Against a peaceful valley

backdrop, the golf course

begins at your doorstep and

crosses meandering

streams and waterscapes

that come into play on ten

of the holes.

FOUR SEASONS RESORT, AVIARA

THE AVIARA GOLF CLUB AT the FOUR SEASONS AVIARA

Architect: Arnold Palmer

Tour stops: Sun Microsystems Par-Three Challenge

Par: 72

Bermuda fairways, bentgrass/Poa Annua greens

Yardage/Rating/Slope:

Palmer (silver) tees

7,007/74.2/137

Back (aqua) tees

6,591/71.8, 78.2*/130, 140*

Middle (white) tees

6,054/68.9, 75.4*/121, 130*

Forward (yellow) tees

5,007/69.1*/119*

*Women's ratings

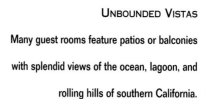

UNBOUNDED VISTAS

Many guest rooms feature patios or balconies with splendid views of the ocean, lagoon, and rolling hills of southern California.

LEGENDARY BEAUTY

Beautiful landscaping, rock work, and waterfalls dominate the spectacular Four Seasons Resort, Aviara.

PASS THE SUNSCREEN

The ever-present California sun provides perfect afternoons for sunbathing, a soothing swim, and a refreshing drink beside the pool.

Whether the Four Seasons, Aviara, will mature into a beloved classic remains to be seen. Four Seasons certainly sets a high standard. And when they opened Aviara in 1997, their goal was to create nothing less than a modern-day legend. Set on a flourishing hilltop Aviara overlooks the Pacific and Batiquitos Lagoon. Rolling valleys embrace a golf course at peace with a famed wildlife preserve.

Aviara has five restaurants, all with alfresco dining, but the big draw is Vivace, showcasing Tuscan cuisine. Venetian plaster walls in burnt orange, dramatic floral arrangements, and a Roman stone fireplace set the cozy mood. Chef Marco Cavuto refined his skills in Milan and

"We provide our guests with a daily pin placement sheet; using this tool makes hitting the greens a little easier."

—Bill Crist, Head Golf Professional, Four Seasons, Aviara

CARLSBAD, CALIFORNIA

FOUR SEASONS RESORT, AVIARA

RESORT RATING:

CHALLENGE	★★★★
BEAUTY	★★★★½
LODGING	★★★★½
CUISINE	★★★★
AMENITIES	★★★★½

blends Italian cooking with contemporary light dishes. Seafood is his forte and smoked tuna, Maine lobster, Dungeness crab, and Pacific salmon are some of the star ingredients he uses, often bringing them to perfection in a wood-fired brick oven.

No less a golfer than Arnold Palmer designed the Aviara Course, and it took nearly a decade to construct because of his ecological concerns and an intense desire to protect the natural wetlands. The course is crafted around the topography of three valleys, with wildflowers growing to the edges of the greens and fairways. Waterfalls and streams are positioned as water hazards. The adjacent lagoon is home to 130 species of shorebirds and waterfowl.

The Southwest's year-round celebration of the natural surroundings is just one of many reasons to make it the golfing destination of choice. But within the region, the abundance of spectacular resorts makes for difficult decisions—or many return trips to America's golden country.

FLOWERSCAPES

Aviara's Arnold Palmer–designed golf course is routed through the incredible topography of three coastal canyons. Hole 17 is the longest hole on the course.

THE MAGNET

Views of the Pacific Ocean draw so many guests to Aviara's lobby picture window that it has come to be known as "the magnet."

CONCENTRATION

The Four Seasons Resort, Aviara's numerous water hazards require a sure drive and clear mind.

ANCIENT PLEASURES

BY ALICE RINDLER SHAPIN

MILLIONS OF YEARS ago deep in the Pacific Ocean, a massive explosion ripped open the sea's floor. Clouds of white steam spewed miles into the air, launching tons of fiery molten rock and heralding the birth of the Hawaiian Islands. Over the next several million years, the islands grew, and a unique array of fauna and exotic tropical flora made its way to them via wind, wing, water, and, more recently, man.

And to Hawaii's shores came waves of Polynesians, Asians, and Europeans, bringing their customs and culinary delights. Early inhabitants wove mystical legends that are still told today. And together the settlers melded into a rich international culture and a relaxed, friendly lifestyle.

The Hawaiian Islands consist of six major islands: Oahu, Maui, the Big Island, Kauai, Lanai, and Molokai. Sun-drenched and cooled by the trade winds, the golfing favorites, Maui, Kauai, Lanai, and the Big Island, parade endless displays of nature's wonders. It's a land of diversity: Hawaii boasts steep emerald cliffs, stark forbidding lava fields, gushing waterfalls, erupting volcanoes, pristine beaches—some white, some black, and some pink—lush rainforests, and snowcapped volcanoes, all ringed by the crystal clear turquoise waters of the Pacific. It's paradise— prime real estate for tony resorts and the world's most spectacular golf courses.

The best of Hawaii's resorts sit on the edge of the ocean and offer front-row seats to fiery sunsets and panoramic views of the Pacific. Relax, forget your jacket and tie, and instead don a colorful Hawaiian shirt and shorts and dine alfresco on fresh fish and other succulent fare. Unwind at the grand spas and enjoy a potpourri of treatments. And be spoiled for life—play golf on the islands, the place where the PGA Tour's year begins.

Maui, the Magic Isle, has an uncanny ability to dazzle and soothe almost simultaneously. Excitement runs the gamut, from driving up to the eerie, moonlike crater of the ten-thousand-foot summit of dormant Haleakala Volcano to navigating the road to Hana, with its fifty-two serpentine miles that wind around six hundred curves and fifty-four one-lane bridges. Long considered to have some of the world's most pristine and award-winning beaches, Maui's reef-lined coastal waters are playgrounds for snorkelers, divers, swimmers, kayakers, and windsurfers. But for many, the real lure is West Maui, the "Golfing Coast." It's where the modern-day legendary golfing gods, Robert Trent Jones, Sr. and Jr., Arnold Palmer, Ben Crenshaw, and Jack Nicklaus imprinted their style and vision.

Lush and brilliantly green, the vast lands of Kapalua stretch from the top of the highest peak in the West Maui Mountains and gently slope to the edge of the azure Pacific. Fingerlike lava peninsulas reach out to the deep blue ocean and seem to embrace it. Luxurious and grand, the Ritz-Carlton, Kapalua, is more than just another pretty hotel.

THE RITZ-CARLTON, KAPALUA
KAPALUA GOLF CLUB

PLANTATION COURSE
Tour stops: PGA Mercedes
Championships
Architects: Bill Coore,
Ben Crenshaw
Par: 73
Bermuda fairways and greens
Yardage/Rating/Slope:
Blue tees
7,263/75.2/142
White tees
6,547/71.9/135
Red tees
5,627/73.2*/129*

BAY COURSE
Architects: Arnold Palmer,
Francis Duane
Par: 72
Bermuda fairways and greens
Yardage/Rating/Slope:
Blue tees
6,600/71.7/138
White tees
6,051/69.2/133
Red tees
5,124/69.6*/121*
*Women's ratings

PARADISE PLAYGROUND

Overlooking the clear, blue
Pacific and nearby island of
Molokai, the Ritz-Carlton
offers tennis, golf, award-
winning restaurants, and a
multitude of water sports.
The hotel concierge can
arrange snorkeling, scuba
diving, kayaking, boogie
boarding, deep-sea fishing,
and anything else a
guest can imagine.

PACIFIC BREEZE

The Ritz-Carlton, Kapalua,

remains a destination for travelers

with fine dining in mind.

It's a place whose foundation is built on service to its guests and preservation of the sacred land. Employees have the responsibility to *malama ka `aina* (care for the land) and respect its *kapu* (regulations). And this began even before the Ritz was built. It was during the excavation for the hotel that the most important historical site at Kapalua, the Honokahua burial grounds, was unearthed. As the significance of the discovery became apparent, the entire hotel was redesigned and moved uphill from the burial site. This dedication to preserving and protecting Kapalua's past continues with "Sense of Place" tours of the sacred area.

Today the lavish and inviting Ritz-Carlton

"On the greens, remember that the grass grows toward Lanai and Molokai. When the ball slows down, it tends to drift in that direction, breaking toward the channel . . .

RITZ-CARLTON, KAPALUA

RESORT RATING:

CHALLENGE	★★★★½
BEAUTY	★★★★★
LODGING	★★★★★
CUISINE	★★★★½
AMENITIES	★★★★½

MAUI, HAWAII

sits high above the shoreline of a gleaming lei of five exquisite bays, two of which are marine life sanctuaries where snorkelers and myriad jewel-tone Hawaiian reef fish happily mingle in crystal waters. The hotel has two six-story wings contoured to the rolling terrain and decorated with fabrics that emphasize beautiful local flowers—hibiscus, orchids, anthuriums, and birds of paradise.

The elegant open-air lobby exhibits a plantation-style architecture with a palette of celadon green, coral, and varying hues of browns, reflecting the mountains and the earth. A pineapple motif, signifying the history of Kapalua as a working pineapple plantation, is used throughout—on the wallpaper, in the carpets, and on the ironworks of the lanais that overlook the pool. Mini-pineapples are even

between the two islands."

—DAVID PRITCHETT, HEAD GOLF PROFESSIONAL, PLANTATION COURSE

woven into the massive tropical floral arrangements that adorn the lobby. The theme continues in the lobby lounge, where guests can sip the specialty drink, a pineapple martini—a blend of vodka and pineapple juice.

A staircase leads from the lobby down to a tropical garden that is accentuated by a soothing tri-level pool complete with a cascading waterfall. Friendly servers greet guests with complimentary ice water and slices of sweet pineapple, or guests can treat themselves to the red-and-white "Lava Flow," a mixture of strawberry puree and coconut. Other flavorful experiences await guests at the Banyan Tree restaurant, which specializes in eclectic Asian cuisine with a Hawaiian twist, and the Beach House, which is known for its awesome Maui onion rings.

Just a quick shuttle ride from the hotel is the crown jewel of the resort, the expansive Plantation Course. This course plays through 240 acres of natural beauty and demands a pilgrimage across jagged ridges and plunging jungle ravines. Teeing off high on the slopes of the West Maui Mountains, players are treated to a panoramic view of the green valley below and the blue ocean beyond. In January another distraction is added—humpback whales and dolphins splashing offshore.

Providing the ultimate golf challenge, this course forces golfers to play every shot in their bag, as they are repeatedly confronted with thick, heavily vegetated ravines and sloping terrain. A unique aspect of Hawaii golf is that the steady trade winds were factored in when laying out the courses. A prime example is the Plantation Course's par-four uphill-into-the-wind 304-yard number 14, which is more of a challenge than the downhill-downwind 663-yard par-five finishing hole. And even with that yardage, Tiger was on the green in two. It's something to shoot for.

HEAVEN ON EARTH
The Ritz-Carlton, Kapalua's Fitness Center and Spa offers several massage therapies, including Lomi Lomi, a customary Hawaiian massage.

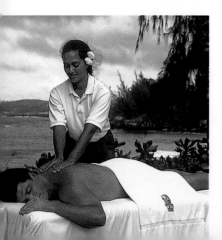

NEW HAWAIIAN CUISINE

The Anuenue Room at the Ritz-Carlton, Kapalua,

gained critical acclaim for such specialties as

rack of lamb and caramelized salmon.

KAPALUA BAY HOTEL

Experience gracious, plantation-style comfort in an intimate setting.

• Indulge your every desire in a luxurious suite with your own lanai, sculpted "tea for two" bathtub, and swift room service at your beck and call twenty-four hours a day.

• Dine in exotic splendor, where tropical drinks are fresh, light, and fizzy, fish come fresh from the Pacific, and desserts are mouth-watering.

• Discover activities uniquely Hawaiian, from diving and snorkeling in Kapalua Bay to hiking the slopes of the West Maui Mountains.

MAJESTIC MAUI

The Kapalua Golf Club hosts the PGA Mercedes Championships and a host of luminaries on its Plantation Course. Learning to use the trade winds and gain direction may take time—a good excuse for an extended visit.

After a round, players can head down to the long stretch of uncrowded beach to watch the changing colors in the sky as the day draws to a close. Guardian of the land, and master of service, the Ritz-Carlton, Kapalua, embodies the tranquility that is Hawaii.

Down the road is the Kapalua Bay Hotel. And what a difference a multimillion-dollar renovation makes. The Kapalua Bay's lobby has recently gone from enclosed and ordinary to WOW! Visitors walk in and come face to face with the blue Pacific and the neighboring islands of Molokai and Lanai. Native koa wood, a huge nine-foot warrior statue, palms, and flowers continue the Hawaiian theme. Earthy and minimalistic, here the natural beauty is king.

The rooms' lanais provide a heavenly spot for a quiet breakfast. Room service rolls in a feast of eggs, fresh mango, luscious pineapple, and rich, bold Kona coffee.

The hotel, terraced into the hillside, overlooks one of the world's best beaches. The sheltered waters of the bay promise a peaceful swim, while farther out, kayaks bob in the waves and snorkelers tag along with schools of fish. In the butterfly pool, the temperature never strays from eighty-one degrees, and novice scuba divers may be spied wandering below the surface. And on shore, red-earth trails lead into a wilderness rife with native plants and birds found nowhere else on earth.

Hard as it may be to pry oneself away from a poolside chaise, no golfer can resist playing the Bay and the Village, distinctive layouts that have been decorated with awards and accolades. The Bay Course meanders through the West Maui Mountains, up hills, through palms, down ravines, through thick stands of ironwood trees, and around pineapple fields. The course rolls gently to the sea with all putts breaking to the ocean. Twisting, turning, and winding high into the mountains, Kapalua's Village Course offers a trek through historic groves of Cook pines and eucalyptus. With panoramic views from holes 5, 6, 7, 8, and 9, the course has a spectacular lake that marks its high point, presiding over pineapple fields and lush green gorges.

Playing is certain to make any golfer ravenous, especially in view of the quiet pleasures of dining at Kapalua. Open to soft tradewinds that lift off the waves, the Bay Club reveals the virtues of fish fresh from the Pacific. And at the Plumeria Terrace, sunlight sparkles on the surface of the butterfly pool, tropical drinks come in bright, fizzing colors, and the desserts are dangerously delectable.

Located south of Kapalua on Maui's sun-kissed southwestern coastline is the sprawling 1,500-acre Wailea resort. There one can transcend the mundane and revel in the extraordinary at Kea Lani Hotel, Hawaii's only luxury, all-suite resort. Perched on twenty-two magnificent lush tropical acres fronting the famed Polo Beach in Wailea, the hotel is comprised of spacious one-bedroom suites and private, oceanfront split-level two- and three-bedroom villas.

"The trade winds are always a factor in Hawaii golf, so you need to know how to hit the ball lower. Don't fight the wind. Make the wind your friend."
—KITT FELTE, HEAD GOLF PROFESSIONAL, BAY COURSE

KAPALUA BAY HOTEL

MAUI, HAWAII

RESORT RATING:

CHALLENGE	★★★★½
BEAUTY	★★★★½
LODGING	★★★★½
CUISINE	★★★★
AMENITIES	★★★★

NO LESS THAN THE BEST
Built near a still-active pineapple plantation, the Kapalua Bay Hotel offers everything that an island paradise is supposed to: swimming, hiking, lei-making and hula-dancing lessons, ocean views, and fine dining.

KAPALUA BAY HOTEL
KAPALUA GOLF CLUB MAUI, HAWAII

VILLAGE COURSE
Architects: Arnold Palmer,
Ed Seay
Par: 71
Bermuda fairways and greens
Yardage/Rating/Slope:
<u>Blue tees</u>
6,608/73.3/139
<u>White tees</u>
6,011/70.4/134
<u>Red tees</u>
5,083/70.9*/122*
*Women's ratings

BREATHTAKING HOLE

The most dramatic hole on
the Arnold Palmer and Ed
Seay–designed Village
Course is unquestionably
hole 7, with a 150-foot
elevation drop from
tee to green.

But way before guests retreat to their grand suites, Kea Lani, Hawaiian for "Heavenly White," makes a bold statement. Its gleaming white turreted exterior is a spectacular sight against the clear blue skies of Wailea and the turquoise sea. Inside, its open-air lobby, elegantly adorned in Mediterranean décor with Italian marble flooring, high vaulted ceilings, and large paintings depicting Hawaiian ancestry, radiates a warm, relaxed ambience.

What sets Kea Lani apart from other resorts are the distinctive accommodations that offer all the comforts of home and more. In the suites, floor-to-ceiling windows open to double-width lanais with breathtaking views. And when only the super-grand and exclusively private will do, there are the 1,000- to 2,200-square-foot villas. Guests enjoy all the amenities of the suites, plus a washer-dryer, a gourmet kitchen, grocery service at the touch of a button, and a sundeck outfitted with a barbecue grill and the pièce de résistance, a private plunge pool.

Beyond the villas, the pools, palms, and the Pacific Ocean come together at the main lagoon-pool complex. Three crystalline swimming pools—two lagoon-style pools that traverse two levels and are connected by a 140-foot water slide and a separate adult pool—Jacuzzis, a swim-up bar, and Polo Beach offer a wealth of tempting diversions. Blue and white umbrellas and cabanas dot the pool and beach area, shading guests from the hot afternoon sun. But if you just happen to get too much sun, the Spa Kea Lani's Ti-leaf Aloe Cooling Wrap is the perfect cure. And for a treatment that's inherently Hawaiian, the spa looked to a traditional treatment practiced by the Kahunas for over four hundred years and developed the "Iliili Stone Therapy." The combination of the warm and soothing heated lava stones and a massage works wonders on today's super-stressed bodies.

After being soothed in the spa, guests can stroll the perfectly manicured grounds, enjoying mango and huge banana trees, birds of paradise, colorful hibiscus, graceful palms, waterfalls, cascading fountains, and lush hanging vines. And Kea Lani has something extra—an on-site organic garden. The produce graces many of the savory dishes prepared by the resort's creative chefs.

While at Kea Lani, enjoy award-winning Wailea golf, which boasts lush scenery and a course for all playing levels. Weekend golfers will appreciate the Blue Course's eighteen holes, which amble across the lower foothills of Mount Haleakala. The wide, manicured fairways woven through the resort offer a picturesque view of Wailea while sporting a lovely array of cooling fountains, quiet lakes, exotic blossoms, and shallow coral sand bunkers.

Along this stretch is the expansive Grand Wailea Resort Hotel and Spa. Saying it's elegantly flamboyant may seem like an oxymoron, but at Grand Wailea, fine art, fine dining, and lush tropical gardens go hand in hand with energy and opulence. The forty-acre Grand Wailea is more than a luxury resort, it's a world unto itself—an adventure waiting to unfold.

RESORT RATING:

MAUI, HAWAII

CHALLENGE	★★★★½
BEAUTY	★★★★½
LODGING	★★★★½
CUISINE	★★★★
AMENITIES	★★★★½

KEA LANI HOTEL

FAMILY FUN

World-class service and an array of activities make the Kea Lani Hotel one of the best golf destination choices for travelers with kids in tow.

KEA LANI HOTEL

Grocery service at the touch of a button, a private plunge pool, and a garden sundeck are among the many amenities at Kea Lani, Hawaii's only all-suite resort.

• Enjoy spacious accommodations in every suite or villa, including a full gourmet kitchen, entertainment center, and lavishly large marble bathrooms.

• Dive into an exotic lagoon, swim up to the bar for a refreshing drink, or plunge down a 140-foot water slide.

• At Spa Kea Lani, experience a wealth of nurturing therapies and products from around the world, some unique to Hawaii.

• Whether you're a novice or expert, try snorkeling or scuba diving at Molokini Crater, Lanai, and coastal Maui for a crystal-clear view of marine life.

FUN, HAWAIIAN STYLE

Along with the water sports and beach activities one would expect from Hawaii, Kea Lani offers an array of activities that seem endless, from golf and tennis to a world-class spa.

GOLFING

KEA LANI HOTEL
WAILEA GOLF AND
TENNIS CLUB
MAUI, HAWAII

GOLD COURSE
Architect: Robert Trent Jones, Jr.
Tour stops: 2001 Senior
Skins Game
Par: 72
Tifton 328 fairways,
Tifdwarf greens
Yardage/Rating/Slope:
Back tees
7,087/73.0/139
Gold tees
7,067/73.0/139
Blue tees
6,653/71.4/136
White tees
6,152/69.0/131
Red tees
5,442/70.3/121

BRAINS AND BRAWN

Although the Wailea Golf
Club's Gold Course is
known for its rugged
terrain, it is also
considered a "thinking
player's course," requiring
strategy and finesse from
those who play it.

"The Gold's been called a 'thinking player's course'. You've got to club yourself right, know your distances, and factor in elevation changes on the course. But at the same time, the course gives you some options, and that's one reason it's so much fun to play."

—RICK CASTILLO, HEAD GOLF PROFESSIONAL, WAILEA GOLD COURSE

FOUR TEMPTING CHOICES

Kea Lani's restaurants offers distinctive flavors and atmosphere.
Nick's Fishmarket Maui serves premier seafood, while more casual
settings include Caffe Ciao, a delicatessen, and a poolside grill.

The open-air lobby showcases an atrium featuring nine immense bronze sculptures that depict human figures of exaggerated proportions created by contemporary artist Fernando Botero. These are only a sampling of a $30-million art collection scattered throughout the property.

Five restaurants specializing in Pacific Rim–inspired cuisine are certain to satisfy even the most discriminating epicurean. Humuhumunukunukuapua'a (named after the state fish), a floating seafood restaurant, is a cluster of banana-leaf thatched-roof huts fashioned in the South Seas style. It sits in the middle of a 700,000-gallon saltwater lagoon teeming with Hawaiian fish. Interlaced

RESORT RATING:		MAUI, HAWAII
CHALLENGE	★★★★	
BEAUTY	★★★★⯪	
LODGING	★★★★⯪	
CUISINE	★★★★⯪	
AMENITIES	★★★★⯪	

GRAND WAILEA RESORT

HOTEL AND SPA

throughout the grounds is a network of lagoons, home to one of the largest collections of koi, some costing over one thousand dollars each. Sculptures of copper, bronze, and wood add interest to the maze of gardens that overflow with exotic plants and flowers.

Of course, while at the Grand Wailea, a must-play is the naturally rugged Wailea Gold, the most difficult layout of the trio. For eighteen holes, sloping fairways, indigenous Hawaiian grasses, prehistoric lava rock walls, and ninety-three strategically placed bunkers will dictate players' club selection. And after or before a

DINNER ON THE WATER

Culinary enthusiasts are delighted by each of the resort's six restaurants, one of which floats in a lagoon filled with Hawaiian fish and spiny lobsters, caught and prepared to order.

round, they can stop at the Sea Watch restaurant for breakfast, drinks, lunch, or dinner. The food is mouthwatering and the location, providing a sweeping view of the ocean, is priceless, as are the incredible sunsets.

Down the beach from the Grand Wailea is the Four Seasons Resort, Maui at Wailea. Besides being greeted in the traditional Hawaiian way with a lei of fresh, delicate orchids of white and purple for the women and green ti-leaves for the men, guests get a refreshingly cool washcloth.

OUTDOOR MUSEUM

Grand Wailea Resort boasts innumerable aquatic facilities, plus the ever-present Pacific and majestic Wailea Beach. Guest wings are surrounded by six enchanting art gardens, home of a $30-million permanent art collection.

SPECTACULAR SCULPTURES

The most prestigious pieces in the resort's collection are the nine bronze sculptures by Fernando Botero.

LUSH BEAUTY

Exotic plants surround Wailea Golf Club's Emerald Course, making for a round of golf rife with tropical splendor.

CAMP GRANDE

The "Children's Resort," a special haven for the younger set, offers hikes, nature walks, and special activities like lei making, clay sculpting, and T-shirt dying.

"One reason the Emerald is so popular is that it has four to six tee boxes on every hole, which means players can tailor the course to their playing ability. Casual golfers can use the regular tees; players who want more challenge can play farther back."

—RICK CASTILLO, HEAD GOLF PROFESSIONAL, WAILEA EMERALD COURSE

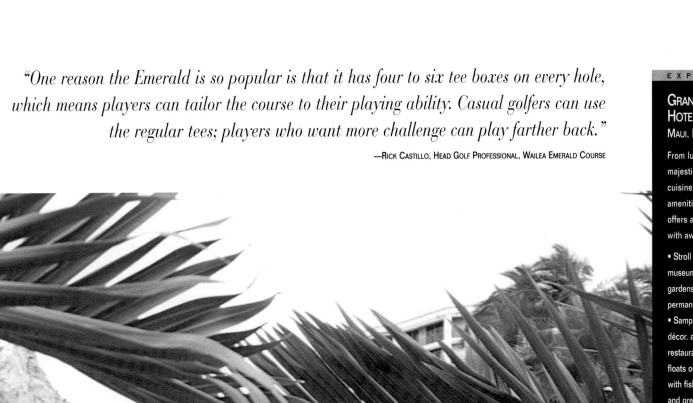

FOUR SEASONS RESORT, MAUI AT WAILEA

Superb service and elegant accommodations create an atmosphere for nurturing the body, relaxing the mind, and rejuvenating the spirit.

• Pamper yourself with Four Seasons service, from soothing massage and facials to land and water sports and a complimentary all-day children's program.

• Relax in a poolside cabana, where attentive staff members bring you chilled Evian spritzes and refreshing iced towels.

• Enjoy luxurious amenities in every room, from the well-stocked tea and coffee service with fresh beans and a grinder, to a refrigerated bar filled with tropical juices.

• Feel like part of paradise from your spacious lanai, with its views of the Pacific, mountains, or gardens—perfect for sunning or alfresco dining.

POSITIVELY PAMPERED

Paths wind past shimmering fountains toward the Four Seasons Resort, Maui at Wailea's poolside cabanas, where attentive staff members bring guests Evian spritzes and chilled towels.

The resort's charm lies in its tranquil, elegant beauty. The entire resort is designed to have the indoors and outdoors flow together, ensuring the greatest enjoyment of the magical sights and sounds of the ocean. The view from the Lobby Lounge provides the first glimpse of the alluring water. Nightly, live music and the mesmerizing view make the lobby lounge one of the best spots in the resort from which to watch the sensational Maui sunsets.

But just as the sun touches the horizon, another show begins. A torch lighter, garbed in Hawaiian shorts, ti-leaf necklace, and headdress, deftly blows the ceremonial conch shell, which sounds much like a throaty trumpet. Then he runs throughout the resort, igniting the many torches that will light up the approaching night and bathe the pool area in a romantic glow.

Seasons restaurant provides a dramatic ocean view. The music of a Hawaiian trio floats through the open-air restaurant as guests savor the artistically presented, luscious fish prepared with local ingredients. Closer to the water's edge is Ferraro's at Seaside. By day, the umbrella-shaded patio serves casual fare, including the fabulous crunchy Maui chips and colorful tropical drinks. At night, under a canopy of stars, Ferraro's rolls out a menu of Pacific Italian cuisine.

Sleep was never more enticing than at the Four Seasons Resort, Maui at Wailea. Soft down pillows, specially made beds with pillow tops, and a light blanket slipped between two perfectly laundered sheets "guarantees" the sweetest dreams.

MAUI, HAWAII	RESORT RATING:	
	CHALLENGE	★★★★
FOUR SEASONS RESORT, MAUI	BEAUTY	★★★★⯨
	LODGING	★★★★⯨
	CUISINE	★★★★
	AMENITIES	★★★★
AT WAILEA		

Golfers awake refreshed and ready for a grand eighteen holes of play. Regal palms, rich landscaping, and a profusion of tropical blossoms add lovely hues and delicious fragrances to the Emerald Course's pristinely manicured tropical garden-like setting. The opening hole, with a 210-degree view of the Pacific is a preview of what's to come on this course that does not demand long drives.

The Four Seasons Maui activity roster is extensive, with everything but golf included in the price of the room—even the kid's program. Guests can exercise inside on state-of-the-art equipment or head outdoors. Tennis comes with an ocean view, as do a series of outdoor treadmills with individual TV monitors.

Set against the blue surroundings, crisp white cabanas overlook either the ocean or the larger fountain pool

with its two Jacuzzis and the waterfall pool. Plush towels are abundant. At Four Seasons, Maui, the mantra seems to be pamper, pamper, pamper.

Just minutes from Wailea, the Maui Prince Hotel is nestled on a white sandy beach along a secluded cove within the 1,800-acre Makena resort. Elegantly understated, the lobby overlooks a lagoon at the base of the center atrium. And surrounding this waterfall lagoon is a carpet of plush grass. On most days, brides dressed in billowy white gowns and young men in tuxes say their vows here.

AWARD-WINNING

Legendary service and exceptional amenities have earned this resort the AAA Five Diamond Award each year since its opening. From incredible architecture to certified dive classes, the Four Seasons seems to have it all.

GOLFING

FOUR SEASONS RESORT, MAUI AT WAILEA
WAILEA GOLF AND TENNIS
MAUI, HAWAII

BLUE COURSE

Architect: Arthur Jack Snyder

Tour stops: 1990–1992 LPGA Women's Kemper Open

Par: 72

Bermuda fairways, Tifton 328 greens

Yardage/Rating/Slope:

Blue tees

6,758/71.6/130

White tees

6,152/68.9/125

Red tees

5,291/70.3/118

ORIGINAL SPLENDOR

The first of the three courses at Wailea Golf Club, the Blue Course meanders through much of the resort community.

"From tee to green, it's a pretty easy course. What you see is what you get—no tricks, no blind shots. The problem for most people is the putting surface. Pay attention to where the ocean is in relation to the putt, because everything breaks toward the ocean."

—RUSTY HATHAWAY, HEAD GOLF PROFESSIONAL, WAILEA BLUE COURSE

HAWAII ALFRESCO

Ferraro's, a more casual dining option at Four

Seasons, Maui, serves light meals throughout the day.

Drinks and entertainment are available at dusk.

THREE IN ONE

By day, Ferraro's at Seaside serves casual fare and appetizers.

Sunset finds an Italian duo offering a musical accompaniment to

the cocktails, and nightfall brings Italian cuisine and ocean views.

DELIGHTFUL TO LOOK AT

The 380 guest rooms and suites are exceptionally

spacious and beautifully furnished. Each opens onto

one or more lanais, and nearly all offer ocean views.

RESORT RATING:

MAUI, HAWAII

CHALLENGE	★★★★⯪
BEAUTY	★★★★⯪
LODGING	★★★★
CUISINE	★★★★
AMENITIES	★★★★

MAUI PRINCE HOTEL

EXPERIENCING

MAUI PRINCE HOTEL

A civilized oasis on the wild end of
Maui sweeps into forest, green-
mounded cinder cones, vast
expanses of lava, and beaches that
go on forever.

• Settle into immediate serenity
from the moment you arrive, when
a seashell lei is draped over your
shoulders and you are
warmly welcomed.

• Enjoy breathtaking sights from every
room, where the doors open onto an
Asian meditation garden and the lanai
overlooks the ocean.

• Relax on a quarter-mile of white
sand beach or sample the many
ocean activities.

• If vigorous activity is what you
prefer, visit the tennis
center, play volleyball, or
try your hand at croquet.

The tropical lagoon that starts in the center of the atrium lazily meanders outside into the lush garden by Cafe Kiowai. In this paradisiacal setting, with the beach and ocean not far off, the aromas of coffee, eggs, bacon, sweet rolls, and fresh fruit fill the morning air. The beach soon becomes a hub of activity. Early risers suit up with fins and mask to explore the magical waters of Makena Beach. Others get into shape with a morning jog. And on the sandy shore the catamaran Kai Kanai, filled with snorkelers, sets sail for the calm protected waters of the island of Molokini, with its abundance of rainbow-colored marine life.

A top draw at the Maui Prince Hotel is its two championship courses, each exhibiting its own personality and sculpted on the western seaside flank of Haleakala Volcano. The North Course plays at a higher elevation than the South Course, which stretches to the shimmering ocean's edge. Both designs feature lots of fairway bunkers, undulating, lightning-fast greens, and an abundance of stunning scenic distractions.

With entrancing mountain views of Haleakala Crater and sweeping views of the Pacific Ocean, the North Course feels more like a nature walk than a golf course. Throughout, Hawaiian rock walls remain where they were found and natural gullies and stream beds are left intact. For those willing to take chances, there are many risk/reward holes, where a great shot gets you a par or birdie, while a bad one sends you to bogie-land. The South Course embodies the spirit of Makena—serenity and tranquility. It features natural, rolling fairways and greens with breathtaking ocean and mountain views. Two favorite holes, 15 and 16, play along the Pacific.

Just a short plane hop or a ferry ride from Maui lies an even more secluded tropical getaway, the island of Lanai. The sparsely populated island is the Hawaii that people dream of— wild, breeze-tossed, outrageously beautiful—with ancient temples hidden in the hills, miles of untouched beaches, and crystal-clear waters that shelter exotic tropical fish. The Lodge at Koele, a sprawling inland resort with only 102 rooms, combines the sophistication and ambience of a traditional English country manor with the charms and untamed beauty of Lanai.

Banks of blue plumbago and yellow shrimp plants bloom near an inviting veranda, where guests relax in wicker chairs. The sloping hillside is filled with a collection of magnificent palms, fruit trees, and Japanese gardens where guests are welcome to pluck a sweet, ripe mango, banana, citrus, jackfruit, or guava fruit right from the tree. The focal point of this grand mountain lodge is the Great Hall, with high-beamed, thirty-five-foot ceilings, two huge fireplaces, comfortable large-scale furnishings in earth tones and a variety of art objects, both local and imported. Here halls and walls are galleries for Lanai's artists.

MAUI PRINCE HOTEL
MAKENA GOLF COURSE

Architect: Robert Trent Jones, Jr.

NORTH COURSE
Par: 72
Common Bermuda fairways,
Bermuda greens
Yardage/Rating/Slope:
Black tees
6,914/72.1/139
Blue tees
6,567/70.4/136
Orange tees
6,151/68.4/132
White tees
5,303/70.9*/128*

SOUTH COURSE
Par: 72
Common Bermuda fairways,
Bermuda greens
Yardage/Rating/Slope:
Black tees
7,017/72.6/138
Blue tees
6,629/70.7/134
Orange tees
6,168/68.5/129
White tees
5,529/71.1*/130*
*Women's ratings

THE MAIN EVENT

The Maui Prince Hotel

whisks guests to the

nearby Makena Golf

Course for thrilling play

on two well-regarded

championship

courses.

DRAMATIC FOCAL POINT

High-beamed ceilings, twin stone fireplaces,

and a rare art collection accentuate the Great

Hall, the centerpiece of the Lodge at Koele.

FLOWERING GARDENS, SPRAWLING BANYANS

The Lodge at Koele's grounds are a tranquil setting for quiet walks

and peaceful contemplation. The reflecting pool fronting the resort

showcases its well-manicured lawns and gardens.

PENULTIMATE DRAMA

The spectacular hole number 17, an

Experience at Koele signature hole,

requires golfers to navigate wooded

ravines and more than a two-hundred-

foot elevation drop from tees to green.

The magnificent display of local artwork continues in the Lodge at Koele's guest rooms. Stencil paintings of native flora decorate ceilings and floors, and each guest room door bears a small painting of native Lanai flora. Fine wood furniture, some rooms with four-poster beds, and local artwork make guests feel as though they are weekending at a friend's luxurious country estate.

Award-winning restaurants show off the fresh flavors of the Pacific: island seafood, poultry, game, fruits, and vegetables are the stars of the show. In the Formal Dining Room a crackling fireplace adds to the warmth, while the casual Terrace

THE LODGE AT KOELE

LANAI, HAWAII

RESORT RATING:	
CHALLENGE	★★★★
BEAUTY	★★★★½
LODGING	★★★★★
CUISINE	★★★★½
AMENITIES	★★★★

Restaurant provides views of the resort's exotic gardens.

The Lodge at Koele offers some unique activities: horseback riding, an eighteen-hole putting course, croquet, lawn bowling, sporting clays, and an archery range. It's also the gateway to Lanai's wilderness, where wooded trails, wild turkeys, and deer abound.

But for golfers the true gem of the resort is the much-touted Experience at Koele course. A highland course, the Experience leads players through mist-kissed forests and steep valley gorges, and is made even more magnificent by surrounding lakes, streams, and waters. Hole 6, a long 512-yard par-five, is one of the course's most spectacular. From the tee, golfers feel like they are "on top of the world" with vistas of Maui and Molokai. Hole 8, the signature hole, is a 390-yard par-four that drops 250 feet to a wooded gorge below, the deepest and most magnificent one on the island. As challenging as it is beautiful, the Experience's number 15, a 387-yard par-four, has players teeing off across a bevy of waterfalls.

SADDLE UP

The stables at the Lodge at Koele provide the perfect starting point for exploring the surrounding hillside and experiencing Lanai's rich ranching history.

GOLFING

THE LODGE AT KOELE
THE EXPERIENCE AT KOELE
LANAI, HAWAII

Architects: Greg Norman,
Ted Robinson
Par: 72
Bermuda fairways,
bentgrass greens
Yardage/Rating/Slope:
Tournament tees
7,014/73.3/141
Champion tees
6,628/71.5/134
Resort tees
6,217/69.7, 77.3*/130,146*
Forward tees
5,425/66.0,
72.6*/123, 130*
*Women's ratings

TWO GREAT COURSES

Along with Jack Nicklaus's Challenge at Manele, the island of Lanai hosts a second championship course, the Experience at Koele.

"The Experience at Koele is unique in Hawaii in the sense that there's a little bit of elevation and bentgrass greens, much like many mainland courses. With water features and small, deep traps around the greens, shooting to the middle is always a good idea."

—BRENDAN MOYNAHAN, HEAD GOLF PROFESSIONAL, EXPERIENCE AT KOELE

TRADITIONAL ELEGANCE

Warmed by a crackling fireplace, the Formal Dining Room

serves island seafood, exquisitely prepared poultry and

game, and the freshest fruits, herbs, and vegetables.

ISLAND FRESH

The award-winning Ihilani Restaurant offers a romantic setting for sampling the freshest seafood, fruits, and vegetables, seasoned with herbs from the hotel's gardens.

THE MANELE BAY HOTEL

Set high above a spectacular white sand beach, you'll find intimate courtyards filled with lush tropical gardens, abounding waterfalls, and the tranquil pools of an earlier time.

• Explore historical sites where ancient petroglyphs are inscribed on boulders and unique colorful rock formations became the Garden of the Gods.

• Sunbathe on Hulopo'e Beach and watch spinner dolphins play offshore, or snorkel among colorful tropical fish in the clear warm waters.

• Saddle up at the stables for an exhilarating ride or play tennis, go hiking, or take aim at sporting clays.

• Celebrate Hawaii's regional cuisine in a variety of delectable dining experiences with dazzling views to match.

SHOWCASE OF LANDSCAPE DESIGN

Hawaii's cultural influences are apparent in the lush grounds surrounding the hotel. Guests can wander through jasmine trees in the Chinese Garden, stroll over to pristine Hulopo'e Beach, or enjoy a cool drink and spectacular views beside the pool.

PRECIOUS ORIENTAL ARTIFACTS

Public areas at Manele Bay Hotel are lavishly decorated with antiques and art objects, and paintings by local artists and chinoiserie-inspired murals by John Wullbrandt adorn the walls.

Poised high above spectacular Hulopo`e Bay and a sugar-white sand beach is the secluded island retreat the Manele Bay Hotel, a fusion of Kama`aina Hawaiian architecture, Mediterranean romance, and Pacific design. The contrasting colors of the red lava cliffs, the blue sky, sapphire waters, and pristine white-sand beach beautifully frame this grand but intimate two-story seaside villa. At Manele Bay peaceful courtyards are filled with lush tropical gardens, abounding waterfalls, tranquil pools, and aromatic flowers. And a strong Asian presence is felt throughout the resort.

Native art also plays an important role at Manele Bay. David H. Murdock, Chairman of

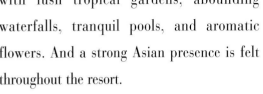

LANAI, HAWAII	RESORT RATING:	
	CHALLENGE	★★★★☆
THE MANELE BAY HOTEL	BEAUTY	★★★★★
	LODGING	★★★★☆
	CUISINE	★★★★☆
	AMENITIES	★★★★

the Board and Chief Executive Officer of Castle & Cooke, Inc. (developer of the island resorts), gathered artists and craftspeople of Lanai to enhance the island flavor at the hotel. Streaming through oversized windows in the lobby, sunlight bathes the hotel's interior, a showcase for a vast collection of spectacular local art and Asian antiques. Great murals of island legends hang in the lobby, subtle petroglyphs grace the corridor ceilings, and Pacific Island crests are in the library, a lovely quiet spot filled with books about Lanai, Hawaii, and the Pacific Rim.

TARGET-STYLE

Hole 11 on the Challenge at Manele typifies this truly target-style course, where keeping the ball in play may mean keeping it out of the Pacific.

Just below the hotel is its pool, and beyond lie the magnificent crescent beach and the bay. A favorite for snorkelers, the undisturbed coral reefs are home to fish, octopi, sea stars, and lobsters. And the clear waters also draw humpback whales and fun-loving dolphins showing off their antics.

Manele Bay, a treasure of a destination, offers superior dining experiences. The intimate Ihilani (Heavenly Splendor) specialty dining room features a Hawaiian monarchy theme and a French Mediterranean menu.

The main dining room, impressive Hulopo`e Court, is designed in a Mediterranean motif and showcases dramatic ocean views and innovative Hawaii regional cuisine highlighting fresh island-grown products.

For golfers, the Challenge at Manele is nirvana. Carved from lava cliffs hundreds of feet above the crashing surf, it's a Jack Nicklaus–designed masterpiece. Built on one hundred acres of oceanside terrain, the Challenge is a target-style golf course, where every hole guarantees breathtaking views of the ocean and neighboring islands.

On number 12, the signature hole, a par is coveted, for the "fairway" is a surging ocean 150 feet below the tee. Hole 13 is a great vantage point for viewing humpback whales in the winter and spring and spinner dolphins all year. And number 17 is one of the most challenging ocean holes and dramatic tee shots in golf. While there are no bunkers, the fairway is narrow and you must carry the cliffs. The second shot, downhill to a cliffside, kidney-shaped green that is defended by a large mound and a bunker in front, offers no relief. The Challenge at Manele is like everything else at the resort—beyond words.

Off to the west lies the oldest of the Hawaiian islands, Kauai. Romance, adventure, and intrigue—Hollywood fabricates it all. But when it comes to location, even Hollywood knows that nothing beats the real thing. For that they head to Kauai, with its incredibly dramatic backdrops. Over fifty blockbuster productions have been shot here, including *South Pacific*, *Raiders of the Lost Ark*, *Indiana Jones and the Temple of Doom*, and *Jurassic Park*. The Princeville Resort is located on the very spot where *South Pacific* was

"The course is built on land that slopes toward the ocean, so every single hole has an unobstructed view of the Pacific. It's a target-style course, so the key to playing and scoring it well is driving it well."

—DOUG STEPHENSON, HEAD GOLF PROFESSIONAL, CHALLENGE AT MANELE

DELECTABLE DINING

Ocean views and informal meals are served at the Pool Grille, the cliffside Golf Clubhouse, and on the terrace at Hulopo`e Court Restaurant.

filmed, atop a remote rich green bluff that overlooks Hanalei Bay and the famed "Bali Hai."

This sophisticated 250-room hotel seems much smaller than expected as you approach the resort. But once you're inside, the Princeville Resort reveals its secret. The grand European-style reception lobby, filled with rich antiques and reflecting the island's Hawaiian lifestyle, is at the top of the hotel, with its luxurious rooms built into the side of the cliffs below.

FAMILY FUN

Hulopo`e Beach beckons young and old alike. Younger guests can participate in tidepool walks, Hawaiian crafts, and other supervised children's activities.

OCEANFRONT ENCLAVE

The Manele Bay Hotel rests atop ancient, windswept lava cliffs overlooking the brilliant blue ocean. Hawaiian architecture blends with Mediterranean and Pacific designs to create a seaside villa filled with cascading waterfalls and intimate courtyards, just steps away from Hulopo`e Beach.

OCEAN VIEWS FROM EVERY HOLE

Acclaimed one of Hawaii's greatest courses, the Challenge at Manele was designed by Jack Nicklaus and overlooks the hotel, bay, and ocean.

THE MANELE BAY HOTEL

THE CHALLENGE AT MANELE
LANAI, HAWAII

Architect: Jack Nicklaus
Par: 72
Bermuda fairways and greens
Yardage/Rating/Slope:

Nicklaus tees
7,039/73.3/132

Gold tees
6,684/71.6/129

Blue tees
6,310/69.8/125

White tees
5,847/67.8, 73.2*/122, 129*

Red tees
5,024/64.0, 68.8*/114, 119*

*Women's ratings

QUITE A CHALLENGE

Even when the Challenge at Manele course lives up to its name in less-than-pleasant ways, the scenery and sheer thrill of being there makes the experience worthwhile.

A PRINCELY RETREAT

Built in a series of tiers on the side of a cliff, Princeville Resort commands one of Hawaii's most spectacular views.

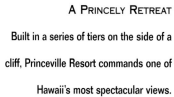

GOLFING

PRINCEVILLE RESORT
PRINCEVILLE GOLF CLUB

PRINCE COURSE
Architect: Robert Trent Jones, Jr.
Par: 72
Bermuda fairways,
Tifton 328 greens
Yardage/Rating/Slope:
Prince tees
7,309/75.3/145
Championship tees
6,960/73.7/142
Alii tees
6,521/71.7/138
Resort tees
6,005/69.3/133
Princess tees
5,338/72.0/127

MAKAI COURSE
Architect: Robert Trent Jones, Jr.
(Note: Three nine-hole
courses—the Lakes Nine,
Ocean Nine, and Woods
Nine—combine into three
18-hole courses.)

OCEAN/LAKES COURSE
Par: 72
Common Bermuda fairways,
Tifton 328 greens
Yardage/Rating/Slope:
Blue tees
6,886/73.2/132
White tees
6,306/70.5, 75.2°/127, 127°
Red tees
5,516/66.9, 69.9°/120, 116°

OCEAN/WOODS COURSE
Blue tees
6,875/72.9/131
White tees
6,365/70.4, 75.4°/126, 127°
Red tees
5,631/67.0, 70.4°/119, 116°

LAKES/WOODS COURSE
Blue tees
6,901/72.5/129
White tees
6,357/70.1, 75.3°/125, 127°
Red tees
5,543/66.3, 69.6°/117, 115°
*Women's ratings

A GRUELING TEST

In designing the courses at Princeville Golf Club, Robert Trent Jones, Jr. utilized existing hazards to create a labyrinth of ravines, jungles, and natural streams.

MORNING, NOON, OR NIGHT

The outdoor terrace at the Café Hanalei offers dramatic views of Hanalei Bay.

The hotel's interior design draws upon the brilliant colors of Kauai's lush, diverse landscape—greens from the rainforests, yellows of hibiscus, reds of the ohia flower, and sand from the Hanalei Bay tidepools. In each bathroom is the "magic" window, which—with just a flip of a switch—changes from clear to opaque.

Dining options are as magnificent as the scenery. Above the gentle breaking waves and offering a secluded view of the fiery sunsets, an oceanside cabana, complete with white tablecloth and flickering candles, sets the scene for the ultimate romantic dinner. Cafe Hanalei is a favorite for its stunning views and its luscious cuisine, while the Living Room, by the lobby, serves afternoon tea, cocktails, and nightly "pupus" (hors d'oeuvres).

Just as the fabled Bali Hai "calls you," the two Princeville Resort courses tucked between the sea and 4,421-foot-high Mount Namolokama entice and captivate. The twenty-seven-hole Makai Course is really three courses in one, with each nine—the Ocean, the Lakes, and the Woods—having a distinct, scenic flavor that's reflected in its name.

But the real challenge plays out on the Prince, a rugged course that chugs uphill, jumps ravines, and careens downhill like a roller coaster. Here there's no need for architectural gimmicks—Mother Nature has taken care of it all. Holes are bordered or bisected by jungles, deep perilous gorges, and creeks that have flowed here for thousands of years. Hole 12, Eagle's Nest, is a 390-yard par-four that has golfers teeing off one hundred feet above a slender fairway lined by a dense jungle. If the fairway is found by a precise drive, then the approach shot is headed to a green set in an amphitheater of natural ferns and tropical foliage with Anini Stream guarding all sides and the rear. And hole 13, aptly named Waterfall, is a 418-yard par-four whose target fairway is cut through tropical jungle to a landing area two hundred yards away. The green is tucked into the corner of a stream created by a cascading waterfall that pours from an ancient lava flow. The Prince requires accuracy, every shot you have in your bag, and extra balls.

Down the eastern coast of the island is the Kauai Marriott Resort and Beach Club. With the airport only five minutes away, guests can start enjoying the good life minutes after they land.

Located on the oceanfront on Kalapaki Beach, fronting Nawiliwili Bay, the resort has 356 rooms and vacation ownership suites. Kalapaki Beach forms its own cove at the foot of Nawiliwili Bay with inviting stretches of soft, sandy white beach. With the sun up, windsurfers, kayakers, and sailors take to the blue waters, while snorkelers plunge in for underwater exploration. Swimmers can splash around in the bay or head to the 26,000-square-foot pool.

PRINCEVILLE RESORT

KAUAI, HAWAII

RESORT RATING:

CHALLENGE	★★★★½
BEAUTY	★★★★½
LODGING	★★★★½
CUISINE	★★★★
AMENITIES	★★★★

"At the Makai Course, remember the names of the three different nines—they describe exactly what you'll find there. You'll get into pine trees on the Woods, . . . carry over water on the Lakes, and drop 150 feet down to sea level on the Oceans."

—LARRY LEE, HEAD GOLF PROFESSIONAL, PRINCEVILLE GOLF CLUB

WALLS OF GLASS

Pacific Rim cuisine is featured at Café Hanalei, where views are as spectacular inside the café as they are on the terrace.

"On the Kiele Course, save your strokes for the last two holes. They're fairly tough, facing into the trades and surrounded by water."

—KENNETH KIMURA, OPERATIONS
MANAGER, KAUAI LAGOONS GOLF CLUB

RESORT RATING:	
CHALLENGE	★★★★☆
BEAUTY	★★★★☆
LODGING	★★★★
CUISINE	★★★☆
AMENITIES	★★★★

ARTISTIC ACCENTS

Kauai's cultural heritage and aloha spirit are evident throughout the resort, from beautifully clad staff members to artwork and sculpture that grace the grounds.

Reminiscent of the Hearst Castle pool, it incorporates an island of royal palms, swim-up soothing whirlpools housed in separate areas, Roman columns, and waterfalls cascading from the reflecting pool above.

Duke's Canoe Club along the ocean serves up a good time and great food. Lining the walls of this casual restaurant/lounge are photographs of legendary Duke Kahanamoku and other famous Hawaii beachboys. And breakfast by the pool will satisfy even the hungriest guest with a sumptuous buffet of fresh island fruits, omelettes, and French toast.

Next to the Marriott Resort is Kauai Lagoons, with two award-winning courses. The

LIHU'E, HAWAII

KAUAI MARRIOTT

RESORT AND BEACH CLUB

Mokihana, a very playable resort-type course, features outstanding views of Mount Waialeale, the extinct volcano that created the island of Kauai. But it's Kiele that gets golfers' adrenaline flowing. The course has golfers hitting along cliffside fairways to greens that precariously hang over the craggy coastline and over imposing ravines filled with tropical fruit trees and a series of lagoons.

To navigate the course, players should think about it in terms of its two nines. The front is more difficult; but on the back nine, magnificent ocean views create some formidable distractions.

The signature hole, number 16, is a 330-yard, par-four where the ocean borders the left side of the fairway, which perilously slopes downhill and is usually downwind. The green, built on a small peninsula that juts into the churning sea, has a picturesque lighthouse nearby. As if the course didn't have enough interest, each hole has a unique affiliation with an animal or mystical being and is marked at the tee box by a white marble statue. Of course, the eighteenth hole features the Golden Bear, in tribute to the golfer who masterminded the course.

STEP INTO PARADISE

Guests are warmly welcomed as they step into

the lobby, where the authentic décor reminds

visitors of Hawaii's timeless traditions.

GOLFING

KAUAI MARRIOTT RESORT AND BEACH CLUB

KAUAI LAGOONS GOLF CLUB

ARCHITECT: JACK NICKLAUS

KIELE COURSE
Par: 72
Bermuda fairways and greens
Yardage/Rating/Slope:

Gold tees
7,070/73.7/137

Blue tees
6,674/71.4/131

White tees
6,164/69.1/125

Red tees
5,417/66.5/123

WATER WONDERS

One of Hawaii's largest swimming pools

resides in the Kauai Marriott, bordered

by five soothing whirlpools and a series

of waterfalls cascading from the

reflecting pool in the Aupaka Terrace.

BACK NINE BEAUTY

Kiele's signature hole is on the back nine. At 330

yards, the par-four hole number 16 ends on a green

that juts into the sea. Panoramic views include a small

lighthouse that protects the inner harbor.

KAUAI MARRIOTT RESORT AND BEACH CLUB
KAUAI, HAWAII

Experience the irresistible combination of gracious Hawaiian hospitality and luxurious accommodations.

• Spend hours on secluded Kalapaki Beach, a quarter-mile-long white sand beach.
• Glide through the seas by kayak, windboard, or sailboat, or plunge into scuba diving, snorkeling, or fishing.
• Relax at one of Hawaii's largest swimming pools, surrounded by five soothing whirlpools and four cascading waterfalls.
• Play tennis, take a hike, ride a horse, or explore the nearby wonders of Wailua Falls and Waimea Canyon.

FULL CIRCLE

A quarter mile of white sand beach and two spectacular golf courses form a nearly perfect circle, with the Kauai Marriott at its center.

YOUR CHARIOT AWAITS
Most guests at the Kauai Marriott Resort and Beach can't wait to jump in their golf carts and hit the Kauai Lagoons Golf Club.

SOOTHING AND SERENE
In the heart of the Kauai Marriott and surrounded by a tropical garden forest featuring indigenous flora, ponds, and waterfalls, the Garden of Kalapaki is an ideal setting for elegant events.

KAUAI MARRIOTT RESORT AND BEACH CLUB

KAUAI LAGOONS
GOLF CLUB

MOKIHANA COURSE
Par: 72
Bermuda fairways and greens
Yardage/Rating/Slope:

Gold tees
6,960/73.1/127

Blue tees
6,578/70.9/122

White tees
6,136/68.8/117

Red tees
5,607/67.0/116

ON THE EDGE

The golf courses at Kauai
Lagoons Golf Club edge
the beautiful and pristine
Kalapaki Bay.

GOLFERS' WARNING

One of the biggest difficulties in golfing on Kauai is maintaining concentration despite breathtaking distractions like eighty-foot cliffs and the stone ruins of ancient places of worship.

EXPERIENCING

HYATT REGENCY KAUAI RESORT AND SPA

Guests experience the ambience of a classic Hawaiian resort, where volcanic cliffs and ribbon waterfalls form a garden paradise like no other.

• Enjoy fresh seafood under a thatched roof on a romantic lagoon island, or sample lavish buffets overlooking Keoneloa Bay.

• From snorkeling and scuba diving to swimming and windsurfing, find uncounted ways to celebrate the sun.

• Sip tropical beverages beside a sparkling pool or take a romantic stroll along beautiful Poipu beach.

• Unwind with a Turkish steam, sauna, whirlpool, and open-air lava rock showers in the spectacular Anara spa and fitness center.

PALM-STUDDED

At the Hyatt Regency Kauai Resort and Spa, no building stands taller than the tallest coconut tree, a tribute to the natural beauty of the rolling mountains and pristine tidal pools.

Situated on Kauai's south side, the Hyatt Regency Kauai Resort and Spa is a lavish 602-room hotel, located on fifty meticulously landscaped oceanfront acres. Elegant but casual, the resort is built into a hillside overlooking beautiful Keoneloa Bay.

This side of the island enjoys sunshine just about all year. The Resort's five-hundred-yard white sand beach draws swimmers, snorkelers, and windsurfers. With two pools and swimming lagoons, the Hyatt satisfies everyone. For a leisurely swim there's the sheltered pool, while the "action" pool, with waterfalls, a 150-foot water slide, and volleyball, provides true excitement. And five acres of meandering saltwater swimming lagoons offer a tropical diversion.

At the PGA Grand Slam, only the winners of the Master, the U.S. Open, the British Open, or the PGA Championship get to compete at the Poipu Bay Golf Course, adjacent to the Hyatt Regency. But guests are lucky—they need no credentials to play. The Poipu Bay Course is backed by lush emerald mountains and sculpted

KOLOA, HAWAII	RESORT RATING:	
	CHALLENGE	★★★★
HYATT REGENCY KAUAI	BEAUTY	★★★★✫
	LODGING	★★★★✫
	CUISINE	★★★★
RESORT AND SPA	AMENITIES	★★★★✫

from a rolling plateau eight stories above the expansive blue waters of the Pacific. This ocean links-style course features seven holes with water hazards and ancient Hawaiian *heiau* (sacred places), and includes over thirty-five acres of colorfully landscaped tropical plants and flowers within its 210 acres. And even the most focused golfer might have trouble concentrating among nature's parade of native nene geese, rare Hawaiian monk seals, green sea turtles, and humpback whales.

Leaving the lush island of Kauai and arriving on the Big Island, some might wonder why they made the journey to a place resembling the surface of the moon. For miles and miles there's nothing but barren exposed black lava rock that's virtually free of vegetation and other forms of life. But then, like a mirage are elegant resorts strung like precious pearls. The contrast is intoxicating—jet black lava, emerald green grass, and tall palms, all poised against the sapphire ocean. And set in their midst are some of the best golf courses in the world.

The grande dame of the area, Mauna Kea Beach Hotel sits on sixty oceanfront acres along the shimmering Kohala Coast with the tallest mountain on earth from base to peak, Mauna Kea, crowned in snow, looming behind it. Classically elegant, the luxury hotel with concrete and teak walls exhibits a priceless collection of 1,600 Asian and Pacific Island pieces.

A GARDEN PARADISE

This classic Hawaiian resort is set on fifty acres of lush tropical gardens and meticulously manicured courtyards teeming with rare birds and tropical wildlife.

HYATT REGENCY KAUAI RESORT AND SPA

POIPU BAY GOLF COURSE
KOLOA, HAWAII

Architect: Robert Trent Jones, Jr.
Tour stops: PGA Grand Slam
of Golf
Par: 72
Bermuda fairways and greens
Yardage/Rating/Slope:
<u>Championship tees</u>
6,959/73.4/132
<u>Forward tees</u>
5,241/70.4/122

GRAND SLAM

Since 1994, the links-style
golf course designed by
Robert Trent Jones, Jr. has
been home to the PGA
Grand Slam of Golf, one of
the world's most exclusive
tournaments.

"Typically our golf course involves a bit of a breeze throughout the day, so if in doubt, go with the longer of two clubs. Our typical grain direction is the same as the wind, making downwind putts relatively quick, and into the wind relatively slow."

—MICHAEL CASTILLO, HEAD GOLF PROFESSIONAL, POIPU BAY GOLF COURSE

GARDEN PARADISE

Water dominates the landscaping at the Hyatt Regency Kauai Resort and Spa, which incorporates five acres of natural, beach-rimmed lagoons.

Gilded disciples, antiques from Thailand, greet you at a lobby entrance that opens to blue sky and azure water. Every hallway and corner is graced with something special. The most prized piece is the pink granite Buddha, sculpted in seventh-century India. This five-foot, three-inch figure, imposing yet serene, is positioned according to Buddhist tradition, with his heart above the level of a man's eye.

Outside the hotel, its natural white sand beach is cradled in the arms of Kaunaoa Bay. Towering old coconut palms shade it and expansive green lawns border it. The atmosphere seduces even the most harried traveler to unwind by napping in a hammock, building a sand castle, or floating in the gentle currents beneath wispy clouds.

Now that the Mauna Kea Beach Hotel is a mature property, the resort's trees are tall, the flowers and plantings lush. And traditions have grown up around it—the manta rays that cruise in the night along the shore, the Tuesday night luau, and the lavish Sunday brunch on the Terrace.

RESORT RATING:

CHALLENGE	★★★★½
BEAUTY	★★★★½
LODGING	★★★★½
CUISINE	★★★★½
AMENITIES	★★★★½

MAUNA KEA BEACH HOTEL

KOHALA COAST, HAWAII

The cuisine at Mauna Kea is a symphony of epicurean pleasures. Hawaii regional cuisine, a blend of the classic culinary traditions of Europe and Asia, nuanced with American flair and based on the overwhelming bounty of Hawaii's land and sea, is featured at Mauna Kea. Sunday brunch on the Terrace is an extravagant spread of awesome salads, desserts, hot and cold entreés, sushi, plus an assortment of dim sum. At the Gazebo bar the adventurous sip an icy-cold Fredrico, a blend of Jack Daniels and tropical juices that delivers sweetness with a kick.

If it seems almost impossible to have built a resort on a prehistoric lava flow, imagine building a golf course on it. But the legendary Robert Trent Jones, Sr. did. And the techniques he was forced to invent are still used more than thirty years later.

An engineering feat, Mauna Kea Golf Course occupies a heavenly spot. Set atop a five-thousand-year-old volcanic lava flow, the course features ocean views from most of the eighteen greens, undulating fairways, steep greens, uphill holes, doglegs, and 120 strategically placed bunkers—nearly twice those of the typical golf course. And the contrast of rugged jet black lava beds, emerald green fairways, sweeping panoramic views of the blue Pacific, and the snowcapped Mauna Kea is startling.

The par-three third hole is Mauna Kea's most famous and one of the most photographed holes in the world. It plays from a cliffside tee across a frothing blue bay to a cliffside green. Getting across the ocean where the surging Pacific inlet water races to meet the rocky shoreline is just half the battle for golfers; the other is facing the seven bunkers guarding the undulating large green. But as daunting as the third hole is, it's not Mauna Kea's toughest par-three. That's the eleventh. The downhill tee shot drops one hundred feet from tee to green, which is surrounded by four bunkers.

BALMY BREEZES

Oriental art and Robert Trent Jones, Sr.'s legendary golf course grace the Mauna Kea Resort. Ocean breezes can quickly become tradewinds, a crucial factor in playing golf here.

BIG ISLAND MASTERPIECE

On Mauna Kea's third hole, surging Pacific inlet water meets the rocky shoreline, affording one of Hawaii's most spectacular views.

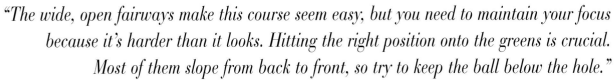

"The wide, open fairways make this course seem easy, but you need to maintain your focus because it's harder than it looks. Hitting the right position onto the greens is crucial. Most of them slope from back to front, so try to keep the ball below the hole."

—SCOTT BRIDGES, HEAD GOLF PROFESSIONAL, MAUNA KEA GOLF COURSE

GOLFING

MAUNA KEA BEACH HOTEL

MAUNA KEA GOLF COURSE
KOHALA COAST, HAWAII

Architect: Robert Trent Jones, Sr.
Par: 72
Bermuda fairways and greens
Yardage/Rating/Slope:

Black tees
7,114/73.6/143

Blue tees
6,737/71.9/138

Orange tees
6,365/70.1/134

White tees
5,277/70.2*/124*

*Women's ratings

A FULL DAY

Guests who play at the Mauana Kea Golf Course like to pack in as full a day of golf as possible, and the temperate climate allows them to do so, even when the shadows start getting long.

EXPERIENCING

HAPUNA BEACH PRINCE HOTEL

With the efficiency of a full-scale resort, this small tropical hideaway boasts a full menu of activities.

• Pamper yourself with the latest in therapeutic massage and a variety of spa treatments, including a poi body wrap.

• Take to the air for a helicopter tour, or explore the clear-blue cove where giant sea turtles lazily drop in for a visit.

• Spend an evening stargazing from your private lanai, or join an astronomer, who shares his knowledge and telescope.

• With five restaurants and two lounges, indulge your every taste and mood, from a casual breakfast buffet overlooking the ocean to a poolside spot for lunch and refreshments.

WHITE SAND WONDER

Atop an exclusive crescent of white sand beach sits the Hapuna Beach Prince Hotel, which offers a full range of activities.

GOLFING HAPUNA-STYLE

An easy walk from the hotel, the par-72 Hapuna Golf Course was designed by Arnold Palmer and Ed Seay and opened in 1992.

AWARD-WINNING BEACH

The Hapuna Beach Prince Hotel is the only hotel on the long stretch of Hapuna to be named America's number-one beach.

Right next door, on the lava coast, is Mauna Kea's sister hotel, the Hapuna Beach Prince Hotel. This dramatic, contemporary low-rise hotel, nestled in natural windswept bluffs overlooking the silky white sands of Hapuna Beach, resonates with the atmosphere of a small tropical hideaway.

Sixteen regal royal palms line the entrance to the hotel. Upon entering the lobby, guests are immediately captivated by the panoramic view of the blue waters of the Pacific. And while they may want to linger, all the generously sized rooms enjoy ocean views. There's even the 8,000-square-foot Hapuna Suite, a private villa, for that ultimate travel fantasy.

HAPUNA BEACH PRINCE HOTEL

KOHALA COAST, HAWAII

RESORT RATING:	
CHALLENGE	★★★★
BEAUTY	★★★★½
LODGING	★★★★½
CUISINE	★★★★
AMENITIES	★★★★

The biggest challenge the Hapuna Golf Course faced at its debut was being compared to the Mauna Kea Golf Course. But Hapuna, very different in design, style, and feel, proved to have its own magic and challenge. Nestled into the dramatic natural contours of the land from the shoreline to about seven hundred feet above sea level, this Scottish links–style course is set on an arid lava hillside with native grasses and shrubs and is practically devoid of trees. Hapuna does more than attract golfers; environmentally sensitive, it draws a variety of birds to the area including the rare pu'eo, Hawaiian owl, and nene.

LOW-RISE LUXURY

The Hapuna Beach Prince rises only a few stories above the surrounding bluffs, yet each room enjoys spectacular views and easy access to all facilities.

A wild course with many undulations, Hapuna presents a variety of harrowing shots that include carries over ravines and untamed natural expanses where jagged lava rocks can easily devour your ball and flesh if you go searching. Add trade winds and tight fairways, and this intriguing course demands accuracy. Even the roller-coaster cart path offers thrills that may have golfers wondering where the grab bar is.

THE ESCAPE BEGINS

Arrival at the hotel begins long before guests get

there, with a winding drive past manicured fairways

and an entry framed by stately royal palms.

"On many courses, bunkers guard the front of the greens and force you to hit the ball high into the air, allowing the trade winds to gobble it up. This course was designed to accommodate the trades; you can play a run-up shot onto every green."

—RONALD CASTILLO, HEAD GOLF PROFESSIONAL, HAPUNA GOLF COURSE

GOLFING

HAPUNA GOLF COURSE
KOHALA COAST, HAWAII

Architects: Arnold Palmer, Ed Seay

Par: 72

Bermuda fairways, dwarf Bermuda greens

Yardage/Rating/Slope:

Tournament tees
6,875 /72.5/134

Championship tees
6,534/70.4/130

Regular tees
6,029/66.8/122

Forward tees
5,067/68.9°/117*

*Women's ratings

AWARD-WINNING GOLF

Aloha magazine rated the Hapuna Golf Course one of the best par-fives in Hawaii in 1998, and *Golf Digest* has given the course its Service Aces Top 50 award.

Prehistoric ponds, a beach with a living reef, dramatic lava sculptures, historic preserves, and ancient sites sat quietly idle and were ignored for years until two dreamers, Francis H. I'i Brown, a golfer of royal Hawaiian lineage, and his friend Noboru Gotoh, became enamored with this beautifully hallowed ground. Their vision became Mauna Lani, a 3,200-acre resort, home to two luxury hotels—Mauna Lani Bay Hotel and the Orchid at Mauna Lani—and two of Hawaii's most famous golf courses, Francis H. I'i Brown North and South, carved out of a volcanic landscape like works of art.

The original course, the Francis H. I'i Brown Golf Course, was split in half, and two nines were added to make two "half new"

THE MAUNA LANI BAY HOTEL

AND BUNGALOWS

courses. Players will be mesmerized by the contrast of colors: emerald green manicured fairways, jet black a'a lava, pure white sand traps, reddish-brown pahoehoe lava, and azure-blue sea. Both courses, framed by the lava, present a unique Big Island experience—hit your ball into the lava field and it will ricochet wildly. If the golfing gods are smiling, your ball may land smack in the middle of the green. But more likely it will be lost forever in a rocky grave where it can be seen but not retrieved. (Never venture into a lava field—you'll trip and cut yourself or rip your clothes. Hardly worth it to recover a ball that's probably fatally scarred.)

STELLAR SELECTIONS
Dining at Mauna Lani Bay includes five distinctive restaurants, ranging from the romantic oceanfront Canoe House to the elegant Bay Terrace.

The South Course, former home of the Skins Game, snakes through the sixteenth-century Kaniku lava field, a relatively young flow of rugged a'a lava. Two of its most striking and scenic holes are numbers 7 and 15, playing along the ocean. number 7, a downhill par-three where on-shore wind comes into play, has golfers teeing off to a large two-tiered green. But any shot to the left will land in sand, lava, or the Pacific.

AT YOUR SERVICE

The ultimate in accommodations at Mauna Lani Bay are the five private bungalows, with two master bedrooms, three baths, private swimming pool, whirlpool spa, and round-the-clock butler service.

EXPERIENCING

THE MAUNA LANI BAY HOTEL AND BUNGALOWS

The Mauna Lani is a treasure trove of restored archaeological sites, fishponds, petroglyphs, and cave dwellings.

• Experience the spirit of aloha from the moment you arrive, when you're greeted by name and presented a fresh flower lei and a glass of chilled tropical juice.

• Tour the ancient fishponds and petroglyphs with the resident Hawaiian historian, or help feed the reef sharks, manta rays, and tropical fish on a tour with the staff marine biologist.

• Become certified in scuba diving and explore spectacular underwater sea caves, archways, and lava tubes.

• Float in the peaceful waters on a view board raft, or don fins, mask, and snorkel to see reef fish and green sea turtles.

• Visit Mauna Lani Spa with its unique menu of treatments, from Hawaiian stone therapy to Watsu and oceanside massages.

LAVA-BOTTOM GREENS

The North Course's signature hole is the charming par-three number 17, whose green lies at the bottom of a deep lava bowl.

WARM WATERS

Guests of the Mauna Lani Bay Hotel and Bungalows can step off the resort grounds and into tranquil Pacific waters.

A BEAUTIFUL CHALLENGE

The South Course's hole 7 is a picturesque par

three, framed by the ocean on the left and a salt-

and-pepper sand dune on the right.

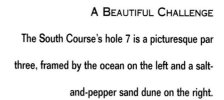

GOLFING

MAUNA LANI BAY HOTEL AND BUNGALOWS
FRANCIS H. I'I BROWN GOLF CLUB

Architect: Nelson and Haworth
Tour stops: 1980 Senior
Skins Game

SOUTH COURSE
Par: 72
Bermuda/sea Pas Palum
fairways and greens
Yardage/Rating/Slope:
<u>Black tees</u>
6,938/72.8/133
<u>Blue tees</u>
6,436/70.5/128
<u>White tees</u>
6,025/68.3/124
<u>Gold tees</u>
5,128/69.6/117

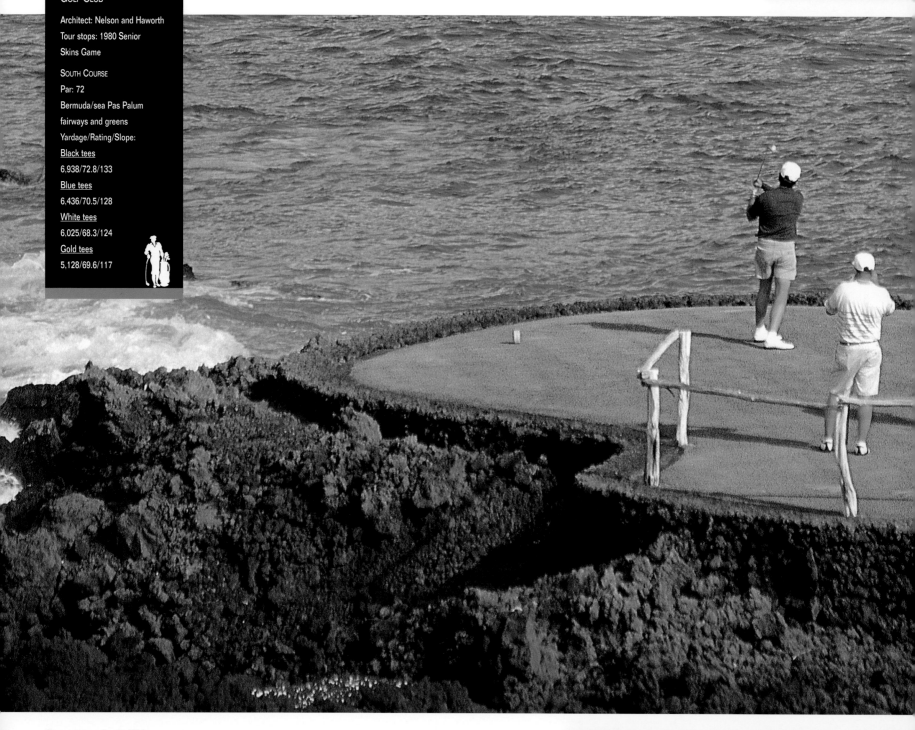

BUILT ON A LAVA FLOW

The South Course's over-the-water number 15 is one of

the most photographed golf holes in the world.

TROPICAL RETREAT

The 350 guest rooms and suites are

beautifully appointed in cool white

and beige, with plush furnishings

and private lanais.

The signature number 15 is a challenging par-three. The tee-off area puts golfers face to face with a 196-yard carry over the surging ocean to a two-tiered large green with a salt-and-pepper sand dune on the right and a feathery grove of kiawe trees as a backdrop.

Only minutes from the courses is the Mauna Lani Bay Hotel. Simple elegance and clean unencumbered lines

define this luxury hotel. Once inside, instead of heading to the usual registration counter, guests are given a glass of chilled tropical juice and escorted to sit at a teak desk to complete their check-in much as they would conduct a private business transaction.

The interior of the hotel reflects its Oriental influence. A huge open atrium with towering palms reaches to the sky above, while a meandering lagoon stocked with koi, stingrays, and sharks winds its way through the hotel. A Plexiglas waterfall provides a perfect backdrop for pictures. And the brightly blue tiled staircase leads to a landing where grass-skirted dancers perform the hula, while musicians play the ukulele and guests sip exotic island drinks.

Delicate potted orchids, dark wood, indirect lighting, and mat-like carpet in the rooms radiate an atmosphere that makes you want to remove your shoes immediately. A private lanai overlooking the ocean beckons guests to stop and sit a while, feel the gentle breeze brush against their skin, listen to the waves roll in, and watch the moonbeams dance on the black sea.

Dining is an integral part of the Mauna Lani experience. The romantic Canoe House hugs the ocean, affording diners a magnificent view of Kohala Coast sunsets. The interior theme revolves around the single most important artifact of Hawaiian fishing culture—the Hawaiian canoe. Suspended from the ceiling is a koa fish canoe, while the entire back wall depicts an ancient petroglyph field. On the menu are such delectable dishes as nori-wrapped tempura ahi with wasabi soy sauce and Asian relish, wasabi lobster tempura on a stick with Japanese cucumber, pickled plus salad in a two-mustard butter sauce, and gratinée of bananas and macadamia nuts in Kahlúa.

"The South Course features wide fairways, a colorful contrast between the lava and the grass, and not many trees. Most people try to hit high and avoid the lava, but you need to play low shots when the trade winds are blowing."

—STEVEN HOOKANO, HEAD GOLF PROFESSIONAL, FRANCIS H. I'I BROWN GOLF CLUB

ANCIENT FISHPONDS

The essence and spiritual center of the Mauna Lani Resort is the Kalahuipua'a fishponds, which date back to 250 B.C. and are still home to countless fish.

RESORT RATING:

CHALLENGE	★★★★
BEAUTY	★★★★★
LODGING	★★★★☆
CUISINE	★★★★☆
AMENITIES	★★★★

KOHALA COAST, HAWAII

THE ORCHID AT MAUNA LANI

Guests can take the shuttle to the Orchid at Mauna Lani, a classically elegant hotel placed in the center of Hawaiian splendor. This affords them an unparalleled set of options to occupy their time. One night they might dine in an ornate restaurant and the next, eat under the stars with sand at their feet.

It's easy to restore both body and soul at the Spa Without Walls, where the activities and treatments are at the ocean's edge. The white sand beach acts like a giant "floor" for yoga while the pounding surf rolls in. Tai chi classes take place under the shade of palm trees, "power walks" through ancient lava flows, and aqua aerobics in the oceanfront swimming pool. And Lomi Lomi massage can be performed in the privacy of a white cabana alongside the shores of Puaoa Bay, or a no-oil Thai massage in loose-fitting clothing on a floor mat of a wooden teahouse, nestled adjacent to trickling waterfalls and lush tropical gardens. Even tennis takes a different form at the Orchid. "Beyond Tennis" is an innovative approach that focuses development of the mind, body, and spirit rather than technical proficiencies.

Guests can learn about Hawaii's past from "Beach Boys." From the turn of the century to the late 1950s, spirited, ocean-wise, and charming local boys gathered on the beach and shared their knowledge of the ocean and the Hawaiian culture with visitors. In the spirit of the tradition, throughout the day the Orchid's Beach Boys demonstrate weaving using coconut and hala fronds, lei making, and outrigger canoe paddling, and take guests on historic hikes.

For a change of pace, guests can return to the sea aboard a traditional double-hulled sailing canoe. The Hahalua Lele and Flying Manta Ray offer short coastal journeys with information about Hawaii's legends, folklore, traditions, and customs.

Golfers who know about Hawaii's offerings will want to play Mauna Lani's splendid North Course. Draped over ancient lava flows, the North Course emphasizes rolling fairways and thick kiawe forests, which often come into play as hazards. For added interest, a 230-acre protected archaeological district lies on the northern boundary, while herds of feral goats frequent the course. At the par-three seventeenth hole, players stand on an elevated tee and drive the ball 132 yards to a short fairway and green surrounded on all sides by lava, forming a deep black canyon.

Back in the 1940s, when wide-eyed visitors arrived by steamship and on prop planes, they were struck by the exotic nature of the islands, the gentle nature of the people, and the easy living. It is this magical era of yesteryear that the exclusive Four Seasons Resort, Hualalai has re-created.

Named for the volcanic mountain that formed this lava coastline, Hualalai is beautifully secluded in historic Kaupulehu, an area rich in Hawaiian culture and history.

RESORT WITHIN A RESORT

The Orchid at Mauna Lani is set within the 3,200-acre Mauna Lani resort community.

INVITING ATMOSPHERE

The Orchid at Mauna Lani houses the upscale, innovative Grill, where local seafood, game, and produce are the stars of the show.

THE ORCHID AT MAUNA LANI
KOHALA COAST, HAWAII

Whether it's golf, tennis, snorkeling, historic hikes, or relaxing in a hammock, you'll find every imaginable luxury here.

• At the "Spa Without Walls," learn tai chi under the palm trees, take a power walk through ancient lava flows, or experience Hawaii's ancient techniques and treatments.

• Climb into a traditional double-hulled sailing canoe and hear Hawaii's legends, folklore, and traditions while enjoying the scenic Kohala Coast.

• Delight in a culinary symphony of artistic presentation and world-class cuisine, from oceanfront lunches to upscale dining under a canopy of stars.

• Step out onto your private lanai and relax to the sounds of nearby waterfalls and sights of the ocean, mountain, or lush tropical gardens.

LAZY LAGOON

The white sand lagoon fronting the hotel offers a myriad of ocean activities, such as snorkeling, scuba diving, sunset sailing, and deep-sea fishing.

THE ORCHID AT MAUNA LANI

FRANCIS H. I'I BROWN
GOLF CLUB
KOHALA COAST, HAWAII

Architect: Nelson and Haworth
Tour stops: 1980 Senior
Skins Game

NORTH COURSE
Par: 72
Bermuda/sea Pas Palum
fairways and greens
Yardage/Rating/Slope:
Black tees
6,913/73.2/136
Blue tees
6,601/71.7/133
White tees
6,086/69.4/129
Gold tees
5,383/70.6/120

DANGEROUS BEAUTY

A tidal pond, sand, and

heliotrope trees create

picturesque but harrowing

hazards on the

North Course's

nineth hole.

The low-density resort occupies a stunning ebony lava landscape, edged by the sapphire Pacific and framed by lush tropical flowers and trees. Throughout, ancient trails, petroglyphs, and fish ponds have been preserved.

But what sets Hualalai apart from the other resorts along this coast is that there's no one central structure and no hallways to proclaim it a hotel. Instead, the hallways to the guest rooms are meandering rock paths and the elegant rooms are in two-story bungalows arranged in coastal crescents.

The intimate lobby, in rich dark mahogany and teak, opens to a magnificent view of the Pacific Rim. An inlaid-wood floor shows the various islands of the Pacific. And towering

RESORT RATING:		KAILUA-KONA, HAWAII
CHALLENGE	★★★★	
BEAUTY	★★★★★	**FOUR SEASONS RESORT**
LODGING	★★★★★	
CUISINE	★★★★⯨	
AMENITIES	★★★★	HUALALAI

above, a live coral reef acquarium replicates the marine environment directly in front of the resort.

While the resort offers five different pools, the 2.5-million-gallon natural free-form scuba and snorkeling aquarium is sure to grab guests' attention. Carved from an ancient lava flow, it's stocked with 3,500 fish and three spotted eagle rays, and is only steps away from the ocean.

With so many world-class amenities, it may be hard to say which is the crowning glory of Hualalai. But in the golfing world, there is only one right answer: the Jack Nicklaus Course, site of the Senior PGA Tour's MasterCard Championship. Open only to resort homeowners and guests of the Four Seasons, this perfectly manicured course, where fairways look like greens, takes golfers on a journey through lava walls and along the edge of the ocean.

AWE-INSPIRING SETTING

A 1996 addition to the Kona Coast, the Four Seasons Resort, Hualalai, adds a sense of the new to historic Kaupulehu, where beautiful surroundings combine with traditional Hawaiian hospitality.

SMOOTH SAILING

The Tifdwarf grass on the Jack Nicklaus signature course at

Hualalai Resort Golf Club makes for relatively smooth

greens and immaculate putting surfaces.

GOLFING

FOUR SEASONS RESORT, HUALALI
HUALALAI RESORT GOLF CLUB

Architect: Jack Nicklaus
Tour stops: Senior PGA
MasterCard Championship
Par: 72
Bermuda Tifdwarf fairways
and greens
Yardage/Rating/Slope:
Mahope tees
7,117/73.7/131
Championship tees
6,632/71.5/126
Regular tees
6,032/68.9, 74.0*/121, 125*
MUA tees
5,374/66.3, 70.4*/116, 118*
*Women's ratings

RESORT TOUR

The Jack Nicklaus–

designed Hualalai Resort

Golf Club starts at an

oasis, winds through the

resort, and ends at

the ocean.

PUNISHING BUT PICTURESQUE

Hualalai Golf Club, below, is golfing at its best, with dramatic ocean

views and challenging lava rock obstacles. Four Seasons Resort,

Hualalai, gives frustrated golfers welcome sanctuary.

While many of the fairways are wide, ninety-five strategically placed bunkers and lava walls add to the challenge of the course.

The two holes that will be etched in golfers' minds forever are numbers 7 and 12. On hole 7, a 556-yard par-five, players tee off from the highest point on the course, leaving a second shot that must traverse a ten-yard gap between two imposing lava walls. Hole 12, a 167-yard par-three, is one of the most unusual holes in Hawaii with a large, deep sand bunker in the middle of the green. A perfect ending is the march up the final hole with its clubhouse as the backdrop.

Opulent and theatrical, the mega Waikoloa Beach Resort is unlike any other on the Kohala Coast. It's fantasy, discovery, and adventure. And at the heart of this over-the-top extravaganza is the Hilton Waikoloa Village, pools, lagoons, canals, restaurants, shopping, tennis, golf, and a spa—a virtual Polynesian Disneyland.

To visualize the look, start with ancient Greece, with its huge towering colonnades and gigantic urns. Now add a lagoon stocked with tropical fish, a Venetian canal, and some tall palms. At the Hilton, guests don't have to walk; they can be transported via a sleek mahogany motorized canal boat (built by Disney and shipped "whole" to Hawaii). Or if they prefer, they can climb aboard the Swiss twenty-four-passenger tram and head to the bounty of activities and lodging.

And the Hilton has cooked up some unique pastimes. Dolphin Quest is a program in which guests come face to face with these playful creatures. Water activities are endless. Guests can enjoy snorkeling, paddle boats, kayaks, water bikes and suncats at the Lagoon Beach, have a thrill of a ride down the 175-foot water slide, or swim through a Niagara-like waterfall.

"Our user-friendly Jack Nicklaus signature course welcomes high handicappers and scratch golfers alike. The generous landing areas, relatively flat greens, and immaculate putting surfaces have given many golfers the best scores of their golfing career."

—WADE NISHIMOTO, HEAD GOLF PROFESSIONAL, HUALALAI RESORT GOLF CLUB

FOUR SEASONS RESORT, HUALALAI

KAILUA-KONA, HAWAII

On the Big Island of Hawaii, the Four Seasons Resort is an intimate enclave of beachfront and golf club bungalows.

• Enjoy blissful solitude in a tropical hideaway, where lanais offer spacious access to the open air, bathrooms open onto lush gardens, and ocean views stretch from every guest's room.

• Awake for a swim at sunrise or luxuriate in an oceanfront pool, where chilled towels and Evian spritzers are at your beck and call.

• Snorkel offshore or in the man-made King's Pond, home to nearly three thousand reef fish.

• Rejuvenate with an open-air massage, a workout at the Sports Club and Spa, or match after match of tennis.

• Immerse yourself in Island heritage at the Hawaiian Interpretive Center or learn traditional Hawaiian outrigging from Hualalai's Alaka'i Nalu, the "leaders of the waves."

DECISIONS, DECISIONS

The spectacular pool fronts the ocean at Four Seasons Resort, Hualalai, giving guests the difficult task of deciding where to go first.

"Our Bermuda 328 grass has a little more grain than bentgrass. If you check out the hole, you'll see a brown or worn-out side, which is actually the root side. . . .

RESORT RATING:	
CHALLENGE	★★★⯪
BEAUTY	★★★★
LODGING	★★★★
CUISINE	★★★★
AMENITIES	★★★★

The balls will always break toward the brown side of the cup."

—JAY TAISE, HEAD GOLF PROFESSIONAL,
WAIKOLOA BEACH COURSE

A KINDER COURSE

The Waikoloa Beach Course is a gentler, more fun-filled resort course than its more challenging counterpart, the Kings' Course.

They can also play tennis, indulge at the spa, dine at nine different restaurants, and head to the Kings' Shops for a potpourri of Hawaiian goodies with everything from nuts to pearls, Hawaiian T-shirts to Hawaiian art. And to prepare themselves for real golf at Waikoloa Golf Club, they can try their putters at the eighteen-hole, real grass putting green.

The Beach Course, a fun resort layout, is a contrast of black lava, green fairways, blue ocean, and palm trees. Sacred Hawaiian petroglyphs border several of the holes. But the one hole that draws all the attention is the twelfth, a 497-yard par-five that takes

HILTON

WAIKOLOA VILLAGE

KOHA KOHALA COAST, HAWAII

golfers to the edge of the sea. The Kings' Course is a Scottish-links design, wide open and flat, with enough challenge to get any golfer's game in gear.

But that's what Hawaii offers: a gorgeous setting, year-round golfing, and glorious challenges for golfers at any level. Pair that with exceptional resort amenities, and you've got what Hawaii's always being called: paradise.

UP CLOSE AND PERSONAL

Waikoloa's Dolphin Quest program is popular

with visitors of all ages. Interacting with the

dolphins makes a lasting vacation memory.

HILTON WAIKOLOA VILLAGE

At Waikoloa Beach Resort, visitors find the perfect combination of relaxation and recreation.

• Sample a plentiful array of shopping, dining, and Hawaiian entertainment at the Kings' Shops, with its boutiques, galleries, restaurants, and hula performances.

• For a taste of authentic Hawaii, view dolphins firsthand at the Dolphin Learning Center or take a tour of the petroglyphs and tropical plants.

• Relax on the white sands of Waikoloa or dip into a variety of ocean activities, from snorkeling and scuba diving to surfing and sunset cruises.

• When the lights go down, follow the torches to an exciting Polynesian revue and luau.

SO MANY SHOPS, SO LITTLE TIME

The Kings' Shops offer a wide array of

shopping and dining choices. Resort

apparel, art galleries, jewelry stores, and

a food pavilion are just a few of the

enticing venues waiting to be explored.

BEAUTIFUL AND CHALLENGING

The Kings' Course challenges golfers with huge lava rock

formations, long lakes, and an abundance of white, sandy bunkers.

Each hole includes four sets of tees for golfers of all levels of play.

HILTON WAIKOLOA VILLAGE

KOHA KOHALA COAST, HAWAII

KINGS' COURSE

Architects: Tom Weiskopf,
Jay Morrish

Par: 72

Bermuda fairways,
Tifdwarf Bermuda greens

Yardage/Rating/Slope:

Kings' tees

7,074/73.9/133

Championship tees

6,594/71.3/127

Resort tees

6,010/68.6/124

Forward tees

5,459/71.0/121

WAIKOLOA BEACH COURSE

Architect: Robert Trent Jones, Jr.

Tour stops: LPGA Match Play
Championship, U.S. Open
Qualifying, U.S. Amateur
Qualifying

Par: 70

Bermuda fairways,
Bermuda 328 greens

Yardage/Rating/Slope:

Championship tees

6,566 /71.5/133

Resort tees

5,958/68.6/126

Forward tees

5,094/69.4/119

BEST OF BOTH

The Waikoloa Beach

Course offers

breathtaking views and

challenging play.

WORK OUT THE KINKS

The Hilton Waikoloa Village offers massages for golfers' tired muscles in a seaside cabana.

FUN FOR EVERYONE

Golf at the Waikoloa Beach Resort offers thrilling play to golfers at any level.

RESOURCE INFORMATION

AMELIA ISLAND PLANTATION, Amelia Island, Florida

(888) 261-6161   www.aipfl.com

THE AMERICAN CLUB, Kohler, Wisconsin

(800) 344-2838   www.americanclub.com

ARIZONA BILTMORE RESORT AND SPA, Phoenix, Arizona

(800) 950-0086   www.arizonabiltmore.com

THE BALSAMS GRAND RESORT HOTEL, Dixville Notch, New Hampshire

(800) 255-0600   www.thebalsams.com

BARTON CREEK, Austin, Texas

(800) 336-6158   www.bartoncreek.com

BOCA RATON RESORT AND CLUB, Boca Raton, Florida

(800) 327-0101   www.bocaresort.com

THE BOULDERS, Carefree, Arizona

(800) 553-1717   www.grandbay.com/properties/boulders

BOYNE HIGHLANDS, Harbor Springs, Michigan

(800) 462-6963   www.boyne.com

THE BREAKERS, Palm Beach, Florida

(888) 273-2537   www.thebreakers.com

THE BROADMOOR, Colorado Springs, Colorado

(800) 634-7711   www.broadmoor.com

CALLAWAY GARDENS, Pine Mountain, Georgia

(800) 282-8181   www.callawaygardens.com

CHATEAU ELAN WINERY AND RESORT, Braselton, Georgia

(800) 233-9463   www.chateauelan.com

THE CLOISTER, Sea Island, Georgia

(800) 732-4752   www.seaisland.com

THE COEUR d'ALENE, Coeur d'Alene, Idaho

(800) 688-5253   www.cdaresort.com

CRYSTAL MOUNTAIN RESORT, Thompsonville, Michigan

(800) 968-4676   www.crystalmtn.com

DISNEY'S GRAND FLORIDIAN RESORT AND SPA, Lake Buena Vista, Florida

(407) 934-7639   www.disneyworld.com

ELKHORN RESORT, Sun Valley, Idaho

(800) 355-4676   www.elkhornresort.com

THE EQUINOX, Manchester Village, Vermont

(800) 362-4747   www.equinoxresort.com

THE FAIRMONT SCOTTSDALE PRINCESS, Scottsdale, Arizona

(800) 344-4758   www.fairmont.com

FOUR SEASONS RESORT AND CLUB, DALLAS AT LAS COLINAS, Irving, Texas

(800) 332-3442   www.fourseasons.com

FOUR SEASONS RESORT, AVIARA, Carlsbad, California

(800) 332-3442   www.fourseasons.com

FOUR SEASONS RESORT, HUALALAI, Kailua-Kona, Hawaii

(888) 340-5662   www.fourseasons.com

FOUR SEASONS RESORT, MAUI AT WAILEA, Maui, Hawaii

(800) 334-6284   www.fourseasons.com

GARLAND RESORT, Lewiston, Michigan

(800) 968-0042   www.garlandusa.com

GRAND TRAVERSE RESORT AND SPA, Acme, Michigan

(800) 748-0303   www.gtresort.com

GRAND WAILEA RESORT HOTEL AND SPA, Maui, Hawaii

(800) 888-6100   www.grandwailea.com

THE GREENBRIER, White Sulphur Springs, West Virginia

(800) 624-6070   www.greenbrier.com

GROUSE MOUNTAIN LODGE, Whitefish, Montana

(800) 321-8822   www.montanasfinest.com

HAPUNA BEACH PRINCE HOTEL, Kohala Coast, Hawaii

(800) 882-6060   www.hapunabeachprincehotel.com

HILTON WAIKOLOA VILLAGE, Koha Kohala Coast, Hawaii

(800) 445-8667   www.hilton.com

THE HOMESTEAD, Hot Springs, Virginia

(800) 838-1766   www.thehomestead.com

THE HOTEL HERSHEY, Hershey, Pennsylvania

(800) 533-3131   www.hersheypa.com

HOUND EARS CLUB, Blowing Rock, North Carolina

(828) 963-4321   www.houndears.com

HYATT GRAND CHAMPIONS, Indian Wells, California

(800) 233-1234   www.grandchampions.hyatt.com

HYATT REGENCY BEAVER CREEK RESORT AND SPA, Vail, Colorado

(800) 554-9288   www.beavercreek.hyatt.com

HYATT REGENCY GRAND CYPRESS, Orlando, Florida

(800) 233-1234   www.grandcypress.com

HYATT REGENCY LAKE LAS VEGAS RESORT, Henderson, Nevada

(800) 233-1234   www.hyatt.com

HYATT REGENCY KAUAI RESORT AND SPA, Koloa, Hawaii

(800) 742-2353   www.kauai-hyatt.com

HYATT REGENCY SCOTTSDALE AT GAINEY RANCH, Scottsdale, Arizona

(800) 233-1234   www.hyatt.com

THE INN AT BAY HARBOR, Bay Harbor, Michigan

(800) 462-6963   www.boyne.com

THE INN AT SPANISH BAY, Pebble Beach, California

(800) 654-9300   www.pebblebeach.com

INDIAN WELLS RESORT HOTEL, Indian Wells, California

(800) 248-3220   www.indianwellsresort.com

KAPALUA BAY HOTEL, Maui, Hawaii

(800) 367-8000   www.luxurycollectionhawaii.com

KAUAI MARRIOTT RESORT AND BEACH CLUB, Lihu'e, Hawaii

(800) 220-2925   www.marriott.com

KEA LANI HOTEL, Maui, Hawaii

(800) 659-4100   www.kealani.com

KEYSTONE RESORT, Keystone, Colorado

(888) 222-9298   www.keystoneresort.com

KIAWAH ISLAND GOLF AND TENNIS RESORT, Kiawah Island, South Carolina

(800) 654-2924   www.kiawah-island.com

KINGSMILL RESORT, Williamsburg, Virginia

(800) 832-5665   www.kingsmill.com

LA COSTA RESORT AND SPA, Carlsbad, California

(800) 854-5000   www.lacosta.com

LA QUINTA RESORT AND CLUB, La Quinta, California

(800) 598-3828   www.laquintaresort.com

THE LODGE AND SPA AT CORDILLERA, Edwards, Colorado

(800) 877-3529   www.cordillera-vail.com

THE LODGE AT KOELE, Lanai, Hawaii

(800) 321-4666   www.lanairesorts.com

THE LODGE AT PEBBLE BEACH, Pebble Beach, California

(800) 654-9300   www.pebblebeach.com

THE LODGE AT VENTANA CANYON, Tucson, Arizona

(800) 828-5701   www.wyndham.com

LOEWS VENTANA CANYON RESORT, Tucson, Arizona

(800) 234-5117   www.loewshotel.com

THE MANELE BAY HOTEL, Lanai, Hawaii

(800) 321-4666   www.lanairesorts.com

MARRIOTT'S CAMELBACK INN, Scottsdale, Arizona

(800) 242-2635   www.camelbackinn.com

MARRIOTT DESERT SPRINGS RESORT, Palm Desert, California

(800) 331-3112   www.desertspringsresort.com

MARRIOTT RANCHO LAS PALMAS RESORT, Rancho Mirage, California

(800) 458-8786   www.marriott.com

MARRIOTT RESORT AND BEACH CLUB, Lihu'e, Hawaii

(800) 220-2925   www.marriott.com

MAUI PRINCE HOTEL, Maui, Hawaii

(800) 321-6248   www.mauiprincehotel.com

MAUNA KEA BEACH HOTEL, Kohala Coast, Hawaii

(800) 882-6060   www.maunakeabeachhotel.com

THE MAUNA LANI BAY HOTEL AND BUNGALOWS, Kohala Coast, Hawaii

(800) 367-2323   www.maunalani.com

THE MOUNT WASHINGTON HOTEL AND RESORT, Bretton Woods, New Hampshire

(800) 258-0330   www.mtwashington.com

NEMACOLIN WOODLANDS RESORT AND SPA, Farmington, Pennsylvania

(800) 422-2736   www.nemacolin.com

OCEAN EDGE RESORT AND GOLF CLUB, Brewster, Massachusetts

(800) 343-6074   www.oceanedge.com

OJAI VALLEY INN AND SPA, Ojai, California

(800) 422-6524   www.ojairesort.com

THE ORCHID AT MAUNA LANI, Kohala Coast, Hawaii

(800) 845-9905   www.orchid-maunalani.com

THE OTESAGA, Cooperstown, New York

(800) 348-6222   www.otesaga.com

PGA NATIONAL RESORT AND SPA, Palm Beach Gardens, Florida

(800) 633-9150   www.pga-resorts.com

THE PHOENICIAN, Scottsdale, Arizona

(800) 888-8234   www.thephoenician.com

PINEHURST RESORT, Pinehurst, North Carolina

(800) 487-4653   www.pinehurst.com

POINTE HILTON TAPATIO CLIFFS RESORT, Phoenix, Arizona

(800) 876-4683   www.pointehilton.com

PRINCEVILLE RESORT, Kauai, Hawaii

(800) 826-4400   www.leisurecollection.com

QUAIL LODGE RESORT AND GOLF CLUB, Carmel, California

(888) 828-8787   www.quail-lodge-resort.com

RANCHO BERNARDO INN, San Diego, California

(800) 439-7529   www.ranchobernardoinn.com

THE REGENT LAS VEGAS, Las Vegas, Nevada

(877) 869-8777   www.regentlasvegas.com

RENAISSANCE VINOY RESORT, St. Petersburg, Florida

(800) 468-3571   www.renaissancehotels.com

THE RESORT AT LONGBOAT KEY CLUB, Longboat Key, Florida

(800) 237-8821   www.longboatkeyclub.com

THE RITZ-CARLTON, AMELIA ISLAND, Amelia Island, Florida

(800) 241-3333   www.ritzcarlton.com

THE RITZ-CARLTON, KAPALUA, Maui, Hawaii

(800) 262-8440   www.ritzcarlton.com

THE SAGAMORE, Bolton Landing, New York

(800) 358-3585   www.thesagamore.com

SAWGRASS MARRIOTT RESORT, Ponte Vedra Beach, Florida

(800) 457-4653   www.marriotthotels.com/jaxsw

SEA PINES, Hilton Head Island, South Carolina

(800) 732-7463   www.seapines.com

SEAVIEW MARRIOTT RESORT, Absecon, New Jersey

(800) 205-6518   www.marriotthotels.com

SHERATON EL CONQUISTADOR RESORT AND COUNTRY CLUB, Tucson, Arizona

(800) 325-3535   www.sheraton.com

SHERATON STEAMBOAT RESORT, Steamboat Springs, Colorado

(800) 848-8877   www.steamboat-sheraton.com

SHERATON TAMARRON RESORT, Durango, Colorado

(800) 678-1000   www.tamarron.com

SUN RIVER RESORT, Sun River, Oregon

(800) 547-3922   www.sunriver-resort.com

SUN VALLEY RESORT, Sun Valley, Idaho

(800) 786-8259   www.sunvalley.com

TETON PINES, Jackson, Wyoming

(800) 238-2223   www.tetonpines.com

TREETOPS RESORT, Gaylord, Michigan

(888) 873-3867   www.treetops.com

TURNBERRY ISLE RESORT AND CLUB, Aventura, Florida

(800) 327-7028   www.turberryisle.com

WESTIN INNISBROOK RESORT, Palm Harbor, Florida

(800) 456-2000   www.westin-innisbrook.com

THE WESTIN LA PALOMA, Tucson, Arizona

(800) 228-3000   www.westin.com

WESTIN RESORT, HILTON HEAD, Hilton Head Island, South Carolina

(800) 933-3102   www.westin.com

THE WESTIN MISSION HILLS RESORT, Rancho Mirage, California

(800) 937-8461   www.westin.com

THE WIGWAM RESORT, Litchfield Park, Arizona

(800) 327-0396   www.wigwamresort.com

WILD DUNES RESORT, Charleston, South Carolina

(888) 845-8926   www.wilddunes.com

WILLIAMSBURG INN, Williamsburg, Virginia

(800) 447-8679   www.colonialwilliamsburg.org

WINTERGREEN RESORT, Wintergreen, Virginia

(800) 266-2444   www.wintergreenresort.com

WRITERS BIOGRAPHIES

David G. Molyneaux, travel editor of *The Plain Dealer* in Cleveland, has worked as a newspaper reporter and editor since the 1960s. He covered police, the courts, government, business, economics, and served as city editor and editorial page editor, but he was always looking for an excuse to travel. Assignments have taken him all over the world, including Germany for the fall of the Berlin Wall and South Africa, where he filed an award-winning report after the end of apartheid. As travel editor, Molyneaux often assigns himself to cover cruise ships and Caribbean islands, especially during the harsh Ohio winters. Whenever possible, he packs his golf clubs and works at the game he enjoys playing with his teenage son, who occasionally beats him. Molyneaux is an officer of the Editors Council of the Society of American Travel Writers and is a trustee of the SATW Foundation.

Cynthia Boal Janssens is a travel writer and photographer who lives in northern Michigan. She is a past president of the Society of American Travel Writers and the former travel editor of *The Detroit News*. She has traveled the globe writing for such publications as the *Chicago Tribune*, *Detroit Free Press*, *Boston Globe*, *Portland Oregonian*, and *St. Petersburg Times* in addition to other major newspapers in the United States and Canada. Boal Janssens took up golf about five years ago and has expanded her writing into the field of golf travel. In addition to golf, her writing specialties include luxury travel and small ship cruising.

Cori Kenicer is a San Francisco–based golf and travel writer whose work has been published in leading consumer and trade publications in the U.S. and abroad, including *Luxury Golf, Fortune, Golf for Women, Private Clubs, and Senior Golfer*. Kenicer has served as a selection panelist for *Golf for Women's* top 100 women-friendly courses, and is a member of the Sunriver Resort Women's Golf Forum, a panel to establish national guidelines. A golfer since childhood, Kenicer has competed in international media golf tournaments, earning first place in the Media Cup in Rabat, Morocco, in 1997, where she was also the first female winner of the event.

Larry Olmsted is the editor and founder of *The Golf Insider*, a newsletter devoted to golf travel. He is an active member of the Society of American Travel Writers, and has been the golf columnist for the national newspaper, *Investors' Business Daily*, for five years. He has served as golf columnist for US Airways' magazine and contributing golf editor for *P.O.V.* magazine. Olmsted writes regularly on golf for American Airlines' magazine, *Cigar Aficionado, Playboy, Diversion,* and *LINKS*, and has written for most major golf magazines including *Golf, Golf & Travel, Golf for Women*, and *Luxury Golf*. He currently lives in central Vermont.

Alice Rindler Shapin is a freelance writer in the Washington, D.C., area and is a member of the Society of American Travel Writers. She specializes in golf and travel, and often combines her two loves. Hawaii ranks at the top of her list of favorite places in the world and always draws her back. Rindler Shapin's articles have appeared in national golf magazines as well as major newspapers including the *Washington Post*. She also writes a real estate feature for *Links Magazine*.

Lynn Seldon, a Virginia-based freelance travel writer and photographer, specializes in the southeast U.S. and the Caribbean. He has authored more than a dozen books and hundreds of magazine features. Seldon often covers golf and golf travel in such magazines as *Golf* magazine, *Travel & Leisure Golf, Senior Golfer, Luxury Golf Homes, Golf & Travel*, and many others.

William Tomicki is the editor of *ENTRÉE*, a Santa Barbara–headquartered luxury travel newsletter. He also serves as a travel columnist with the New York Times Syndicate. He is known as a resort expert and an intrepid traveler, always in search of a new experience. Such experiences have included eating piranhas in the Brazilian Amazon, hunting jaguars in Belize, and galloping horses through the royal woods of Versailles. Tomicki is a graduate of the University of Pennsylvania, was a vice president of both Tiffany and Sotheby's, and served with the United States Air Force Reserves during the Vietnam War.

SURVEY PARTICIPANTS

Nina Africano, freelance travel writer

Eric Anderson, travel editor, *Physician's Money Digest*

Geri Bain, travel editor, *Modern Bride Magazine*

James Y. Bartlett, editor, *Luxury Golf* magazine

Harry Basch, freelance travel writer

Cynthia Boal Janssens, freelance golf travel writer

Patricia and **Lester Brooks**, freelance travel writers

J. D. Brown, freelance travel writer

Robert Carey, business golf editor, *Successful Meetings Magazine*

Richard Carroll, freelance travel writer

Ray Chatelin, freelance travel writer

Jay Clarke, travel editor, *Miami Herald*

Judi Dash, syndicated travel writer

Robert Haru Fisher, freelance travel writer

Lois Friedland, freelance travel writer and editor

Bill and **Diana Gleasner**, freelance travel writers

Larry Habegger, executive editor, Travelers' Tales, Inc.

Ann Hattes, freelance travel writer

Mary Ann Hemphill, freelance travel writer

Bill F. Hensley, freelance golf travel writer

Vivian Holley, freelance travel writer

Yvonne Horn, freelance travel writer

Judi Janofsky and **Rich Steck**, freelance golf travel writers

Stephen Jemanok, freelance travel writer

Mitch Kaplan, freelance travel writer

Cori Kenicer, freelance golf travel writer

Jim Kerr, freelance golf travel writer

Barb and **Ron Kroll**, freelance travel writers

Dale Leatherman, freelance golf and adventure travel writer

Florence Lemkowitz, freelance travel writer

Jeff Lesson, host and producer, "Lesson on Golf," CBS Radio (Detroit)

Marcia Levin, freelance travel writer

John S. Long, columnist, *Cleveland Plain Dealer*

Janet McCue, freelance travel writer

Matt McKay, golf and travel writer, *Dallas Morning News*

Maribeth Mellin, freelance travel writer

David G. Molyneaux, travel editor, *Cleveland Plain Dealer*

David Noland, freelance travel writer

Bernie O'Brien, editor and travel writer, *Golf Southern California Magazine*

Larry Olmsted, editor in chief, *The Golf Insider*

Tom and **Joanne O'Toole**, freelance travel writers

Douglas Peebles, freelance travel photographer

Todd Pitock, freelance travel writer

Edward Schmidt, Jr. contributing editor/golf, *Robb Report*

Alice Rindler Shapin, freelance golf travel writer

Shirley Slater, freelance travel writer

Molly and **Adam Staub**, freelance travel writers

Janet Steinberg, freelance travel writer

Linda Stewart, freelance travel writer

Charles Stine, editor, *Florida Golf News*

William Tomicki, travel columnist, New York Times Syndicate

James Wamsley, freelance travel writer

Harry West, freelance travel writer

Deborah Williams, freelance travel writer

PHOTO CREDITS

1990 Golfoto: 206–207, 260–261, 262–263. **1991 Mike Klemme/Golfoto:** 92–93, 268, 270–271, 358, 360–361. **1995 Mike Klemme/Golfoto:** 66–67. **1997 Mike Klemme/Golfoto:** 54–55. **2000 Joann Dost:** 208–209, 209, 218–219, 210. **Al Messerschmidt/JRP:** 8–9, 94–95, 114–115, 116–117, 136–137, 142a, 142b, 144–145, 145. **Amelia Island Plantation:** 106, 106–107, 107b. **Arizona Biltmore Resort & Spa:** 261b. **Arnold Savrann/Lana'i Company, Inc.:** 358a. **Barton Creek Resort:** 150, 150–151, 152a, 152b, 152–153, 153. **Ben Blankenburg/Vail Resorts:** 242b. **Bill Gleasner/The Viesti Collection:** 368–369. **Boca Raton Resort & Club:** 122, 123a. **Boyne Highlands:** 166–167, 167, 168–169. **Callaway Gardens:** 100a, 100b, 100–101, 101. **Cathy Fox Ralphaelson/Houserstock:** 89, 123b. **Chateau Elan Winery & Resort:** 98a, 98b, 99. **Craig Jones/Allsport:** 178–179. **Crystal Mountain Resort:** 174–175, 175, 176–177. **Dave G. Houser/Houserstock:** 24, 43, 45b, 107a, 108–109, 135b, 139, 140–141, 146–147, 187a, 187b, 196, 196–197, 197, 198–199, 214–215, 216–217, 217, 234b, 234–235, 235, 236–237, 243, 244–245, 246–247, 251b, 252–253, 254, 257b, 259, 260, 261a, 263, 278–279, 281, 286, 286–287, 287, 288–289, 289a, 289b, 296b, 297, 298b, 298–299, 302–303, 313, 314, 316, 322b, 322–323, 324–325, 330–331, 335, 346–347, 347b, 348–349, 361, 362b, 362–363, 364–365, 364, 365a, 365b, 370–371, 372, 372–373, 373b, 375a, 376–377, 378–379, 382a, 382b, 383, 384–385, 386a, 386b, 386–387, 387, 388, 393, 398–399, 400, 402, 404–405, 406, 406–407, 407b, 409b. **Dave Richards Golf Photography:** 179, 180–181. **David Leah/Allsport:** endsheet. **David R. Stoecklein Photography:** 190–191. **David Thiemann/Sheraton Steamboat Resort & Conference Center:** 240–241. **Douglas Peebles Photography:** 333, 402–403, 408–409. **Ellen Barone/Houserstock:** 212–213. **Four Seasons Resort & Club, TX:** 146, 147a, 148–149. **Four Seasons Resort Maui at Wailea:** 350–351, 351b, 352–353, 353, 354, 355. **Four Seasons Resort Maui at Wailea/David Franzen:** 351a. **Four Seasons Resort Maui at Wailea/Michael French Photo:** 354–355. **Four Seasons Resort, Aviara:** 328a, 328b, 328–329, 329, 331a. **Gabriel Benzur/Lana'i Company, Inc.:** 362a. **Garland Resort:** 182–183, 183a, 183b. **George Kenicer:** 26–27, 214, 312–313, 366–367, 378, 400–401, 401, 403, 407a, 409a. **Ginny Ganong Nichols/The Viesti Collection:** 72–73, 73a, 73b, 74–75. **Golf Northwest:** 202–203, 200–201. **Grand Cypress Resort:** 132a, 132b, 135a. **Grand Traverse Resort & Spa:** 170, 170–171, 171, 172a, 172b, 172–173. **Grand Wailea Resort Hotel & Spa:** 346, 347a, 348. **Grouse Mountain Lodge:** 201a. **Heinsius photo/Lana'i Company, Inc.:** 358b. **Hershey Resorts:** 30, 30–31, 31a, 31b, 32–33, 33a, 33b. **Hound Ears Club:** 82, 82–83. **Hyatt Grand Champions Resort:** 308, 308–309. **Hyatt Regency at Lake Las Vegas:** 296–297, 298a. **Hyatt Regency Kauai Resort & Spa:** 379, 380–381, 381. **Hyatt Regency Scottsdale:** 278. **Indian Wells Resort Hotel:** 312a, 312b, 314a, 314–315. **Jack Affleck/Vail Resorts:** 242–243, 244b. **Jan Butchofsky Houser/Houserstock:** 201a, 210–211, 211b, 255, 280a, 280b, 282–283, 296a, 322a, 323, 331b. **Jeff Garton Photography:** 256–257, 266–267. **Jeffery Asher/Lana'i Company, Inc.:** 359. **Joe Robbins Photography:** 269b, 420. **Joe Viesti/The Viesti Collection:** 4–5, 29, 61, 234a, 254–255, 324. **Jon Ferrey/Allsport:** 20–21. **Joshua Savage Gibson:** 88b. **Kapalua Bay Hotel/Kapalua Land Company, Ltd.:** 338–339, 340–341. **Kauai Marriott:** 373a, 374–375, 375b. **Kea Lani Hotel:** 342b, 343, 345. **Kiawah Island Resorts:** 88a, 90–91. **Kiawah Island Resorts:** 91. **Kingsmill Resort:** 64, 65a, 65b. **La Quinta Resort & Club:** 225, 300–301, 302. **M. Silver Associates Inc.:** 226b, 227, 228, 229b. **Manele Bay Hotel/Lana'i Company, Inc.:** 363. **Marona Photography:** 230a, 230b, 233a, 233b. **Marriott Desert Springs:** 316a. **Marriott's Camelback Inn Resort, Golf Club & Spa in Scottsdale:** 284, 284–285. **Marriott's Rancho Las Palmas Resort & Spa:** 310–311, 311. **Maui Prince Hotel:** 356a, 356b, 357. **Mauna Kea Resort:** 388–389. **Mauna Lani Bay Hotel:** 390, 391a, 391b, 392b. **Mauna Lani Services, Inc.:** 392, 395. **Michael Kleinberg:** 269a. **Mike Klemme/Golfoto:** 317. **Nathan Bilow/Allsport:** 14–15, 410–411. **Nemacolin Woodlands Resort & Spa:** 34, 35a, 35b, 36–37, 37a, 37b. **Nik Wheeler:** 12–13, 17, 301a, 301b, 384, 390–391, 392–393. **Ocean Edge Resort & Golf Club:** 52a, 52b. **Ojai Valley Inn & Spa:** 318–319, 319, 320–321, 321. **PGA National Resort & Spa:** 124–125, 125a, 125b, 126–127. **PGA West:** 10–11. **Pinehurst Resorts:** 76–77. **Pointe Hilton at Tapatio Cliffs:** 264a, 264b, 264–265, 265, 266a, 266b. **Ponte Vedra Beach Sawgrass Marriott Resort:** 115. **Princeville Resort/Paul Barton:** 368b. **Princeville Resort/Tom Brit:** 368a, 369. **Quail Lodge Resort & Golf Club:** 23, 220a, 220b, 221, 222a, 222b, 222–223. **Rancho Bernardo Inn:** 326–327, 327. **Rankin Harvey/Houserstock:** 147b. **Renaissance Vinoy Resort:** 140. **Reproduced by permission of Pebble Beach Company:** 208, 216. **Reproduced by permission of Pebble Beach Company/Alex Vertikoff:** 215. **Reproduced by permission of Pebble Beach Company/Robert Neimy:** 211a. **Richard Pasley/The Viesti Collection:** 339a, 339b. **Russell Kirk/GolfLinks:** 19, 34–35, 38, 39, 64–65, 77a, 77b, 78–79, 78, 80–81, 133, 134–135, 158–159, 160–161, 162, 162–163, 163, 164–165, 344–345. **Sea Pines Resort:** 96a, 96b, 96–97. **Seaview Marriott Resort:** 56, 56–57, 57a, 57b, 58–59, 59a, 59b. **Sheraton El Conquistador Resort & Country Club, Tucson:** 272, 272–273. **Sheraton Steamboat Resort & Conference Center:** 238–239, 239a, 239b, 240a, 240b. **Steve Bly/Houserstock:** 185. **Sun Valley Resort:** 192a, 192b, 192–193, 193, 194–195. **Sun Valley's Elkhorn Resort:** 191. **Sunriver Resort, OR:** 204, 204–205, 205a, 205b, 206. **Susan Kaye/Houserstock:** 246, 247a, 247b, 248–249. **Tamarron Resort, Durango:** 232–233. **Teton Pines:** 186–187, 188–189, 188. **The American Club and Resort:** 6–7, 155, 156a, 156b, 156–157, 157, 158. **The Balsams Grand Resort:** 40–41, 41. **The Boulders:** 257a. **The Breakers Palm Beach:** 118, 119a, 119b, 120–121, 121a, 121b. **The Cloister:** 102a, 102b, 103, 104–105, 105a, 105b. **The Equinox:** 2–3, 50–51, 51a, 51b. **The Fairmont Scottsdale Princess:** 258, 258–259. **The Homestead:** 70–71, 71. **The Inn at Bay Harbor:** 163. **The Kea Lani Resort:** 342a. **The Lodge & Spa at Cordillera:** 226a, 226–227, 228–229, 229a. **The Lodge at Ventana Canyon:** 274, 274–275, 276–277. **The Mount Washington Hotel & Resort:** 42, 42–43, 44, 44–45, 45a. **The Orchid at Mauna Lani/J. Demello:** 394a, 394b, 396a, 396b, 396–397. **The Phoenician:** 250, 251a, 252. **The Regent Las Vegas:** 290, 291a, 291b, 292a, 292b, 292–293, 294–295, 295. **The Resort at Longboat Key Club:** 138a, 138b, 139. **The Ritz-Carlton, Kapalua:** 334, 334–335, 336, 336–337, 337. **The Ritz-Carlton, Amelia Island:** 110a, 110b, 110–111, 111, 112a, 112b, 112–113. **The Sagamore:** 46, 46–47, 47a, 47b. **The Viesti Collection:** 48–49, 231. **The Walt Disney Company:** 142–143. **The Westin Innisbrook Resort:** 136a, 136b. **Turnberry Isle Resort & Club:** 128a, 128b, 128–129, 129, 130–131. **Vail Resorts:** 242a, 244a. **Westin Mission Hills Resort Hotel:** 304a, 304b, 305, 306–307, 307a, 307b. **Westin Resort, Hilton Head Island:** 94, 95. **Wild Dunes Resort:** 84, 84–85, 85, 86–87, 87a, 87b. **Williamsburg Lodge:** 62, 62–63. **Wintergreen Resort:** 68–69, 68a, 68b.

INDEX

FAIRWAYS

FAIRWAYS

FAIRWAYS

FAIRWAYS

FAIRWAYS

FAIRWAYS

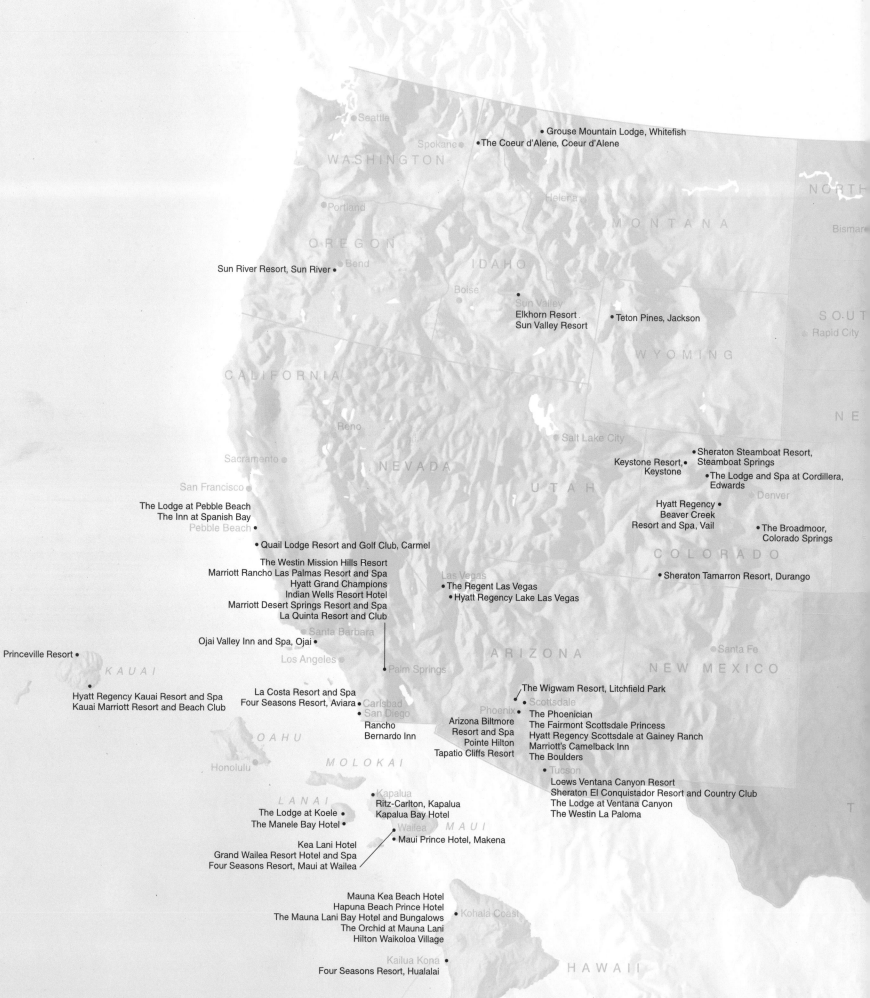